TITANIC

& FASHION

Waanders Publishers, Zwolle   **Kunstmuseum Den Haag**

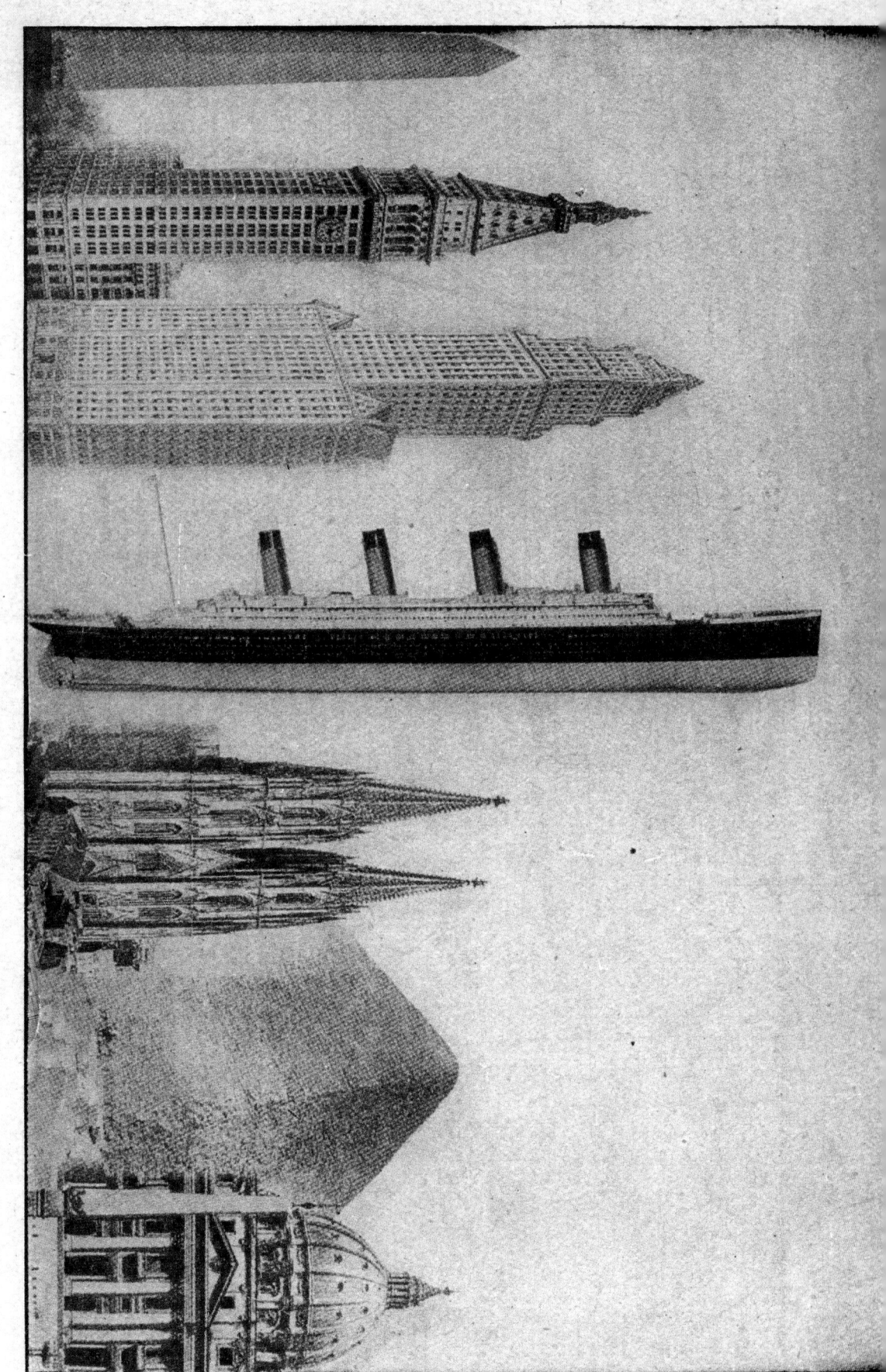

Trunk Rail way, was lost

1. Washington Monument, Washington, 555 feet high 5. Cologne Cathedral, Cologne, Germany, 516 feet
2. Metropolitan Tower, New York, 700 feet high   high
3. New Woolworth Building, New York, 750 feet high 6. Grand Pyramid, Gizeh, Africa, 451 feet high
4. White Star Line's Triple Screw Steamers "Olym- 7. St. Peter's Church, Rome, Italy, 448 feet high
   pic" and "Titanic," 882½ feet long

Contents

Foreword
& Introduction

The legentary sinking of the Titanic (in 1912) is one of the most striking historical events of the modern era. The loss of the allegedly unsinkable ship, sunk by an iceberg shortly before the end of its maiden voyage to New York, is etched into our collective memory. The dream of groundbreaking progress and the notion that a different, better world was within reach, collided with fear of a doomsday scenario that could strike at any moment.

The story of the Titanic chimes with a fascination that is deeply rooted in popular culture, which has been manifested in the form of musicals, exhibitions and films. The best-known example is the 1997 movie epic starring Kate Winslet and Leonardo DiCaprio, which is still a favourite with the public.

Kunstmuseum Den Haag has been given the unique opportunity to show for the first time in the Netherlands original Oscar-winning costumes from the film. Showing them in combination with a variety of items from our museum's own fashion collection dating from the first two decades of the twentieth century, and new perspectives by contemporary designers, has allowed us to paint a vivid picture of this turbulent period of history, and highlight links with the present day.

The years leading up to the First World War (1914-1918) can be seen as the end of an age dominated by the aristocracy and the wealthy classes. As the old order fell apart under the influence of global political tensions, great technological progress and social change, the sinking of the Titanic provided the perfect metaphor. Issues that were current at that time are increasingly matters that concern us today, including the impact of new technology, migration, social inequality, gender inequality and the threat of global war. While fascination with the Titanic generally focuses on the disaster and the wreck, the fashion worn onboard tells the story of people. Consigned to a terrible fate, they either perished or survived, in clothes that symbolised their status, origins and expectations.

Issues that were current at the time – like the impact of new technology, migration, social and gender inequality and the threat of global war – increasingly concern us today. For many of us, the most painful parallel with the Titanic is probably the sea, which plays a tragic and pivotal role at so many level's in today's society.

I am delighted with the contributions made by today's innovative and inspiring makers. Their spectacular creations and 'critical fabulations' are invaluable, offering new perspectives alongside the historical and Hollywood costumes. Here, too, love and the hope of a better future are often the focus, as they were in the film *Titanic*, because we cannot survive without love and hope.

Many people devote a great deal of energy, enthusiasm and emotion to an exhibition like this. I would like to thank all the departments and staff at the museum involved in this project for their teamwork and their dedication to this exhibition (conceived by fashion curator Madelief Hohé), catalogue and programme of public events. Maarten Spruyt and Felipe Gonzalez Cabezas are responsible for the fabulous exhibition design. Jasper Abels and Alice de Groot are responsible for the amazing photography, and Loes Claessens beautifully designed this catalogue, which is published by Waanders Publishers. Cathelijne Blok arranged a number of unique loans of items for the exhibition. I would also like to express my gratitude to all those who have provided items on loan, as well as Fonds21 for its generous sponsorship.

Margriet Schavemaker
Director, Kunstmuseum Den Haag

Margriet Schavemaker

Titanic & Fashion:
The Last Dance

Why an exhibition about the Titanic and fashion? And why now? This exhibition is a response to recent fashions, which have been full of references to the 1910s. Suddenly, romantic dresses and blouses, with plenty of lace and broderie anglaise, appeared in the shops. These lovely, delicate fashions contrast starkly with the world around us, which is growing steadily harsher. Around the world, societies are increasingly polarised. For the first time in many years, the threat of global war is present. People are taking to the streets to protest against war and violence, or to campaign, once more, for women's rights. Have we not seen this all before? Back in the 1910s, the time of the First World War (1914-1918)? Have we learned nothing from history?

Lots happened in the 1910s, a decade that began with boundless optimism. Fashion was alive with new colours and modern ideas. It was the time of radical young designers like Paul Poiret and Gabrielle 'Coco' Chanel. Art, music and dance were alight with wild ideas and innovation. Modern technology made life more fun. The telephone, telegraph, cars, steamships and the first planes made humans feel invincible. And then, in 1912, came reports of a ship, the Titanic, that was said to be unsinkable. It was at any rate reputed to be larger, faster, safer and more luxurious than any ship ever built. On its maiden voyage, it would convey passengers from Britain to the United States in just five days. A trip from the old world to the new, as people saw it then. Britain was at the height of its power, including in terms of the extent of its colonies, and in the United States migrants were founding lucrative companies in cities where skyscrapers were being built. The world on board the Titanic was a microcosm of society. There was spacious first-class accommodation, where the wealthiest spent their time on their pleasure or business trip, generally travelling on a return ticket. There was a small second class, as the middle classes were not so big at the time. The majority of passengers were travelling on a third-class ticket, often a single, on their way to start a new life on the other side of the Atlantic. The ship was designed in such a way that the different classes never encountered each other, though the dogs belonging to first-class passengers were walked on the third-class deck. And in order not to 'mar' the first-class deck, the lifeboats (too few in number) were located on the second-class deck.

We all know how the story ended. The Titanic, the 'unsinkable ship', hit an iceberg in the night of 14 April 1912 and sank. It was a human tragedy, and a majority of the passengers and crew did not survive. A range of books, films and reports have ensured the disaster is imprinted on our collective memory. People are still fascinated by the Titanic, both the reality and the myth. The best-known film about the disaster is without doubt James Cameron's 1997 epic *Titanic*, starring the young Kate Winslet and Leonardo DiCaprio. The film could be viewed online for many years, so younger generations are also aware of it, and it still feels topical today. The story told in the film is partly fictional, and partly an excellent representation of history. The costumes worn in the film were so well made that some of them look like the historical costumes in Kunstmuseum Den Haag's collection. Deborah Lynn Scott, the designer, won an Oscar for best costumes in 1998. Kunstmuseum Den Haag is delighted to be able to share the most important costumes from the film with its visitors in this exhibition, alongside historical costumes from its own collection.

What did one wear on the Titanic? That all depended on who you were, and who you could be or wanted to be. Like society, the boat was divided by rank and station. A gentleman wore a hat, a labourer a cap. Clothes make the man, and when Jack wears a borrowed dress suit in the film, he is treated completely differently. Clothes reflected a person's place in society. Not every woman could wear a silk gown from Paris with fabulous embroidery. Following Paris or London fashions was a sign of opulence in itself. Good-quality, ready-to-wear clothing was increasingly available for the new middle classes, but many people were forced to wear secondhand clothes, or had simple clothing made for them, if they did not make it themselves. And these garments would not be made of lovely silk fabrics, but of practical, washable cotton or linen, and nice warm woollen fabrics. These were materials that the fashionable upper echelons would also wear, but in the form of a bespoke tweed suit, a wool travelling costume or walking costume, clothes for sports and leisure, cotton morning dresses or pretty summer dresses and children's clothes. Leisure and luxury took precedence over necessity and practicality.

This exhibition shows the two sides of the coin: the fashionable costumes worn by the wealthy, and the practical, shabby clothes of those who were not in a position to follow the latest fashions. Most of the garments require little explanation: the social class of the wearer is immediately apparent. In this sense, the 1910s was a decade that was pivotal in fashion history. The focus of the exhibition is the period 1908 to 1918: from the moment when Paul Poiret issued his sensational *Les Robes de Paul Poiret* and Jeanne Margaine-Lacroix showed her 'naked dresses' at Longchamp to the end of the First World War. During this period, which has been rather overlooked, despite the fact that it was revolutionary in terms of fashion history, women's fashions changed ever more rapidly. Corsets were abandoned and vibrant colours replaced the soft, powdery shades of the belle époque. This was the time of rebellious innovators like Paul Poiret and Coco Chanel, and Lucile, the idiosyncratic British designer who survived the Titanic disaster. It was a time when women demanded the vote and people had boundless faith in technological progress. Feminism was manifested in modern, practical costumes, in a society were class difference and exclusion were also perpetuated by fashion. Modern techniques were gaining ground, and the fashion world was bursting with modernity on the eve of the First World War. After the war, women's fashion would change forever.

Since a story about the past is even more compelling in a contemporary context, *Titanic & Fashion* also includes work by several modern designers. Fashion is a mirror of its time, and their work reflects developments in society: issues we are concerned with, that we think and talk about, that perhaps keep us awake at night. The layers created by the combination of film costumes, historical fashion and modern work gives us plenty of food for thought: about the past, and about now. And how, as a society, we want to head into the future.

Madelief Hohé
Curator of fashion and costume, Kunstmuseum Den Haag

Madelief Hohé

Titanic & Fashion: The Film

Titanic: the film costumes

Tirza Westland

Like the film itself, the costumes in *Titanic* have left a lasting impression. We all recall the scene in which the young Rose is introduced. A large car stops, and the driver steps out to open the door for his passenger. We see a white glove with purple details, black shoes and white stockings, a suit of white striped fabric with purple buttons, and, to top it off, a gigantic purple hat with an equally impressive bow in purple and white striped silk. Only once we have seen the entire costume does the wearer lift her head, giving us our first glimpse of Rose, played by Kate Winslet. The costume is introduced before the character.

Director James Cameron elected to show the costume in such detail for good reason. Before anyone utters a word, the viewer immediately forms an impression of the main character. Even those unfamiliar with the fashions of the time would immediately recognise that this was not just any passenger. Her tailored suit, inspired by men's fashion, complete with a starched collar, gives Rose a formal but fashionable look, and at the same time tells us something about her personality. This is a modern woman. It must have been a great honour for the film's costume designer Deborah Lynn Scott to have her work featured so prominently on screen. Her skill was also recognised in the form of the highly prestigious Academy Award (Oscar) for costume design, which she won in 1998.

Clearly, Scott did extensive research for the film, as the costumes are very convincing. They are appropriate to the time in which the story is set, the social status of the people wearing them, the occasion (evening or daytime) and, in the case of the leading roles, even the personality of the different characters. Dressing all the actors and extras was a huge task, on which more than fifty people worked for an entire year.[1] To ensure that the entire thing looked as credible as possible, everyone wore a costume that looked authentic. All the female actors in first class, even the extras, wore a corset under their costume, to ensure that their posture was correct. Jewellery, accessories and matching shoes completed the look. Scott herself appears in the film as an extra. Dressed in a black evening gown and somewhat concealed behind a red fan, she descends the famous staircase to the dining room at the same time as Jack and Rose.

As with most costume dramas, some of the clothes were from costume rental companies, so some of the outfits and accessories can also be spotted in other films and series.[2] However, a large proportion of the costumes were specially purchased and made for *Titanic*. Scott also collected many authentic costumes and accessories for the film.[3] It was quite common and, above all, practical to wear authentic clothing in films. Even today, some costume rental companies have original items, though often they have been altered or adapted.

New costumes were designed and made for the character Rose. This was a challenge, as they had to be a match for the highly sophisticated original costumes from the era.[4] There were also practical challenges: several versions had to be made for some scenes, for example. Twenty-four versions were eventually made of the dress Rose wears on the night the Titanic sinks. One interesting detail: the thin fabric meant that Kate Winslet could not wear a wetsuit under her costume, as the other actors did to protect them from the cold when filming scenes in the water. For Winslet, therefore, it was 'mighty cold', as she herself put it.[5]

A clear source of inspiration can be identified for some of the *Titanic* costumes designed by Scott. The suit in the opening scene, for example. This costume was quite clearly inspired by a suit from the January 1912 issue of French fashion magazine *Les Modes*. The original was a tailored winter suit, a 'costume tailleur pour l'apres midi' to be exact, from fashion house Amy Linker & Co., which specialised in 'tailleurs'. (p.21) According to the caption, it was made of black-and-white striped wool velours, trimmed with velvet and skunk fur ('skungs').[6] Tailored suits such as that worn by Rose were very popular in the 1910s, and there are many examples of similar suits from that time.[7]

Although Rose's suit was not intended to be a precise copy – the fur was omitted, for example – it is striking that the elements that differ from the original also reveal something of the tastes of the 1990s. Above all, the silhouette was changed – presumably to appeal to a modern audience, or simply because a designer is always influenced by the time in which they live. The shoulders are more defined than they would have been in 1912, and the shape of the collar is more reminiscent of a suit from the 1990s. The biggest difference is probably in the height of the bustline, which was quite low in 1912 due to lower corsets. This was probably adapted for the film because the silhouette would otherwise have appeared strange to modern viewers. The make-up and even the hairstyles also betray late-twentieth-century influences, for the same reason. Think, for example, of Rose's highly defined curls, and even what appears to be 'guyliner' (eyeliner) on her fiancé Cal. They are Hollywood stars after all.

The fact that costumes were adapted to modern tastes is also apparent in Rose's coral red evening gown, a white version of which she wears in the final scene. It was probably inspired by a gown by Worth in the collection of the Victoria and Albert Museum in London.[8] Although it is not an exact copy, there are clear similarities, in the form of the tapering embroidered tulle edging in the skirt. The billowing bodice in the original is replaced in the film by a fitted bodice that shows off the figure, more in line with 1990s tastes. It is very appropriate that Rose's gown should be inspired by a design by Worth. For decades, Maison Worth was the best-known fashion house in Paris, and was particularly popular among the American ladies who had the resources to pay its exorbitant prices.[9]

In the film, the costumes serve the same purpose as outfits did in the age of the Titanic: they signal which class a person belongs to. Think, for example, of the scene in which Jack, wearing a borrowed dress suit, makes his entrance in the first-class dining room. He immediately receives a friendly welcome from a steward. When, a day later, he walks around first class wearing his own cloths (corduroy workman's trousers and a shirt), the same steward makes it clear he is not welcome there.

The difference between the clothes of the first- and third-class passengers is huge, mirroring the social distance between the classes. While the first-class passengers change their expensive, sophisticated outfits several times a day, the third-class passengers have fewer costume changes. The clothes they wear are much more practical in terms of their design and materials than those of the people from the higher social classes. Jack, like many of his fellow steerage passengers, generally wears work clothing made of sturdy fabric. Apart from the borrowed outfit, we see him either in a collarless shirt, or in a brown work shirt made of heavy cotton. In both cases, he wears light brown corduroy trousers.

The stark contrast between the clothes worn in first and third class is very noticeable after the first-class dinner, when Rose accompanies Jack to a party below deck. The clothes worn by the steerage passengers are very diverse, as are their backgrounds. While the men in first class all wear the same solemn black dress suits, white ties and waistcoats, the men below deck wear much more varied outfits, although they are mostly in earthy tones. Some of the women in third class wear regional costume and accessories that show where they come from. (p.72) Although Rose's clothes are perfectly appropriate for her life among the social elite, they turn out to be a hindrance in steerage. She kicks off her high heels as she dances, and asks Jack to hold her train out of the way when, in a moment of abandon, she shows that she can stand on her toes.

The development of Rose's character from bored, constrained young lady to self-assured, unprejudiced young woman, is handily reflected in her costumes. There is a world of difference between the stiff suit with the giant hat at the start of the film, and the soft colours and fabric of her gown and her loose hair on the evening of the disaster. The fact that Rose has had enough of her first-class life and the clothes that go with also becomes clear in the scene where she lets Jack draw her. Rose specifically chooses to have herself portrayed naked because, as she says, 'The last thing I need is another picture of me looking like a porcelain doll'. And so one of the best-known moments in this celebrated costume drama is in fact one where no clothes are worn, and an independent modern woman is born.

1 *Heart of the Ocean: The Making of 'Titanic'* documentary (1997).
2 The online platform recycledmoviecostumes.com, for example, has several costumes and accessories worn in films and series before or after Titanic (1997).
3 Emma Robertson, Deborah L. Scott: "The heart of it is always the same", interview in *The Talks*. Accessed via the-talks.com. in July 2025.
4 Idem.
5 *Heart of the Ocean: The Making of 'Titanic'* documentary (1997).
6 *Les Modes*: revue mensuelle illustrée des arts décoratifs appliqués à la femme, 1 January 1912, p. 38. Accessed via gallica.bnf.fr. in July 2025.
7 There is for example a fashion print in *La Femme Chic* of a woman wearing a similar striped travelling costume, and in 1912 there was a picture on the cover of a Molstad&Co catalogue showing a woman in another similar striped suit, complete with large purple hat; Kunstmuseum Den Haag and Museum Nord (Norway) respectively.
8 Victoria& Albert Museum, London, inv.no. T.57-196.
9 Chantal Trubert-Tollu et al., *The House of Worth 1858-1954. The Birth of Haute Couture*, London 2017, p. 28.

The sinking of the Titanic in 1912 was a disaster that attracted global attention, and continues to intrigue many people to this day. Countless stories about the Titanic and its passengers have attained the status of myth, partly as a result of the 1997 film *Titanic*. Many, for example, regard the main characters from the film, Rose and Jack, as actual people, and 'diehard' fans even go so far as to seek 'evidence' of their existence. It is indeed true that some characters in the film were real people, including Margaret ('The Unsinkable Molly') Brown (1867-1932); Bruce Ismay (1862-1937), director of the White Star Line; Thomas Andrews (1873-1912), chief designer of the Titanic; John Jacob Astor (1864-1912), an American businessman, owner of the Waldorf-Astoria Hotel and the richest man on the Titanic; and Lord and Lady Duff Gordon (1862-1931 and 1863-1935 respectively). Lady Duff Gordon was the famous fashion designer Lucile, whose company had branches in London, Paris and New York – but more of her later. (p. 70) So what is fact, and what is fiction?

Titanic: Fact & Fiction

In the film, Jack Dawson ends up on board the Titanic by accident, winning a third-class ticket in a poker game. The character Jack Dawson was born in Chippewa Falls in Wisconsin, United States of America, around 1892. His parents died when he was young. Jack had some artistic talent, and a preference for drawing nudes.[1] In the film he soon meets up with his co-star, first-class passenger Rose Dewitt Bukater, also an American. Rose was born in Philadelphia, Pennsylvania in 1895. In the film she is travelling home from Europe with her mother Ruth to marry her fiancé, one Caledon 'Cal' Hockley, in New York. After the death of Rose's father, the Dewitt Bukater ladies had been left penniless, and Ruth has decided that Rose must marry for money. She regards Cal Hockley, the spectacularly wealthy son of Nathan Hockley, a Pittsburgh steel magnate, as the ideal husband for Rose.[2] However, her daughter wishes to live freely and independently, and hates the idea of marrying for money. In a desperate attempt to escape her situation, she tries to take her own life by jumping off the stern of the Titanic. This is where our two heroes meet … Jack saves Rose and the rest is movie history.

But what is the truth of the situation? Did Rose De Witt Bukater and Jack Dawson really exist? Briefly and simply: no. And that is a fact. At the same time, this is where the myth begins. For there was in fact a J. Dawson on board the Titanic. His given name was not Jack, however.

At Fairview cemetery in Halifax, Novia Scotia, Canada, among the other graves of Titanic victims, is grave number 227.[3] The inscription on the small stone reads: "Dawson Died April 15, 1912". When Dawson's body was recovered from the ocean, it was clear from his clothing that he was a member of the crew. We know that he was wearing dungarees.[4] Stokers and trimmers on a steam-driven ocean liner would wear white canvas dungarees, to ensure that they were more visible in the poorly lit boiler room, and any injuries would also become apparent more quickly.[5] They found Dawson's 'National Sailors and Firemen's Union' card in his jacket pocket.[6] But this J. Dawson was actually Joseph Dawson, born in Dublin, Ireland in September 1888. He grew up in poverty, but his father trained him as a carpenter, and he attended a Jesuit school. After the death of his mother, he and his younger sister were sent to relatives in Birkenhead near Liverpool in England. There, he joined the Royal Army Medical Corps, and went to work at a large military hospital in the small town of Netley near Southampton. One day he met Nellie Priest, sister of a friend who worked as a stoker on an ocean liner, and fell in love with her. He left the army in June 1911 to go and work as a 'trimmer'[7] on one of the large ocean liners of the White Star Line.[8] He departed for his final journey on board the Titanic on 10 April 1912.

After the 1997 movie *Titanic*, grave number 227 became a place of pilgrimage for all Jack Dawson fans who mistakenly believe that their film hero lies buried there.

And what of Rose? Rose is a completely fictional character. Or is she? It turns out that director James Cameron took inspiration for the character of Rose from dada artist Beatrice Wood (1893-1998), who became famous, particularly in later life, for her ceramic art. Cameron read her biography while making preparations for the film.[9] Beatrice Wood, from a wealthy, traditional American family, abandoned her life of privilege to become an artist, just as Rose in the film leaves her old life behind her to lead an independent life, free of her demanding mother. But that is where the similarity ends. So here, too, fact and fiction are intertwined.

[1] Via: Jack Dawson, Titanic Wiki, Fandom Accessed on 2-6-2025.
[2] Via: Caledon Hockley, Titanic Wiki, Fandom Accessde on 2-6-2025.
[3] Number 227 refers to the 227th victim or body recovered after the sinking of the Titanic. Via: The Real Jack Dawson Accessed on 2-6-2025.
[4] "His dungarees and other clothing immediately identified him as a member of the crew when his remains were recovered" Via https://www.encyclopedia-titanica.org/the-real-jack-dawson.html Accessed on 2-6-2025.
[5] Via: https://www.reddit.com/r/titanic/comments/18os5ju/why_did_the_firemen_and_coal_trimmers_on_the/ Geraadpleegd op Accessed on 2-6-2025.
[6] His number and name are given on his union card, and this was how J. Dawson was identified. Via: The Real Jack Dawson Accessed on 2-6-2025.
[7] A 'trimmer' or coal trimmer on a large ship like the Titanic was responsible for moving coal in the engine room's coal bunkers, to ensure it was evenly distributed and the ship thus remained stable. This ensured the ship did not start to list, or even capsize. Via: Kolendrager – 3 definities – Encyclo and via: wat is een trimmer op een schip als de Titanic – Google Zoeken Accessed on: 2-6-2025.
[8] He first spent a few months on the Majestic, a ship built in 1889 for the White Star Line, before joining the crew of the Titanic. Via: The Real Jack Dawson and via: Majestic (ship) – Wikipedia Accessed on 2-6-2025.
[9] Via: Beatrice Wood – Wikipedia Accessed on 2-6-2025.

Marije Blaasse

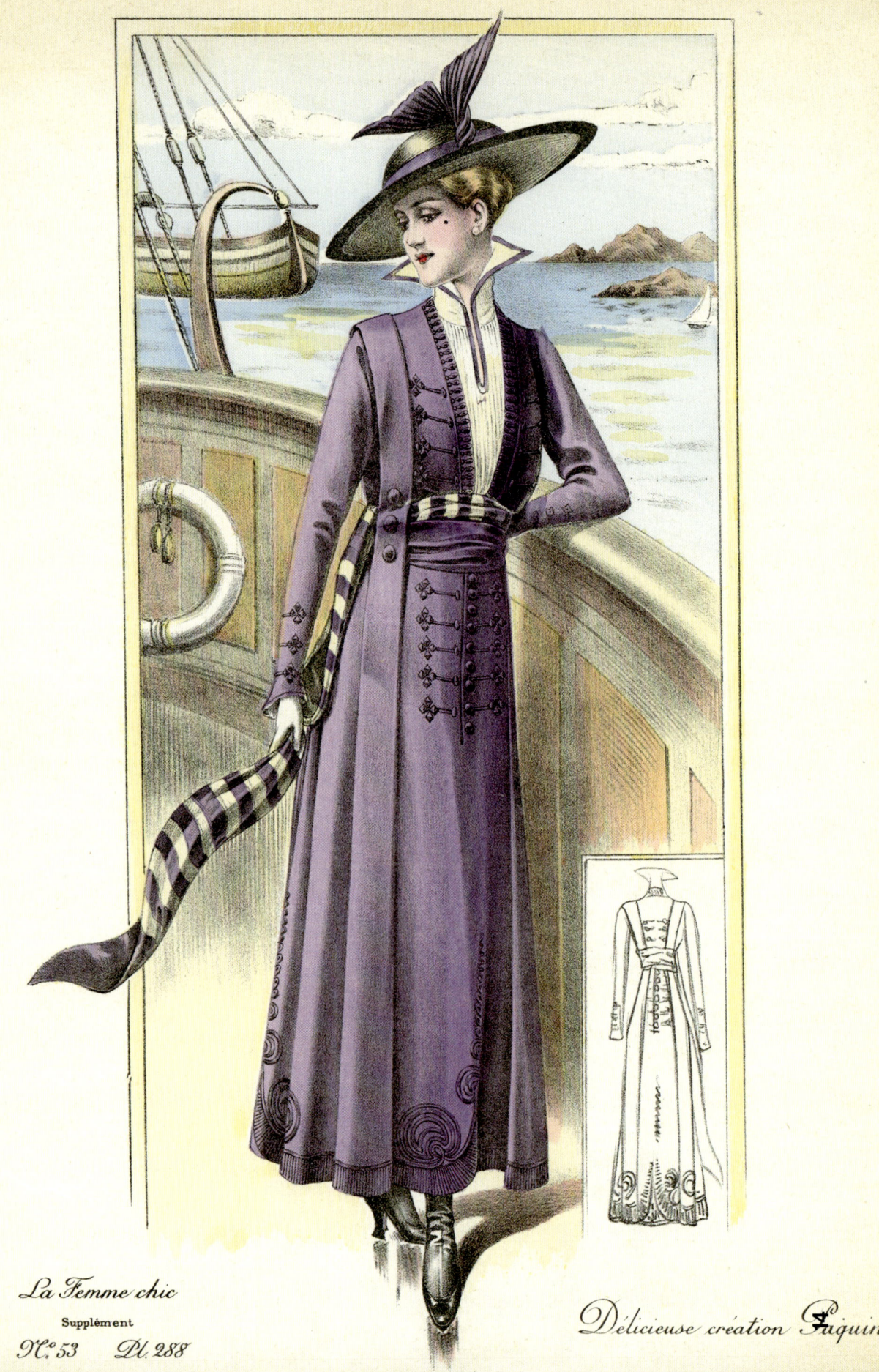

Délicieuse création Paquin.

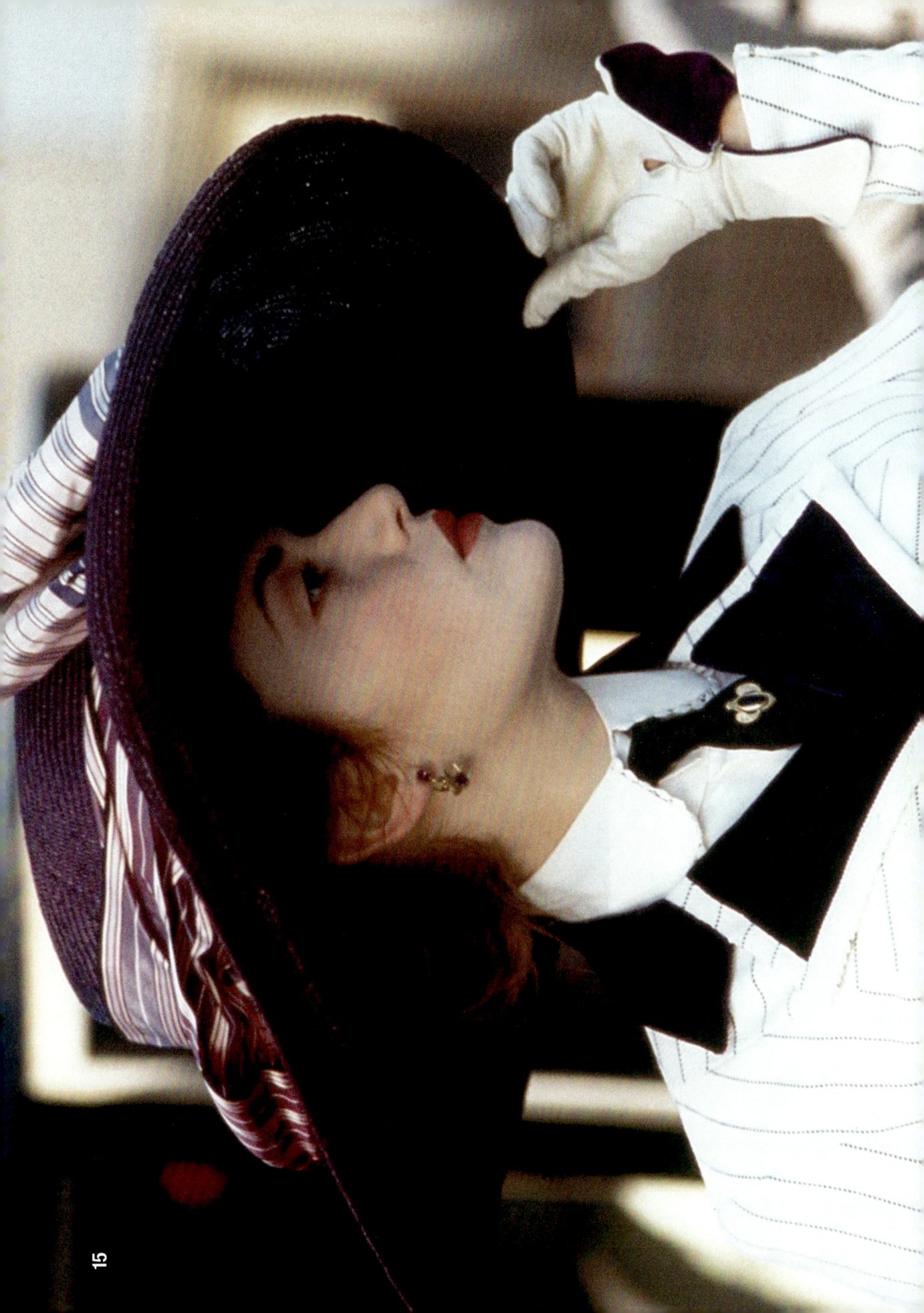

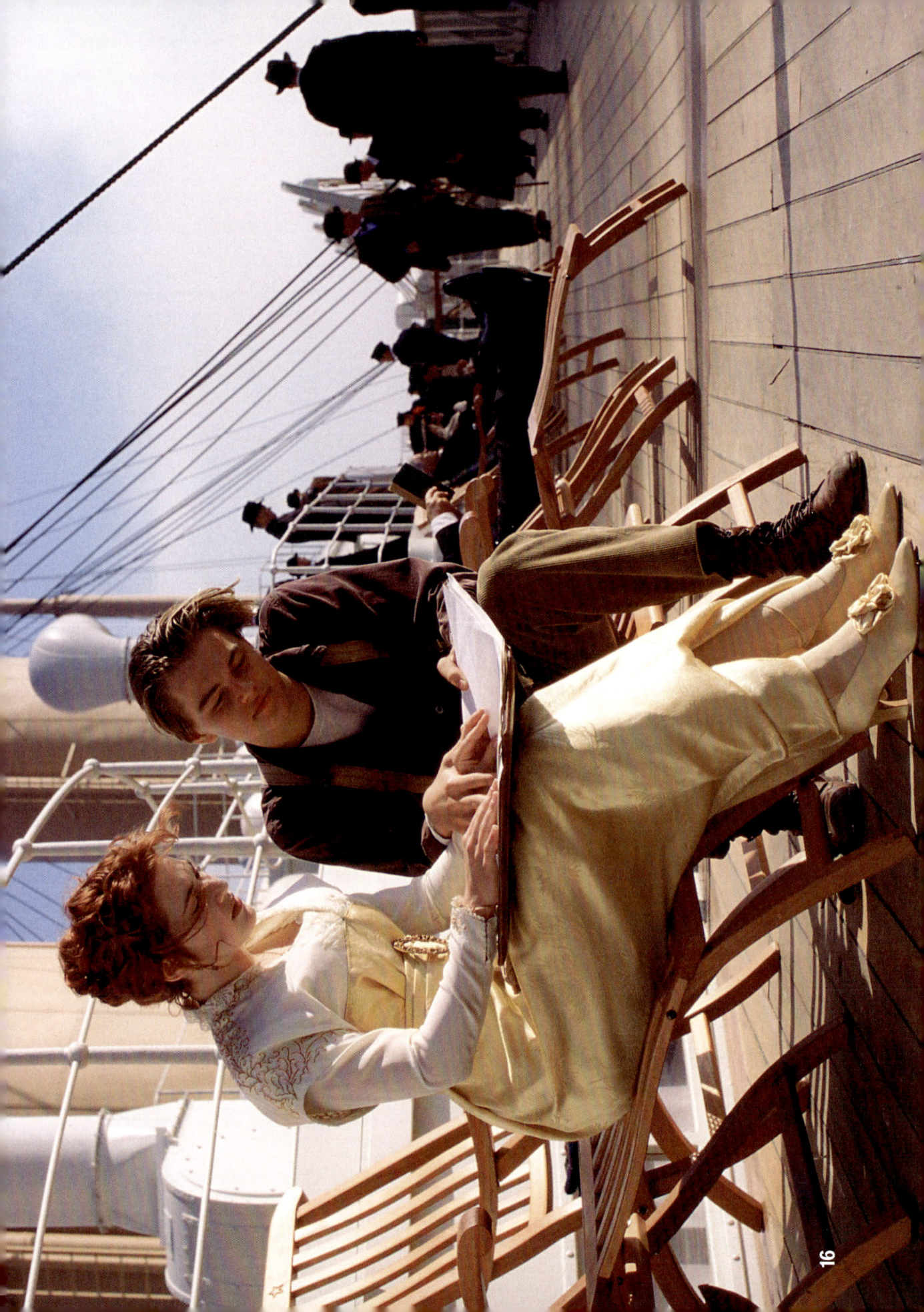

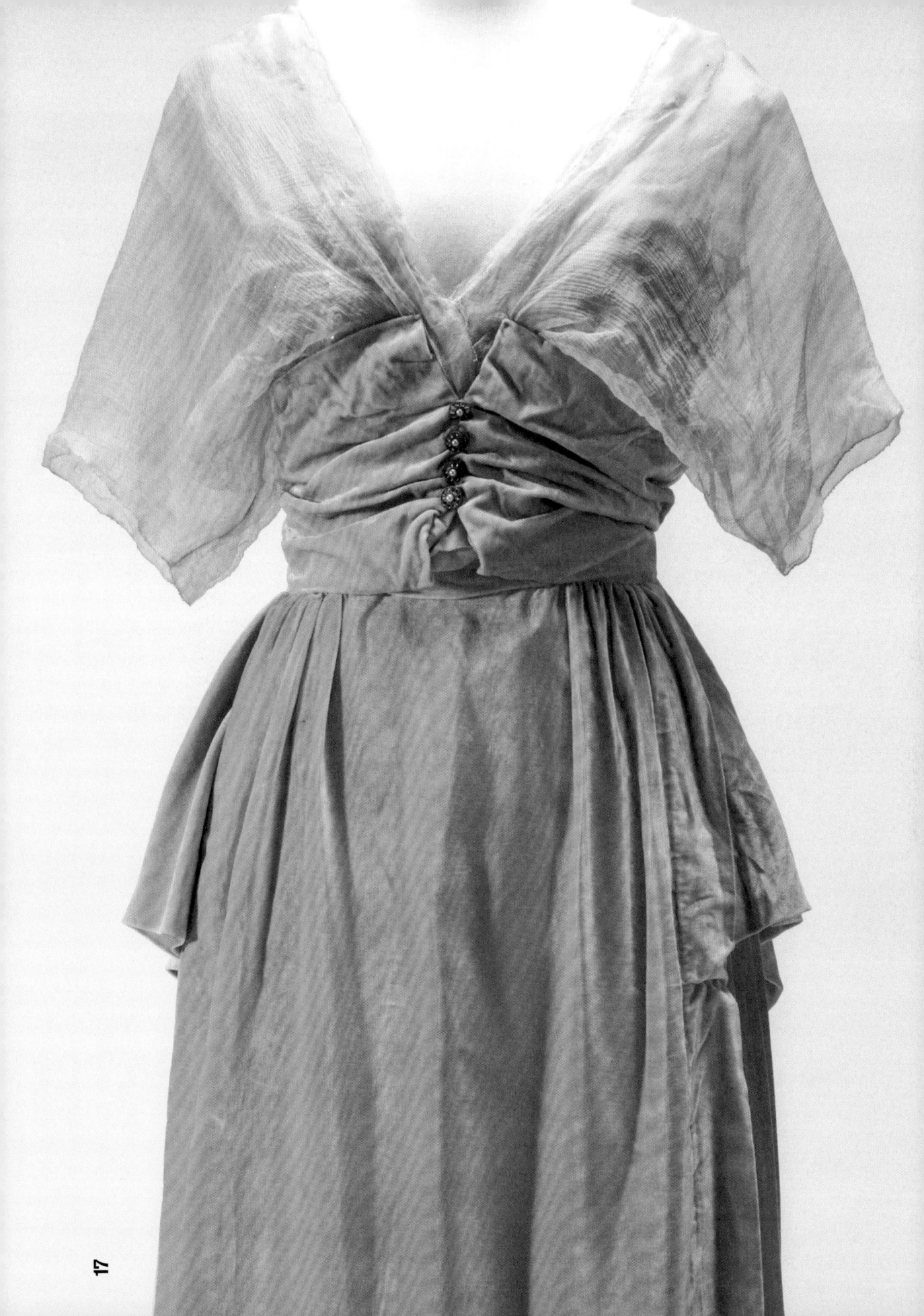

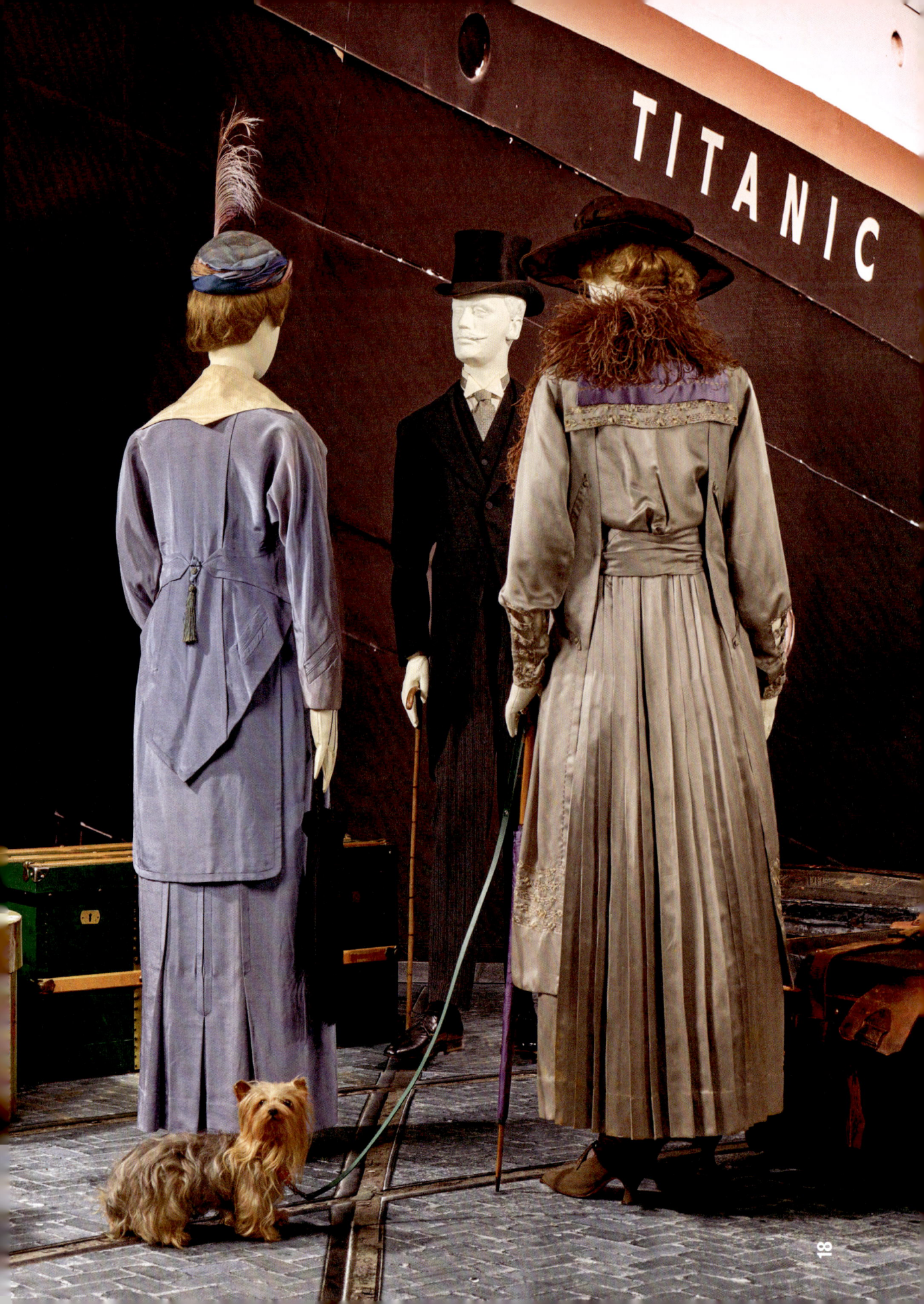

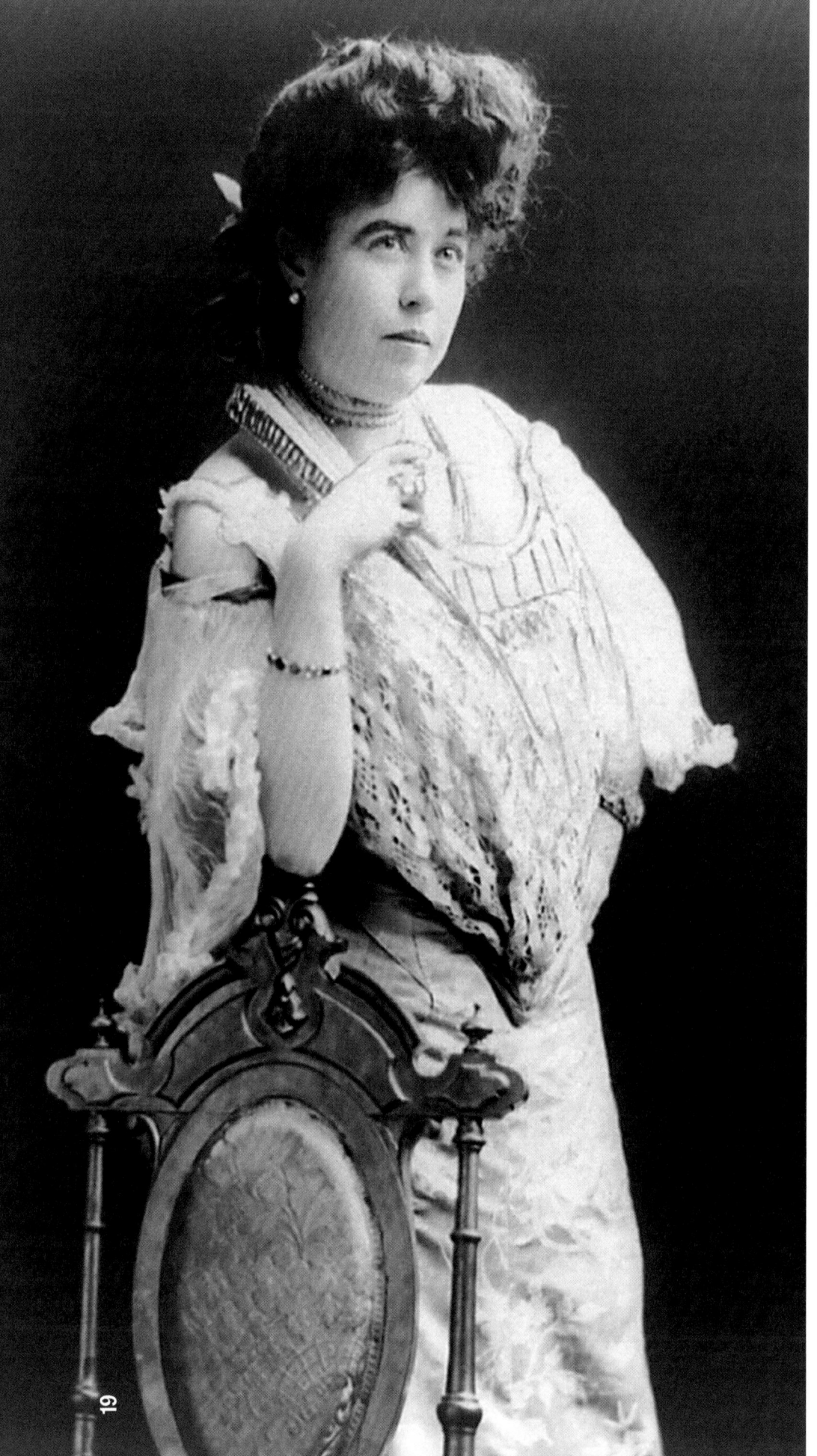

p. 2 Drawing from c. 1912 comparing the size of the Titanic with well-known buildings around the world.

p. 14 Fashion plate featuring woman's tailored suit by Jeanne Paquin, in: *La Femme Chic*, 1915.

p. 15 Kate Winslet as Rose in the opening scene of the film *Titanic* (1997), wearing a modern tailored suit and hat (*Boarding Suit*), based on fashions in 1912.

p. 16 Rose and Jack on the first-class deck of the Titanic in the film of the same name. Rose's day dress is similar to a yellow velvet dress by Gustav Beer in Kunstmuseum Den Haag's collection.

p. 17 Gustav Beer, Yellow silk evening gown with floral motifs embroidered on the bodice, Paris c. 1917-1919. Probably worn by Baroness Ada van Hardenbroek van Lockhorst (1889-1971).

p. 18 Maison de Bonneterie, Woman's suit in lavender silk faille, c. 1913-1914, worn by Adelaide Angelique Mathijsen (1873-1957); Hirsch & Cie, Gown in light grey and lilac satin with embroidery and sailor collar, c. 1915-1917; Morning suit, M.S. de Jong, The Hague, 1913, worn by L. den Beer-Poortugael Esq;; Yorkshire terrier (mounted; this breed was fashionable at the time), on loan from Museon.

p. 19 Photograph of Mrs James J. 'Molly' Brown (1867-1932), one of the survivors of the Titanic, who appears as a character in *The Unsinkable Molly Brown* (1964), *S.O.S. Titanic* (1979) and *Titanic* (1997).

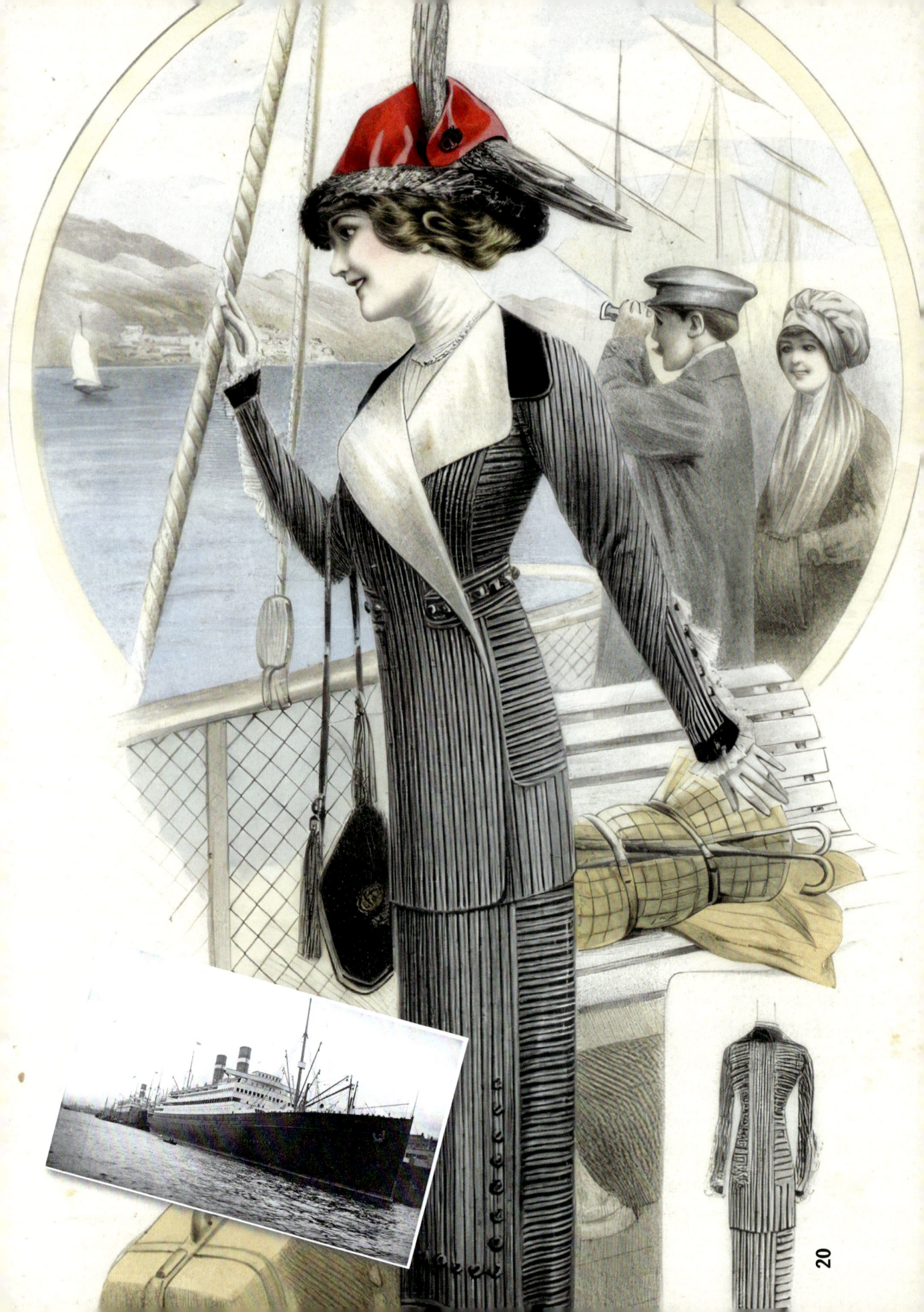

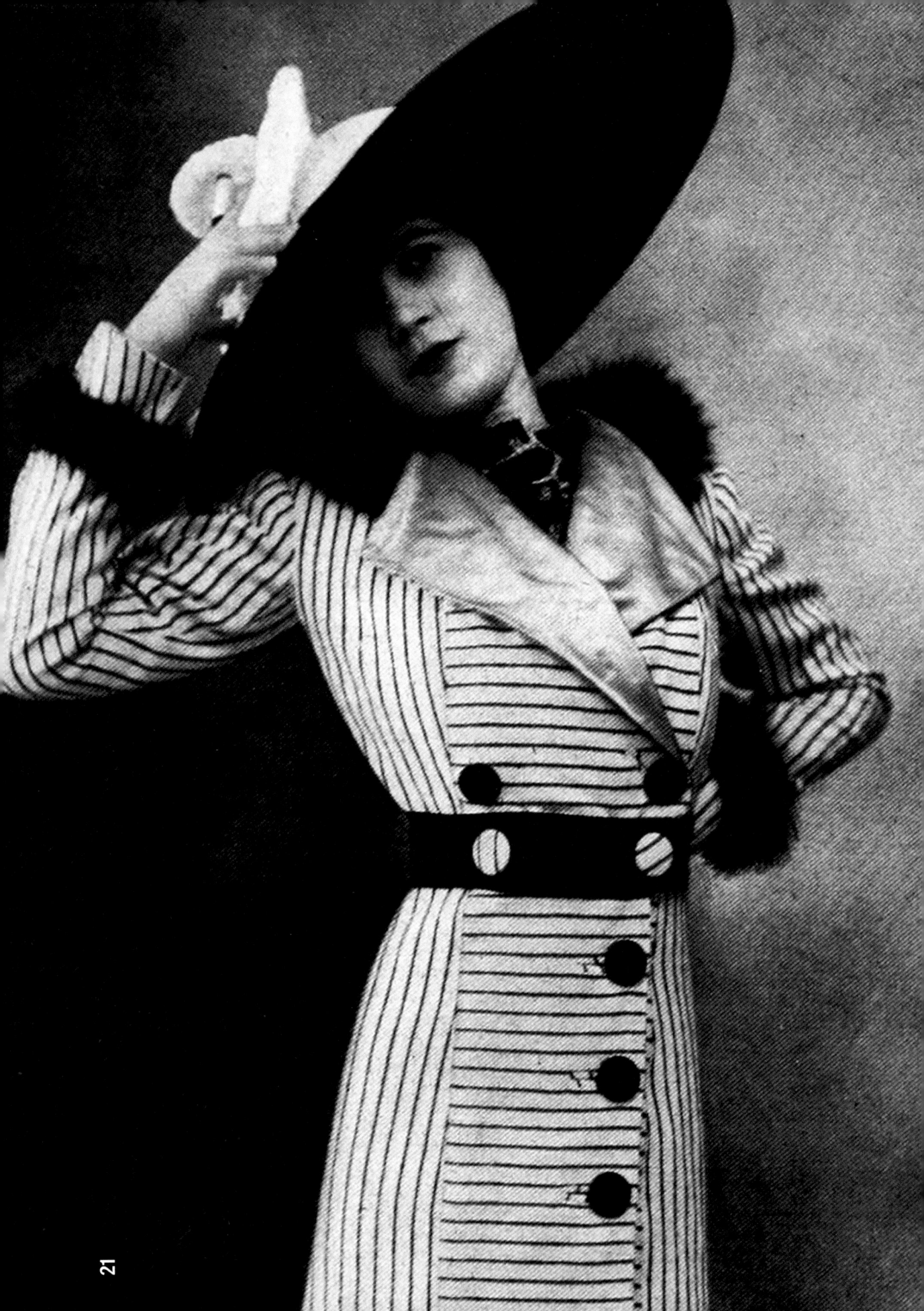

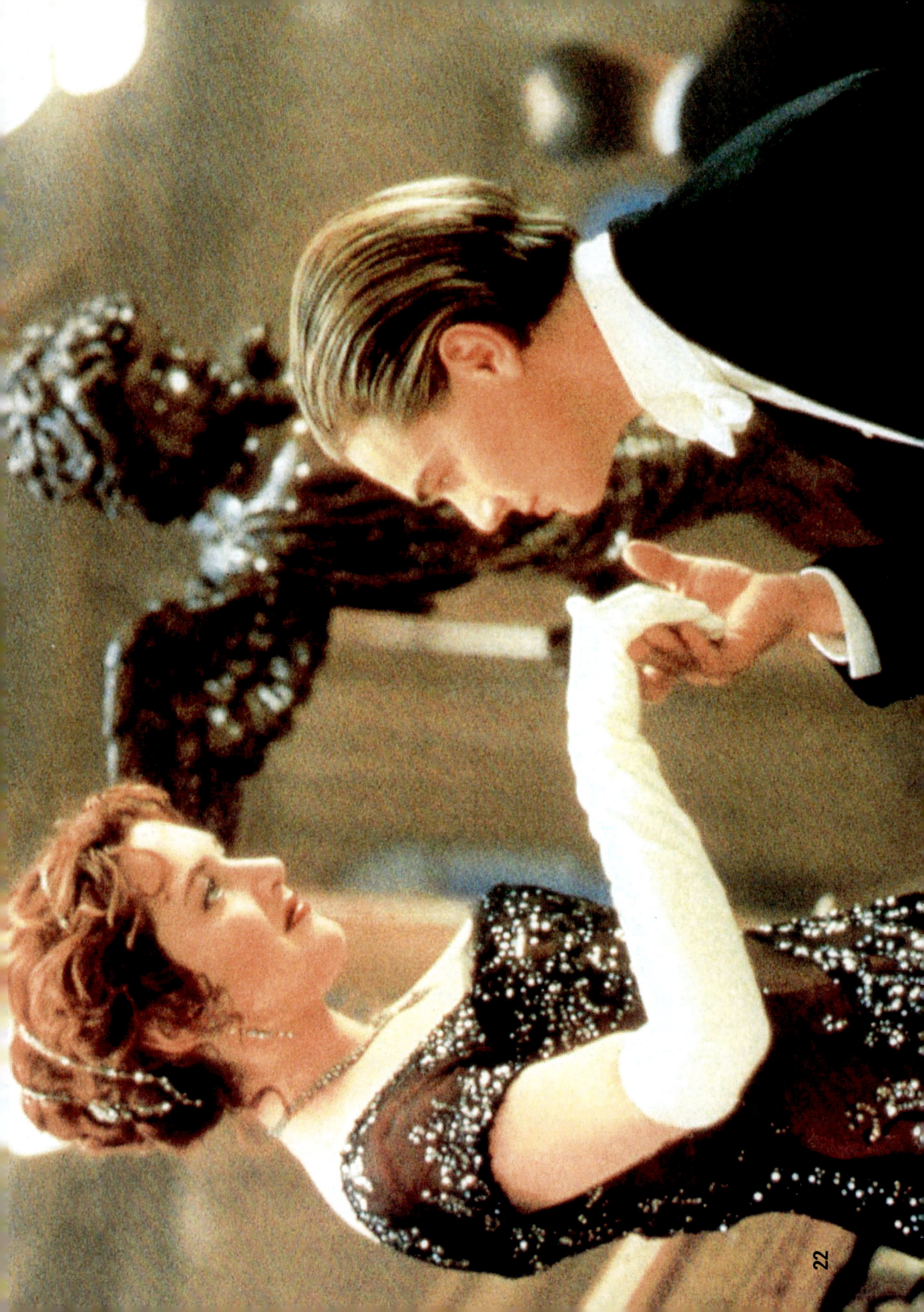

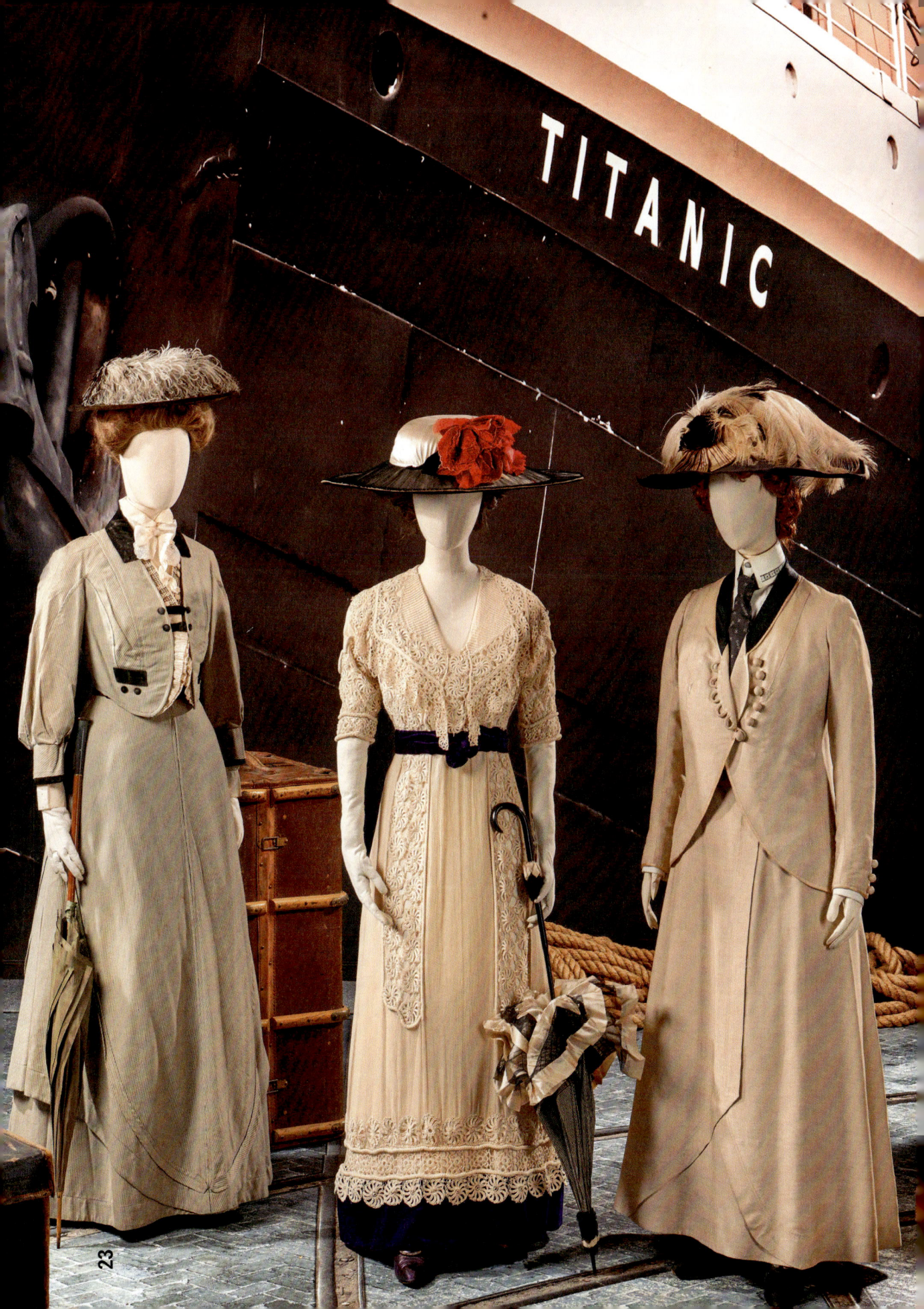

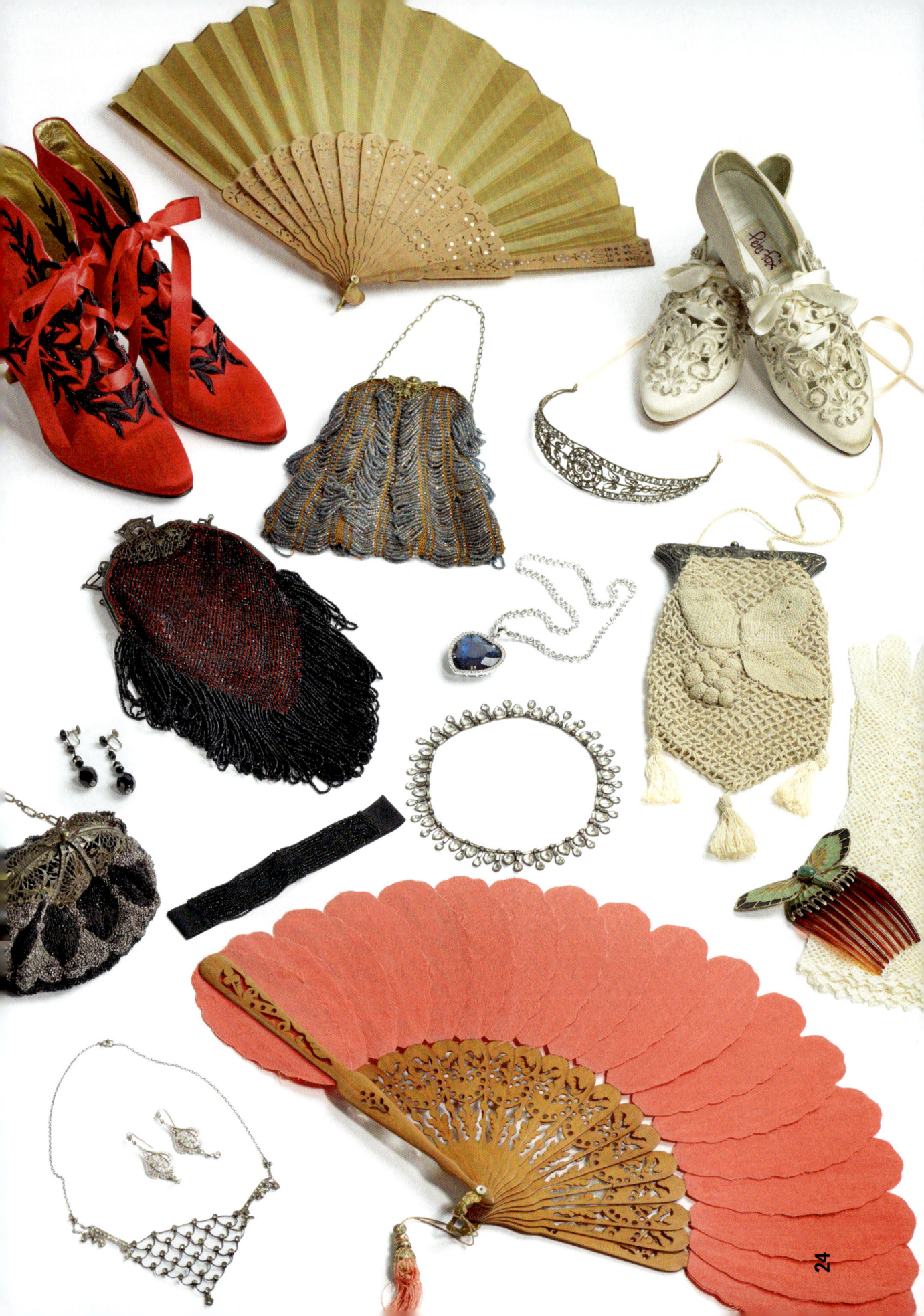

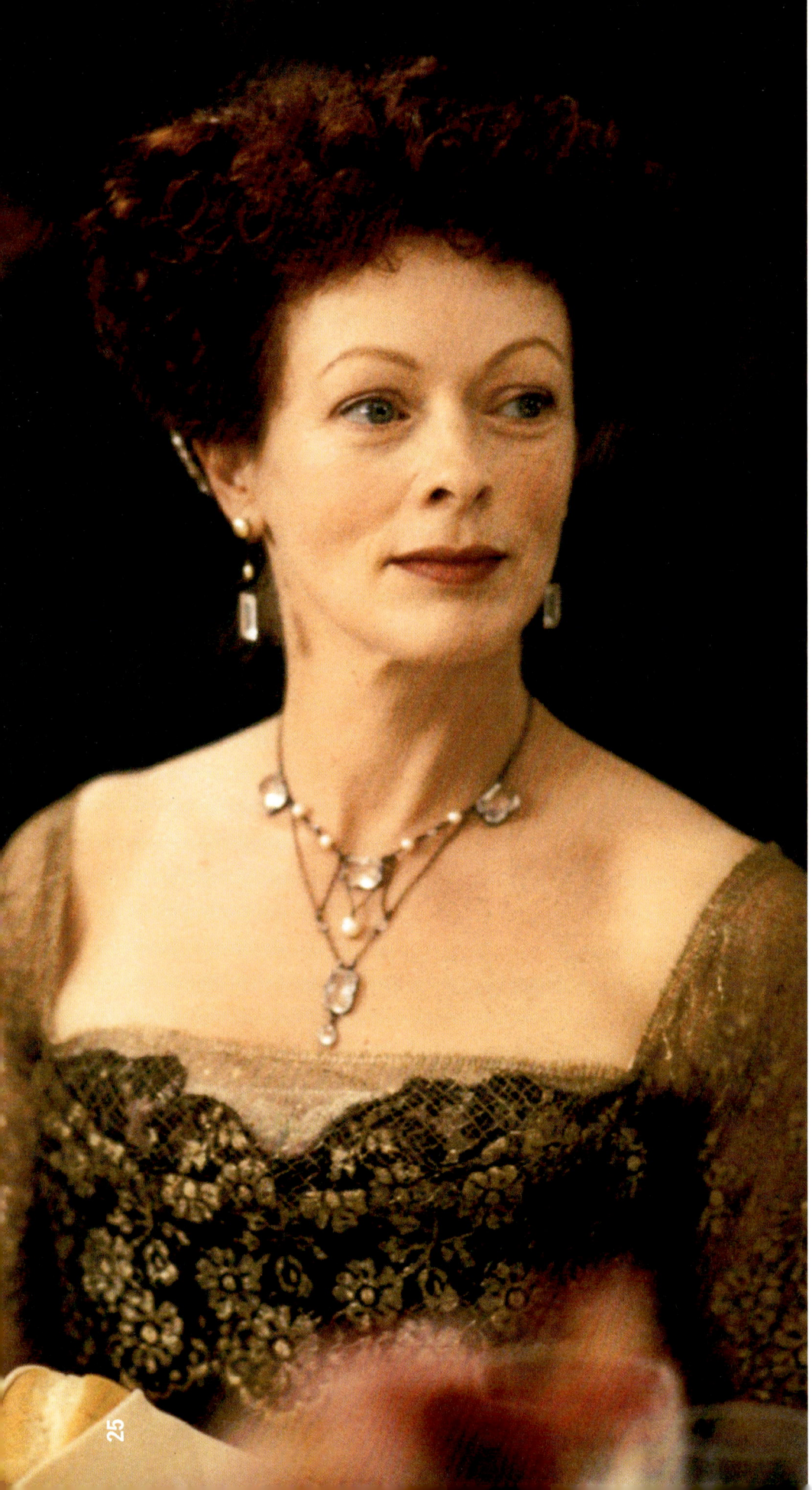

p. 20 Fashion plate, Travel costume on board, in: *La Femme Chic*, 1912, similar to the suit worn by Rose in *Titanic* (1997).

p. 20 The Rotterdam (1908-1939), the Holland-America Line's largest ship, July 1910.

p. 21 Linker & Co, Paris, Tailored suit ('Costume Tailleur pour l'après midi'), January 1912, in fashion magazine *Les Modes*, used as inspiration for film costumes for Rose (Kate Winslet) in the movie *Titanic* (1997).

p. 22 Rose (Kate Winslet) and Jack (Leonardo DiCaprio) in evening dress onboard the Titanic: pink silk evening dress with sequined black tulle, similar to a design by Maison Worth in the collection of the Victoria & Albert Museum, London. Jack borrows a dress suit in order to dine in first class, and combs back his hair in the style of a gentleman.

p. 23 Tailored suit (semi-ready-to-wear) in striped grey-green wool (two different bodices surviving), c. 1906-1909; Afternoon dress in white cotton and purple velvet, c. 1912-1914; possibly worn by Maria Henriëtte Röell-Rutgers van Rozenburg (1872-1923); Seiden Grieder, Zurich / Lucerne, Tailored suit in shantung with matching blouse, c. 1912.

p. 24 *Titanic* (1997) accessories, authentic from the 1910s, made for the film and replicas made after the film's release, courtesy of Robert Minozzo.

p. 25 Frances Fisher as Ruth Dewitt Bukater (Rose's mother) in *Titanic* (1997), wearing a low-cut evening gown.

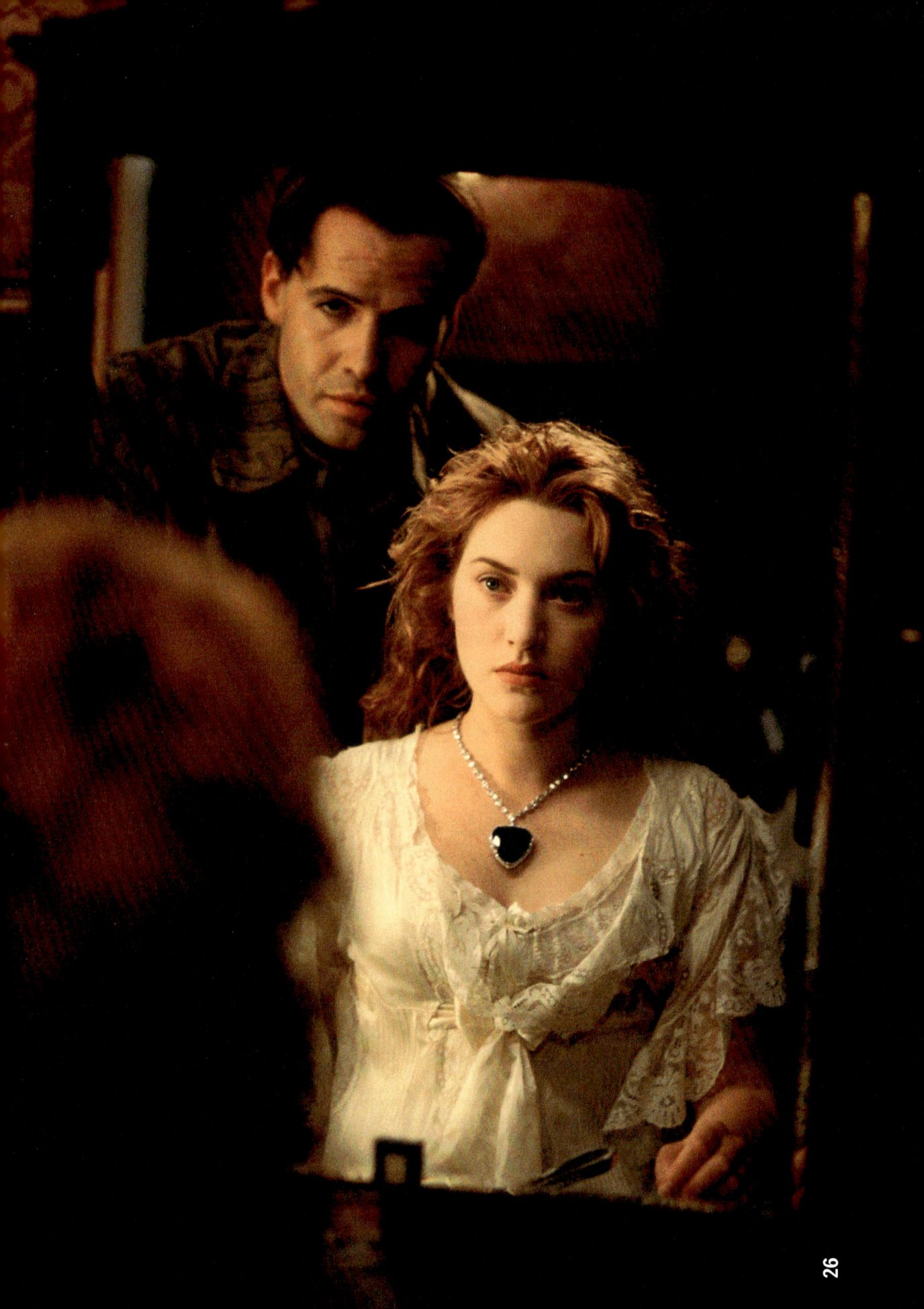

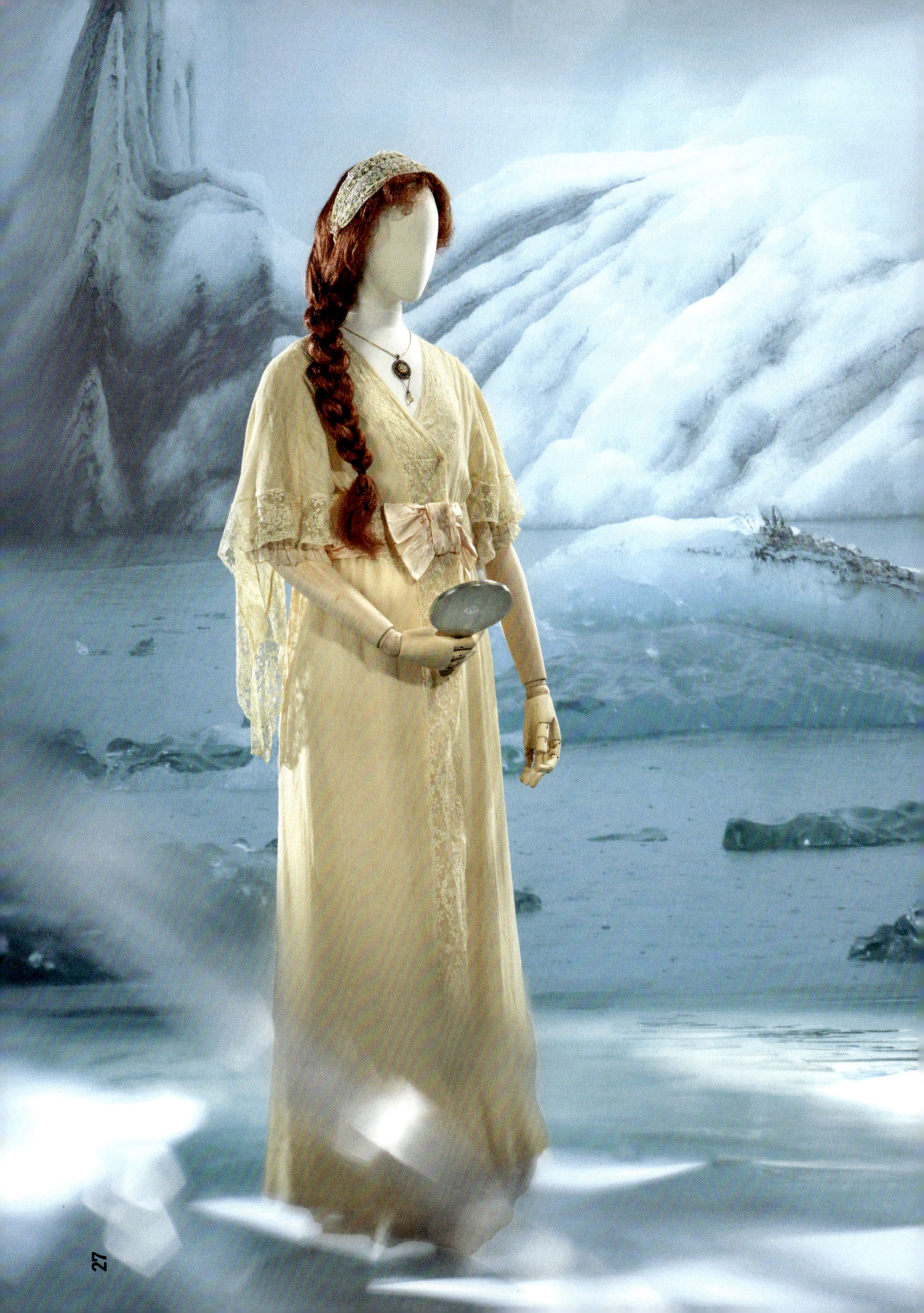

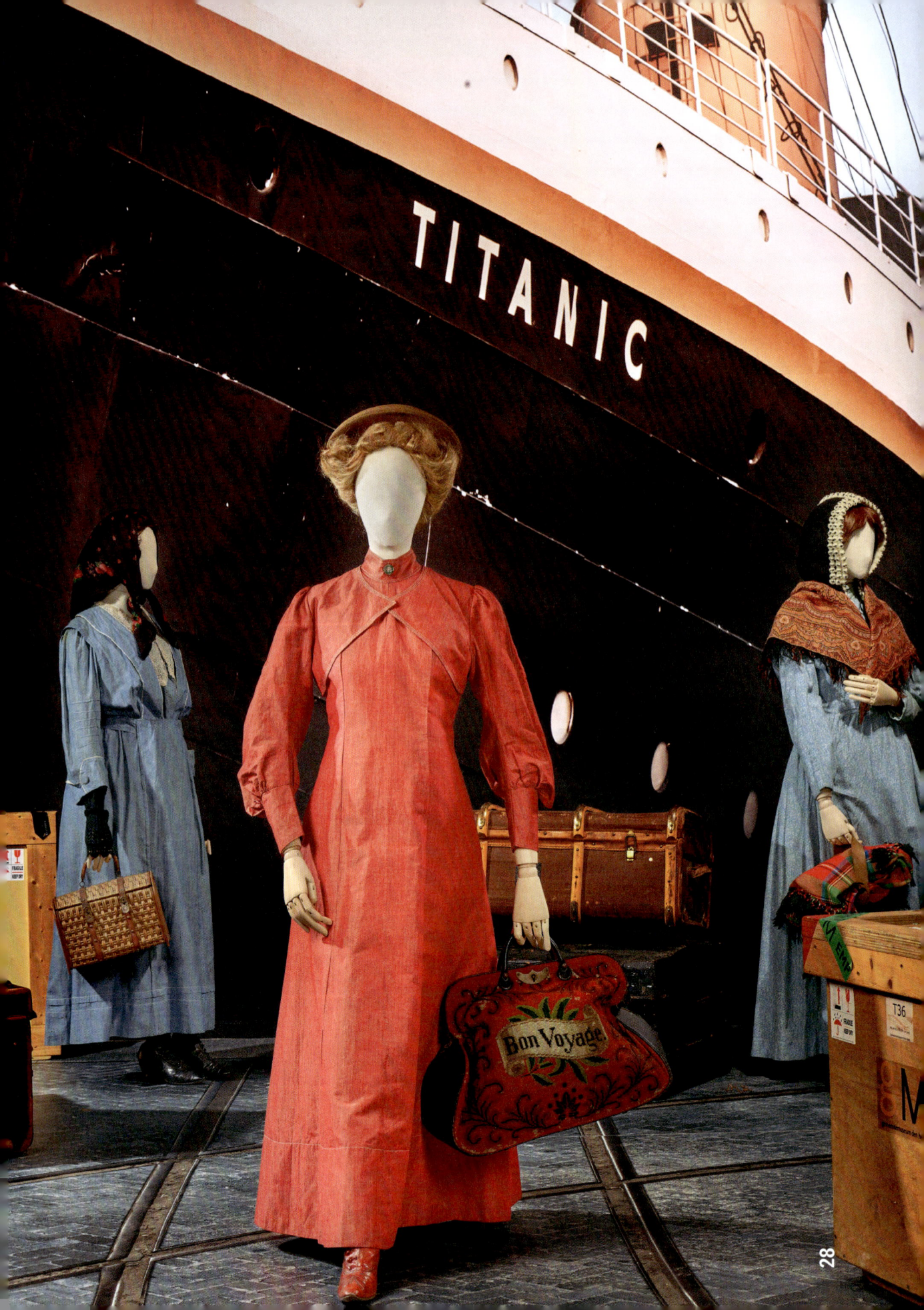

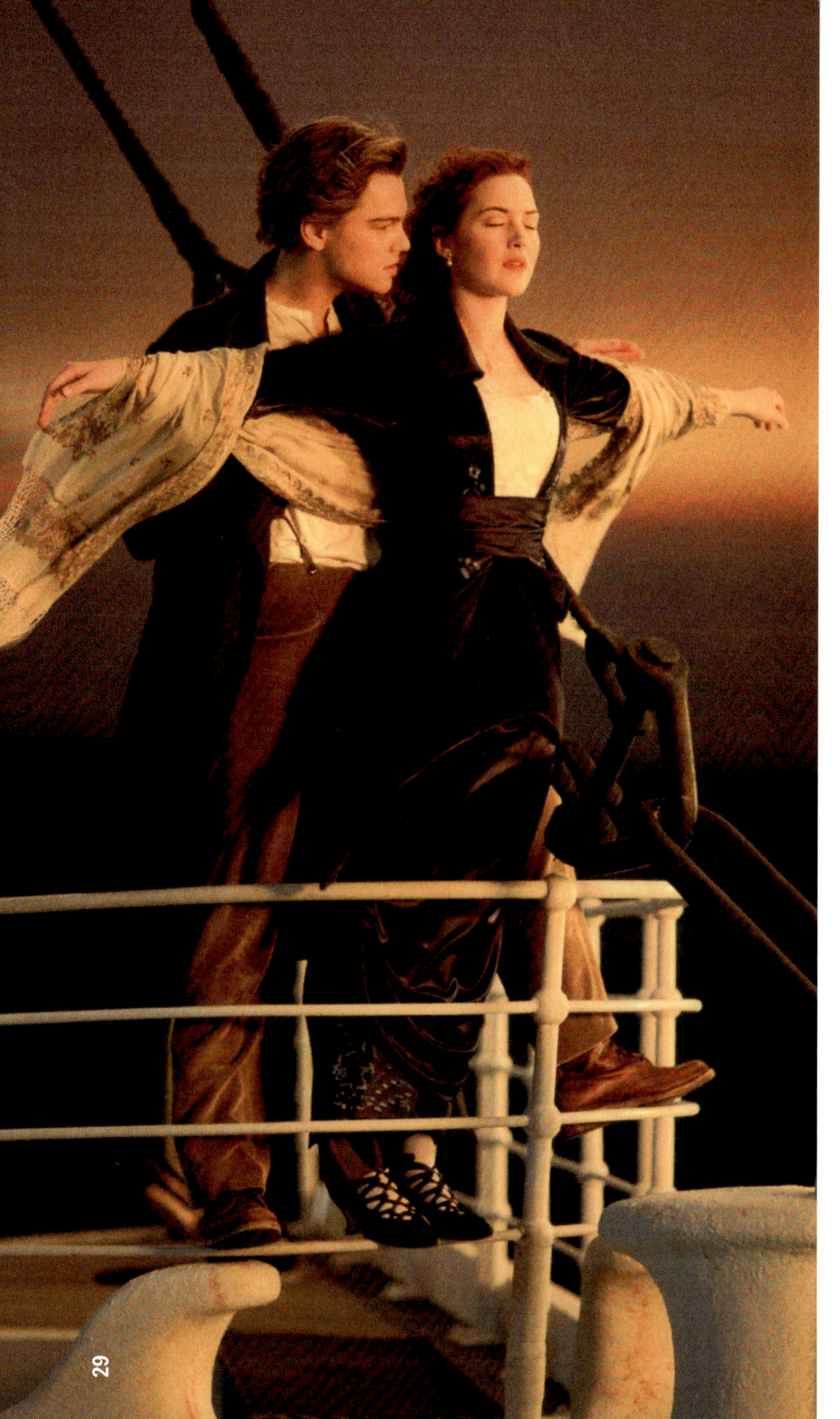

p. 26 Rose (Kate Winslet) and fiancé Cal (Billy Zane); he is hanging 'The Heart of the Ocean' around her neck; she is wearing a negligé that resembles a similar garment in the collection at Kunstmuseum Den Haag (also c. 1912).

p. 27 Negligé in cream wool crepe and machine lace, with a pink silk lining, c. 1912, from the wardrobe of Baroness Ada van Hardenbroek van Lockhorst (1889-1971).

p. 28 Gown in blue 'nurse's cotton', with white lace, c. 1910-1915; Reform dress (also used as maternity wear), red cotton denim, c. 1905; Maid's dress, white and blue printed cotton, c. 1880-1910.

p. 29 Leonardo DiCaprio as Jack and Kate Winslet as Rose in *Titanic*. Jack is wearing corduroy trousers, a shirt and a jacket; Rose is wearing a 'tea gown' (*The Flying Dress*) in indigo velvet and silk.

29

Titanic: A Microcosm of Society

We are dressed at our best and prepared to go down as gentlemen' These are the words for which American businessman Benjamin Guggenheim, son of an influential copper mining magnate, is best known. He died on the night of 14 April 1912, onboard the RMS Titanic. But not before first heroically helping women and children to the lifeboats. When Guggenheim realised that the situation was hopeless, he removed his lifejacket and donned his finest outfit: a black evening suit and top hat. He pinned a red rose to his lapel. 'No one can say that Ben Guggenheim died a coward', a survivor heard him call. He and his driver withdrew to the smoking room. His body was never found.

His daughter Peggy Guggenheim, thirteen at the time of the disaster, was profoundly affected by the death of her father. She inherited a modest fortune and devoted herself to collecting art. It almost became an obsession, part of her grieving process. But the works she acquired – by Picasso, Dalí and Magritte – laid the foundations of one of the most important art collections in the world, which these days can be viewed in Venice.

The story of Benjamin Guggenheim symbolises self-sacrifice, courage and the 'stiff upper lip' of the American and British elite in the early years of the last century. The idyllic image of that fatal night on the Titanic is of women and children waving their husbands and fathers goodbye from the lifeboats, the band playing until the bitter end and the captain speaking encouraging words to his passengers through a megaphone: 'Be brave, be British!' Although the disaster was full of extraordinary and poignant moments, the truth is probably somewhat different.

Yes, the band continued to play to boost morale. The strains of waltzes and ragtime – forerunner of jazz – could be heard until fifteen minutes before the ship disappeared beneath the waves. No solemn hymns, or anthems, as has been written. The music will however have been almost inaudible among the sounds of a dying ship, the exploding boilers, the steam escaping, the crew members shouting orders to each other, and the wooden floors creaking and cracking. Not a single musician survived the disaster and when, two days later, the body of the band leader Wallace Hartley was pulled out of the water, he was still clutching his violin. (The violin sold for a million euro at auction in 2013.) A courageous and heroic story it certainly was.

Historians cannot agree on Captain Smith and his role during the disaster. He was sleeping in his quarters when the ship hit the iceberg, but was soon made aware of the severity of the situation. 'There's water in five compartments', ship designer Thomas Andrews explained to him. Even with all the watertight doors closed, the seawater will simply have flowed over them. Andrews called it 'a mathematical certainty' that the Titanic would sink. From that point on, the captain, who was due to retire after this voyage, was in something akin to a state of shock. He knew there were too few lifeboats onboard for all the passengers. Smith mumbled some orders, initially stationed himself by the lifeboats, but then withdrew. No one heard him calling patriotic slogans through a megaphone from the bridge at any rate. His body, too, was never found.

It was mainly senior officers Murdoch and Lightoller who tried to oversee the evacuation. They each took responsibility for one side of the ship, where the lifeboats would be launched. While Murdoch allowed the occasional man to board a lifeboat, Lightoller adhered strictly to the 'women and children only' instruction, and not a single man made it through. Some of the first lifeboats to be launched were only half full, because they did not know how much weight they could carry. Clearly, too little consideration had been given to an emergency scenario, and the officers were unaware of what the captain already knew: the inescapable fate of the 'unsinkable' Titanic. As the bow plunged further into the water, and the desperation grew, more people were allowed onto each lifeboat. Many women and children from first class had already left by then. But the passengers from third class, whose accommodation was on the lower decks, were still trying to make their way out onto the deck. Many were crushed and drowned.

Tom Veldhuijzen

The men who escaped on the lifeboats and survived the disaster were later subjected to harsh criticism in the press and in public opinion. The best-known example was Bruce Ismay, the director of the White Star Line shipping company. He had frequently referred to the Titanic as unsinkable in press interviews, and in the days prior to the collision had pressed Captain Smith to increase speed on several occasions, so that the press could write of the ship's speedy passage to New York. Captain Smith acquiesced, even though warnings of icebergs already lay on his desk. Ismay got his newspaper head-lines, but not the ones he hoped for. Guggenheim received abundant praise for his heroic death, while Ismay was reviled as a coward for surviving.

It was not, incidentally, just men who sacrificed themselves for others. One poignant example was that of an elderly couple, Isodor and Ida Straus. They were travelling together first-class to America when disaster struck. Given their advanced age, they were invited to board a lifeboat, but as a man Isodor did not want to take another person's place. Ida therefore decided she too would remain on the sinking ship. Her husband begged her to reconsider, but she resolutely declared, 'We have lived together for many years. Where you go, I go.'

When the passengers boarded the Titanic in Southampton, they would have been amazed at the sight that awaited them. Mahogany sculptures and furni-ture, a Parisian salon, a Turkish steam bath and dazzling dinnerware and art. The paint was still fresh and no one had ever slept between the crisp white sheets. Every detail had been taken care of. In first class, members of the British aristocracy, American industrialists and actresses travelled in style from the British Empire to New York, the new world. Like Jeff Bezos, Beyoncé and David Beckham all sitting round the same dinner table.

The early years of the twentieth century were a time of unprecedented opti-mism. The world could be shaped, opportunities for success were boundless, anything was possible. You simply needed to strike gold (literally, in many cases). The passengers in second and third class also dreamed of a better future, a new start in a new country. This was 'la belle époque', as the French so aptly call it. And it was all to be reflected in the RMS Titanic and her two sister ships, the Olympic and the Brittanic, which were to be more luxurious, faster and bigger than ever before. The designers had no illusions, however, that other shipbuilders would soon surpass their achievements – so great was the faith in human progress.

The Titanic was built in a transitional period when the era of British domi-nance was coming to an end. The colonies, and the working class and suf-fragettes, were beginning to grow restless. America was slowly but surely evolving into a financial superpower, calmly biding its time before taking over Britain's dominant role. The world of the British aristocracy was also starting to show some cracks. It is no coincidence that the famous costume drama *Downton Abbey* starts with the Titanic disaster. Many British aristo-crats were desperately clinging on to their stately homes, but the roofs were leaking and they could not afford to heat every room. They had a title, but no money. On the other side of the ocean, there were people with money – huge amounts of it, even – but no title. And the Americans found a title, a 'lordship', very appealing. There were many marriages that united the old and the new world, which elicited some contempt from the British, who saw the Ameri-cans as 'vulgar' and 'ill-mannered' with their newfound wealth.

But times were changing rapidly. The First World War began within three years of the sinking of the Titanic. All optimism about the future was lost in the trenches. Millions of people lost their lives. Revolutions brought global empires to an end. And that is what makes the story of the Titanic so endless-ly fascinating. It is not just the drama, tragedy, heroism and romanticism of a sinking ship; it also symbolises the decline of a class-based society and the advent of a new world order.

'..and prepared to go down as gentlemen'

The endless fascination of the Titanic

A letter from a surviving passenger, a first-class dinner menu, a watch that belonged to a billionaire, a door from the final scene of a feature film: the media is full of such things. And what connects them all? The Titanic, a ship with a neverending history. This passenger liner has always appealed to the popular imagination since it sank during its maiden voyage over a century ago. How so? Why do we continue to remember this particular ship, even though there have been much bigger maritime disasters? Why is the Titanic so firmly rooted in the collective memory?

To understand this, we have to go back in time, to the period before the First World War, an uninhibited time, when anything seemed possible. Though there were of course the constraints of class. If you were wealthy and a member of the upper class, the world was your oyster. If you were poor, part of the lowest class in society, it was almost impossible to escape your situation. But you would not know any different. The world was small to you, while for the wealthy, the sky was the limit.

And then suddenly there was this huge ship, the biggest and most luxurious of all time: the Titanic, built as the second of three sister ships (along with the Olympic, 1911 and the Britannic, 1915) for Britain's White Star Line. The ship represented a movable world for all who sailed on her, from the wealthiest to the poor migrants who were keen to try their luck elsewhere. And this fabulous ship was lost on its very first voyage, in the night of 14 April 1912, after hitting an iceberg. It sank within three hours, taking some 1500 victims to the bottom of the ocean with it. Rank and station were irrelevant in those final hours. Everyone was equal, and everyone fought for survival. The disaster changed the world for good. No more lack of inhibition.

What exactly happened that night? The Titanic was sailing across the North Atlantic and, despite the fact that several ships in the area had warned of icebergs, it ploughed on, full steam ahead, straight into disaster. Later, it was said that nature had beaten humanity, that pride had come before the fall. The collision with the iceberg was of course the immediate cause of the disaster, but there may have been more factors. It is said human error was made in the vessel's construction, and the inexperienced crew made many mistakes during and after the collision. There is also a book that almost seems to foretell the disaster. In 1898 American author Morgan Robertson (1861-1915) published *Futility, or the Wreck of the Titan*. The story told in this novel bears a striking resemblance to the events of fourteen years later associated with the Titanic – the very name is almost identical!

Since this was its maiden voyage, there are few images of the ship itself. Most of the ones that existed were on board and ended up on the ocean floor. This was soon resolved, as its sister ship the Olympic was almost identical. And Captain Edward Smith (1850-1912) of the Titanic had previously captained the Olympic, so moving images of him are from his time on the Olympic.

And where does the idea that the Titanic was practically unsinkable come from? The industry journal *The Shipbuilder* published a detailed description of the vessel in 1911. One section focuses on the watertight sliding doors with which it was fitted. The captain could simply flick an electric switch and close the doors immediately, isolating those compartments from the rest of the ship – making it 'practically unsinkable'. This was picked up on by other media, except that they omitted the word 'practically'. If three or four compartments sprang a leak, the Titanic would still remain afloat. Unfortunately, when the ship hit the iceberg, five compartments were damaged – one too many. Several newspapers that were the first to report the disaster stated that everyone had been rescued. Unfortunately, the reality soon proved to be otherwise. The icy waters did not discriminate. Anyone who ended up in the ocean was lost. Just over 300 bodies were recovered; almost 1200 people disappeared without a trace. It was 'women and children first', so it was mainly male passengers and crew who died. Some 60% of first-class passengers were rescued, around 44% from second class, and 25% from third. The third-class passengers had a smaller chance of survival than those in first

Ron de Brand

and second, not only because more effort was made to rescue the rich than the poor, but also because of the inadequate access to the lifeboats. They were on deck, which was most easily accessible for first- and second-class passengers. The passengers in third class normally had no access to the deck.

After the disaster, many people wanted to know more about what happened, and how the passengers had fared. Who had survived, who had died? What were their stories? Reports began to appear in the newspapers, illustrated with photographs. The public lapped up the news of the celebrities of the day, including millionaire John Jacob Astor, the richest man on board, and businessman Isidor Straus and his wife Ida. And let us not forget 'our' George Reuchlin, the director of Rotterdam's Holland-America Line. They all lost their lives. Reports on other passengers, including famous writers, industrialists and athletes, also helped enhance the 'glamour' of the Titanic, the disaster and the public's fascination.

What were the consequences of the disaster? There were several investigations, in which a number of experts were questioned. This led to recommendations to improve the safety of shipping. Henceforth, there would have to be a place for every passenger on a lifeboat. The Titanic's lifeboats had room for only 1178 of the 2207 passengers. Yet the ship was not operating illegally, as shipping laws were different at the time.

Other shipping accidents that claimed many more victims and had much greater impact followed the Titanic disaster – particularly during the Second World War. Take the Wilhelm Gustloff, for example, which was sunk by Soviet torpedoes in the Baltic in January 1945. It was carrying refugees, soldiers and sailors. According to the most recent estimate, it claimed over 9000 lives, making it the biggest maritime disaster in history in terms of victims on a single ship – but who has heard of it? The story of the Titanic is much more appealing, has been told in countless books and films, and is surrounded by a host of myths and unanswered questions. The Titanic is still a byword for something unexpectedly going wrong. We can all identify with one of the passengers. The story of the Titanic therefore tells us a lot about who we are as people, and that is why it will remain a neverending story.

Whole libraries of books have been written about the Titanic disaster, and it would be impossible to list them all. A selection of interesting titles is given below, however.

Robert D. Ballard, Rick Archbold, Ken Marschall, *The Discovery of the Titanic*, New York 1989.

Bruce Beveridge, Art Braunschweiger, *Titanic: The ship Magnificent*, Stroud 2008, 2 vol.

Cathalijne Boland, *Reuchlin's reis. De Holland-Amerika Lijn en de landverhuizers*, Amsterdam 2023.

Ron Brand, "De kamers op dit schip zijn wel driemaal zoo groot als de salon bij ons thuis',

George Reuchlin, een Rotterdamse passagier aan boord van de Titanic', in: *Rotterdams jaarboekje*, 11th series, vol. 10. (2012), pp. 84-101.

Ron Brand, 'Nederlanders op de 'Titanic'', in: *De Blauwe Wimpel* vol. 67, 2012, no. 4, pp. 142-144.

John P. Eaton, Charles A. Haas, *Titanic: Triumph and Tragedy*, Wellingborough 1986

Edward P. de Groot, *75 jaar Titanic*, Alkmaar 1987 (Republished as *Titanic*, Alkmaar 1996).

Edward P. de Groot, *De Titanic. De ware verhalen*, Alkmaar 2012.

Tom McCluskie, Michael Sharpe, Leo Marriott, *Titanic & Her Sisters Olympic & Britannic*, London 1998.

Dirk Musschoot, *100 jaar Titanic. Het verhaal van de Belgen en de Nederlanders*, Tielt 2011.

There are a few Dutch stories associated with the Titanic, with a number of surprising and unexpected connections. Firstly, there were three Dutchmen on board during the voyage to New York – all in connection with work. They were ship's cook Hendrik ('Hennie') Bolhuis, stoker Wessel van der Brugge, and Johan George ('George') Reuchlin Esq., one of the directors of the Holland-America Line (HAL) in Rotterdam, who was making the voyage out of professional interest.[1] All three lost their lives in the disaster; their bodies have never been recovered. Bolhuis was from Groningen. He trained as a chef and had been working abroad since 1910, at hotels in Brussels, Monte Carlo, Paris, Ostende and London. In 1911 he was employed to work in the kitchen of the à-la-carte restaurant on the Olympic, the Titanic's sister ship, which went into service earlier. In 1912 Bolhuis became one of the 81 staff working in the kitchen on the Titanic.[2] Van der Brugge was born in Delfshaven, lived in several places in the Netherlands, and also briefly in Johannesburg, South Africa. He had been working in shipping since 1906/1907. He was one of the 176 stokers working in the searing heat of the Titanic's boiler room.[3] The stokers continued working after the ship hit the iceberg, to prevent the scorching hot boilers from exploding. Only one in three of them survived the disaster.[4]

George Reuchlin was the son of Otto Reuchlin, one of the founders of the Rotterdam steamship company that later became known as the Netherlands-America Steamship Company (NASM). George was being primed for a role in the family firm, and was destined to follow in this father's footsteps. To learn the business inside out, he worked (and studied) in Bremen, Paris, New York and Vienna, eventually becoming part of the management team in Rotterdam. On 10 April 1912 he took the night boat to Harwich on his way to Belfast, where he boarded the Titanic. There, he had a meeting with Thomas Andrews of Harland & Wolff, which built the Titanic, since NASM had also ordered a ship – the Statendam – from the same shipyard. The Statendam may have been slightly smaller than the Titanic, but it was certainly as luxurious.[5] It was for this reason that George Reuchlin was travelling to New York on the Titanic, to get a taste of what his firm could expect of the Statendam.[6] He was very impressed with what he found on board, and wrote in a letter to his wife Agatha ('Athie') Reuchlin-Elink Schuurman, sent from on board the brand-new ship, 'I have been given a very good outside cabin with bathroom, and am very comfortably installed.'[7]

Sea travel was a dangerous undertaking. Ships were regularly lost. To reassure his wife, George wrote to her regularly by post or telegram during his voyages, to let her know that he was well, and indeed he did so while on board the Titanic. He also wrote two postcards to his oldest children, Henri aged five and Caroline aged three. The cards were posted in Cherbourg and arrived at the family home in Rotterdam after his death. George was also accustomed to sending telegrams while at sea, whenever his ship was in the vicinity of a coastal radio station.[8] He sent Athie a telegram from Harwich, assuring her that he was fine. The final marconigram from George was sent from the Titanic via Cape Race, Newfoundland (Canada) as it passed the coastal radio station on the evening that the ship sank. It read: 'continuing nmoth [smooth] and fair greetings.'[9]

George Reuchlin travelled in a first-class cabin on the Titanic. We do not know exactly which cabin was his. The first-class cabins were the height of luxury, decorated in different styles. The Hague firm of H.P. Mutters & Sons supplied some impressive interiors, twelve in total in various styles, for both the Olympic and the Titanic, as well as furniture for the veranda, the palm court, the smoking lounge and the private first-class deck.[10] They included interiors in a 'modern' style, Louis XVI style, empire style, Queen Anne style and traditional Dutch Style (seventeenth-century style, in other words).[11] George Reuchlin was familiar with Mutters. The firm was a highly reputed supplier of interiors and furnishings, both for buildings and for luxury liners. Mutters had been working on ship interiors for the Holland-America Line

(HAL) since 1888. This was the name used by NASM from 1896 onwards. In 1909 Mutters also supplied some of the interior (panelling, ceiling ornaments and finishings) for the home George had built on Calandstraat in Rotterdam.[12] Since 1896, the HAL had had its ships built by Harland & Wolff in Belfast, as Dutch shipyards were too small for such large vessels. This made the company all the more eager to add a Dutch touch to the interior by ordering from Mutters.

The British shipping company White Star Line also commissioned the firm to supply the interior elements for the Titanic mentioned above. They were made in The Hague and installed on board the Titanic by staff of Mutters around March 1912, at the shipyard in Belfast.[13] There are original photographs of the interiors in The Hague municipal archives. For the cabins in traditional Dutch style, Mutters ordered wall coverings from the Hengelosche Trijpweverij fabric company in Hengelo. The firm supplied printed velvet with a floral motif called *Superbe*, most probably in burgundy. The *Superbe* pattern was printed by the Hengelosche Trijpweverij using an original eighteenth-century roller.[14] (p.61)

Mutters was also invited to supply interiors for the Statendam, the ship ordered by the HAL in 1912.[15] When the First World War broke out in 1914, the ship was still under construction at Harland & Wolff. It was commandeered by the British Admiralty in 1916 for use as a troop ship, sailing under the name Justitia. In 1918 it was torpedoed by a German submarine, so it never served as a civilian passenger ship. Meanwhile, the fittings for a bedroom that Mutters had made for the ship had remained in The Hague. They consisted of two beds and nightstands, a wardrobe, two chairs, a dressing table and stool, and a chest of drawers. They passed into private ownership, and ended up in the collection of the Maritime Museum in Rotterdam. The current upholstery in a floral fabric is a later addition. The original upholstery was ochre-coloured.[16] (p.49)

1 See also Ron Brand, "De kamers op dit schip zijn wel driemaal zoo groot als de salon bij ons thuis": George Reuchlin, een Rotterdamse passagier aan boord van de Titanic' in: *Rotterdams jaarboekje*, series 11, vol. 10. (2012), pp. 84-101.

2 Cathalijne Boland, *Reuchlins Reis. De Holland-Amerika Lijn en de landverhuizers*, Amsterdam 2023, p. 391; https://anderetijden.nl/aflevering/177/Ten-onder-met-de-Titanic accessed in July 2025.

3 https://www.encyclopedia-titanica.org/titanic-victim/wessel-adrianus-van-der-brugge.html accessed in July 2025.

4 'Nieuwe details uit 3D-scans vullen verhaal ondergang Titanic aan', *NOS Nieuws*, 9 April 2025, accessed in July 2025.

5 Boland 2023, pp. 276-278.

6 Boland 2023, p. 12.

7 Boland 2023, p. 279.

8 Boland 2023. P. 11.

9 Boland 2023, p. 287.

10 G.H. Banis, *Hengelo Velours. De Hengelosche Trijpweverij 1901-2001*, Delden 2023, pp. 272-277. Thanks to Gert Banis, who alerted Kunstmuseum Den Haag to this fact.

11 Titus M. Eliëns en A. Joshua van Scherpenzeel, *Koninklijk goedgekeurd: Horrix en Mutters: twee Haagse meubelfabrikanten*, exh.cat. (Gemeentemuseum Den Haag) Zwolle 2010; Banis 2023, pp. 274-277.

12 Boland 2023, pp. 244-246.

13 Banis 2023, p. 273.

14 Banis 2023, p. 266. Mr H.P. Mutters himself attended the launch of the Titanic, but declined an invitation to travel first-class on the ship. If he had travelled on the ship and gone down with it, the history of the famous Hague firm would have been very different. Thanks to Ron Brand for this information, July 2025.

15 Information from the Maritime Museum Rotterdam, with thanks to Irene Jacobs and Ron Brand. The inventory number of the interior is M3724.

16 It was said, as has been recorded at the Maritime Museum Rotterdam, that Mutters made another six to eight similar sets of bedroom furnishings that were installed on the Titanic. According to the donor, the Maritime Museum Rotterdam informs us, details of this order still exist in the Mutters archive, kept at The Hague city archives. Research in The Hague city archives uncovered the fact that the 'modern'-style interior most resembled the light blue set at the Maritime Museum Rotterdam.

Close your eyes and imagine a fortune seeker. Do you see a nineteenth-century European? I do. In Dutch discourse about migration, a fortune seeker ('gelukszoeker') is someone who moves to another place in search of a better life. In 2025, the stereotypical image of a fortune seeker is someone who comes to Europe to start a new life. Yet in the nineteenth and twentieth century, there were millions of people who wanted to leave Europe, believing there were better opportunities elsewhere. These people are perfect examples of the 'fortune seeker' phenomenon.

Whether to move to the other side of the world is a big decision. It is a difficult undertaking nowadays, but it was even more so in the nineteenth and early twentieth centuries (in most cases). The voyage would take days, weeks even, rather than hours. When you arrived, you could not simply take out your smartphone and send a message to your family and friends. You could not facetime or call people whenever you wanted. In all likelihood, you would never see your family or your home again. So what prompted people to take such a step?

Between 1820 and 1920 more than 50 million people emigrated from Europe to the United States, Canada, Australia, Brazil and Argentina.[1] Shipping companies like the Holland-America Line, the Red Star Line and the White Star Line played a vital role in scaling up transatlantic migration. These companies, along with technological developments in steam shipping, made the voyage more affordable, safer and quicker than ever before.[2] The competition between the shipping companies accelerated technological progress and the reduction in prices. Between 1853 and 1913 the average travel time between Liverpool and New York fell from around forty days to just eight days – a reduction of 80%.[3] In 1856 only one in 28 emigrants crossed the Atlantic by steamship. Four years later, it was one in three.[4] Migration was no longer limited to the elite.

Anyone who studies the history of migration will come across the concept of 'push and pull factors'. Push factors are the reasons why someone wants or has to leave their place of origin. Pull factors are what makes someone want to migrate to a particular place.
One example of a push factor for the late nineteenth century European emigrants was the severe agricultural crisis in Western Europe between 1878 and 1895. It was caused by large quantities of grain being imported from North America within a very short period of time, as the introduction and development of the steamship had also made it profitable to transport goods across the ocean. The large imports from North America caused the value of local agricultural produce to plummet.

Farmers in Western Europe were forced to work more efficiently to compete with North American farmers, who seemed to have infinite acres of farmland at their disposal. Those who could afford it introduced agricultural machinery on their farms. This, in turn, meant that fewer workers were needed on the land. Unemployment grew, and people ventured farther and farther from home in search of gainful employment, many of them moving to urban areas, or even emigrating.

The next question was, where to go? The destinations can be explained by pull factors. Nineteenth and twentieth century European emigrants had a rosy image of what they knew as the 'New World'. They saw North and South America as a paradise of boundless possibility. There was enough land 'available' for everyone to farm, there was enough work to earn a decent income, and there was the adventure of the unknown.

But the 'New World' was not new at all. The conversion of more and more land to farmland was accompanied by the forced displacement and oppression of the original inhabitants of this 'New World'. The arrival of newcomers drove the original population ever further westwards. The apparently endless

Lillian Boutros

possibilities, 'available' land and adventure that the migrants imagined cannot be seen in isolation from this process.

Political and religious persecution, and the violence that came with it, was another important push factor among nineteenth and early twentieth century European emigrants. Those who fled such oppression left for the 'New World' with the dream of living in freedom, being able to openly live by their religious or political beliefs. This, in turn, also formed an important pull factor in the destination countries, particularly the United States.
Countless push and pull factors played a role in the large-scale European emigration that took place in the nineteenth and early twentieth centuries. The combination of push and pull factors is like a jigsaw puzzle that looks different for each group and each individual.

Somewhere on the Atlantic Ocean, as passengers on a steamship, these migrants would transform from emigrants to immigrants. They changed from oppressed minorities and economically vulnerable members of society to newcomers in search of a better life. The combination of their economic motives for emigration, their hopes of a life with more freedom, and their adventurous optimism about the 'New World' made these emigrants the prototypical fortune seekers.

[1] Timothy J. Hatton and J. Williamson, *Migration and the International Labour Market: 1850-1939*, London 2005, p. 44.
[2] Torsten Feys, *The Battle for the Migrants: The Introduction of Steamshipping on the North Atlantic and Its Impact on the European Exodus*. Research in Maritime History, Liverpool 2012, p. 67.
[3] Timothy J. Hatton, 'Time on the Crossing: Emigrant Voyages across the Atlantic, 1853–1913', *European Review of Economic History* 28:1, 2024, pp. 120–133.
[4] Torsten Feys, *The Battle for the Migrants: The Introduction of Steamshipping on the North Atlantic and Its Impact on the European Exodus*. Research in Maritime History, Liverpool 2012, p. 51.

Lillian Boutros is assistant curator at Fenix, Rotterdam's new art museum about migration, housed in a historic warehouse. In the nineteenth and twentieth centuries, millions of migrants departed from the quays around this warehouse to the other side of the world.

In a luxury cabin Rose DeWitt-Bukater – the main character in the film *Titanic* – sets out various works of art: a still life by Paul Cézanne, one of Claude Monet's famous water lilies, and a pastel drawing by Edgar Degas. When asked who made one of the paintings she unpacks, an abstracted image of a naked woman, Rose casually answers, 'Something Picasso'. In the background her fiancé affably mumbles that this Picasso character will never amount to anything.

Her art collection ranks Rose among the avant-garde of modern collectors. In the age of the Titanic, the United States was a particularly lucrative market for art dealers like Paul Durand-Ruel, who did indeed tempt the rich elite there to purchase Monet's fairytale images of the water lilies on his pond. Interestingly, appreciation of his work declined shortly afterwards, in favour of the aforementioned Pablo Picasso. Compared with Picasso's radical new approach to perspective and form, Monet's water lilies suddenly appeared decorative, superficial and, therefore, passé. (p.153)

Rose presents as quite the revolutionary art connoisseur; in the film she appears to be in possession of perhaps the most iconic work by Picasso, his famous painting *Les Demoiselles d'Avignon* (1907). Although he made this monumental figure painting well before the Titanic disaster, he did not present it to the outside world until four years after, in 1916. In 1924 the work did indeed end up in the hands of an art collector, French couturier Jacques Doucet, who bought it directly from Picasso. The painting is now in the collection of the Museum of Modern Art in New York, so most definitely not at the bottom of the Atlantic Ocean. The observant viewer will also see that the version Rose nonchalantly carries across the room is smaller than the original, and that the postures and faces of the figures are not all the same. The Degas, featuring a graceful ballerina, is also, on closer inspection, a fairly liberal interpretation of *l'Étoile*, now at the Musée d'Orsay in Paris. Which rather tosses the art-historical accuracy of the film overboard.

The scene is of course intended mainly to define Roses' character. Her progressive tastes – like her wild red curls – reflect her free and passionate spirit. Art explains her class-busting romance with the penniless artist Jack. He, too, is ahead of his time. The sensual nude drawing he makes of his lover on board the ship, at her request ('Draw me like one of your French girls'), is more in the style of 1997 than 1912.

In this respect, *Titanic* as a historical costume drama is also like a portrait of the 1990s. Although the names Monet and Picasso are no less famous, nowadays a director would probably opt to illustrate Rose's liberal attitude with female artists of the time, like Berthe Morisot and Suzanne Valadon. Her short-sighted fiancé would then complain of the waste of money by grumbling that 'those female artists will never amount to anything'.

Art with character

Frouke van Dijke

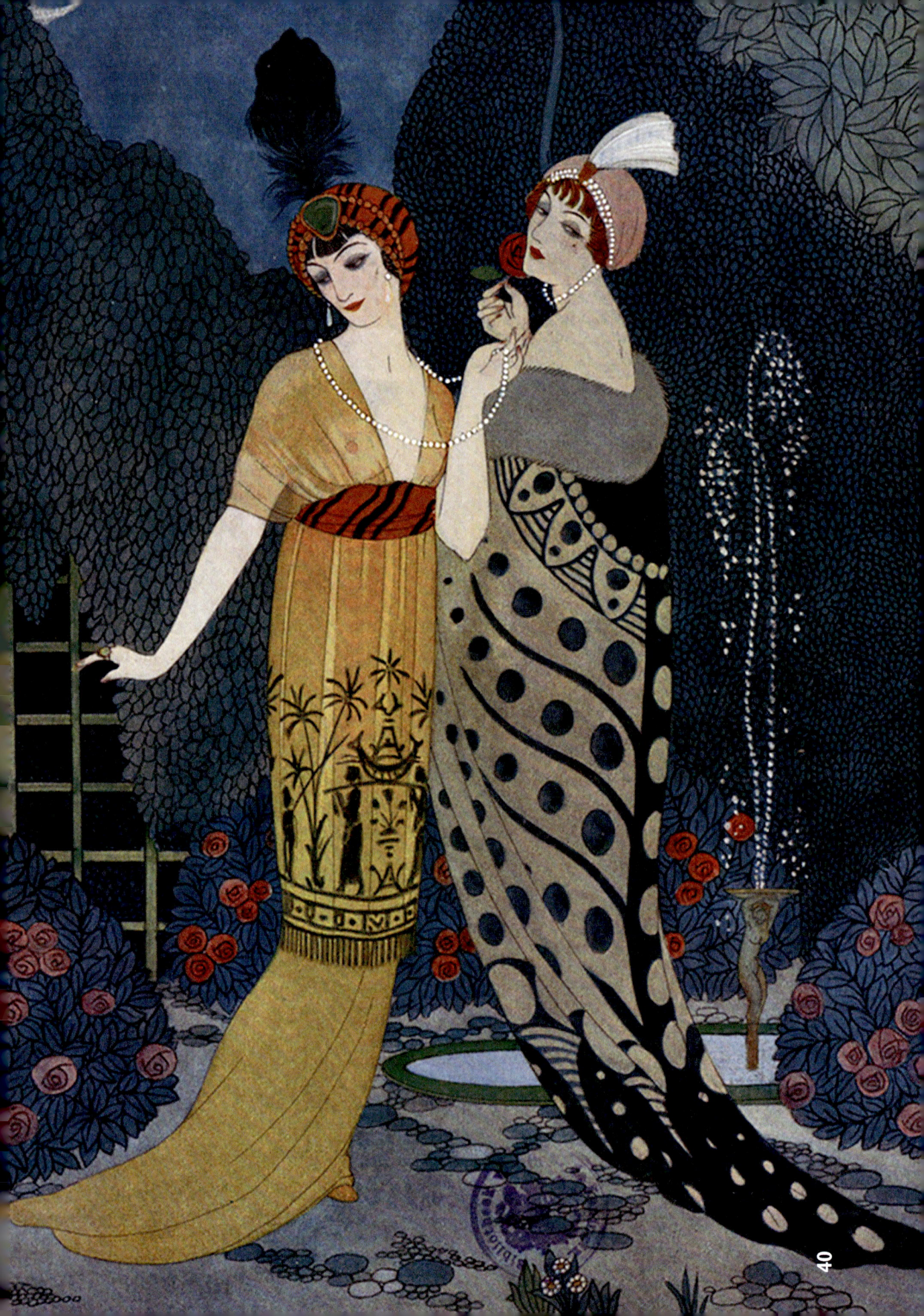

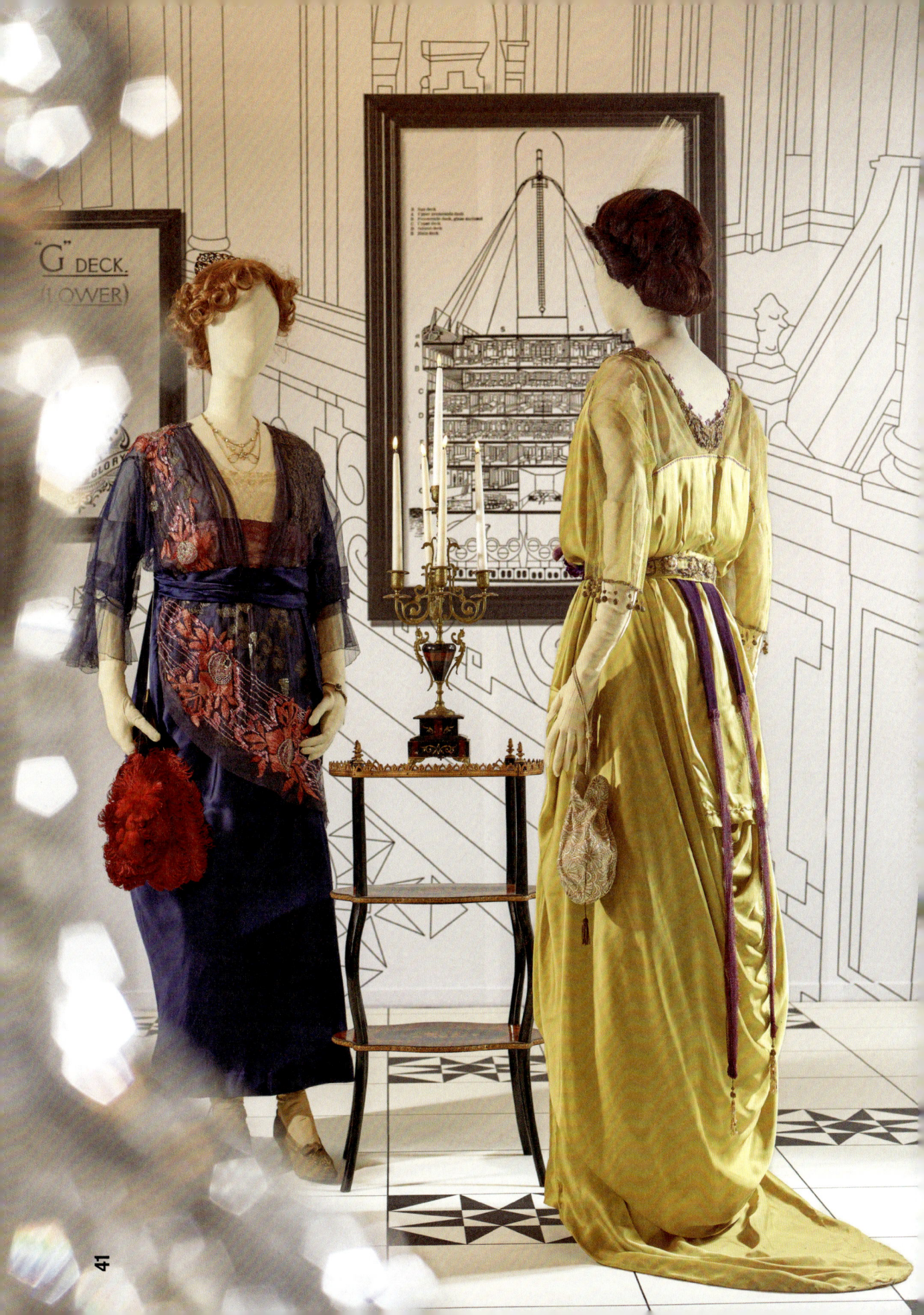

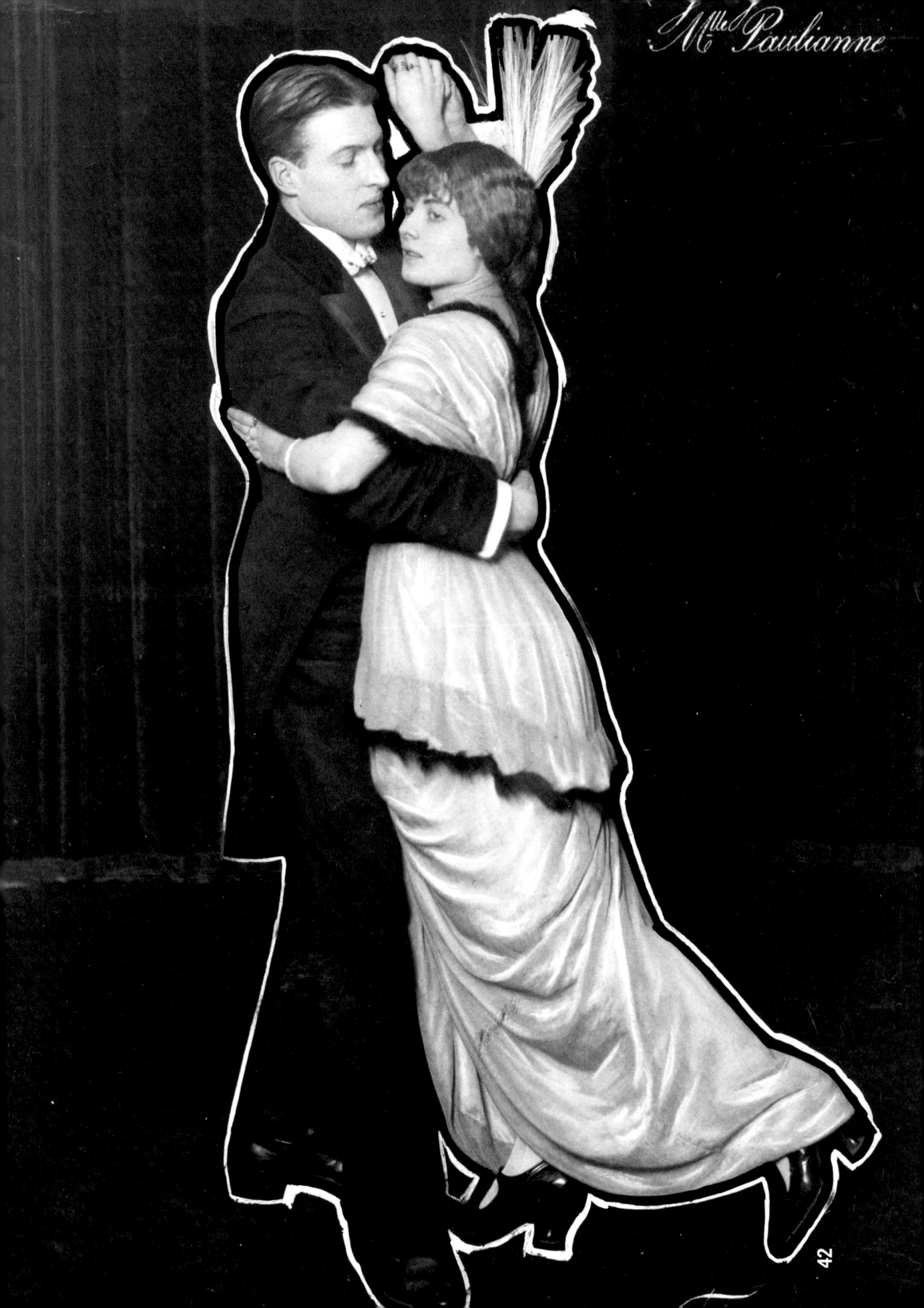

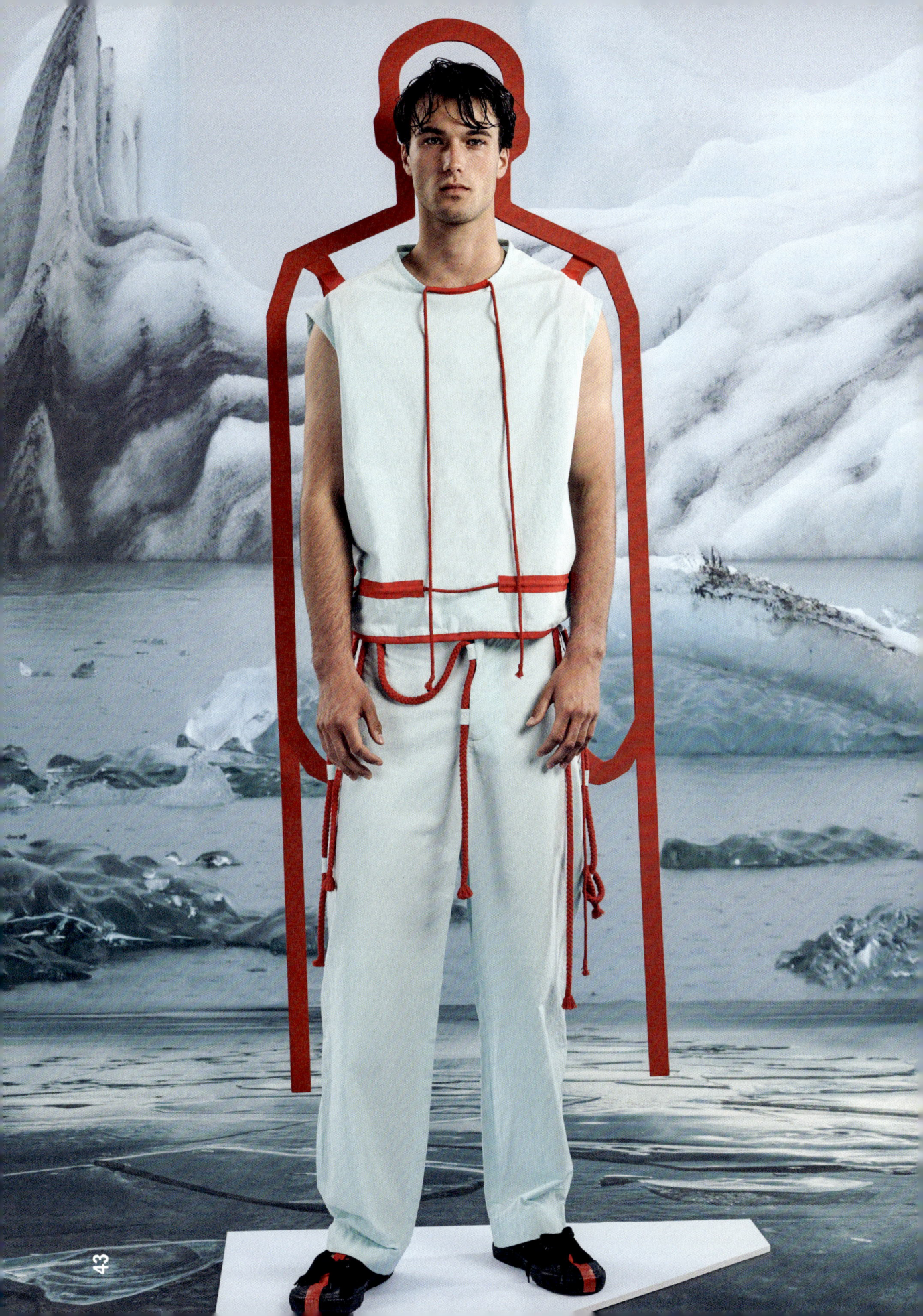

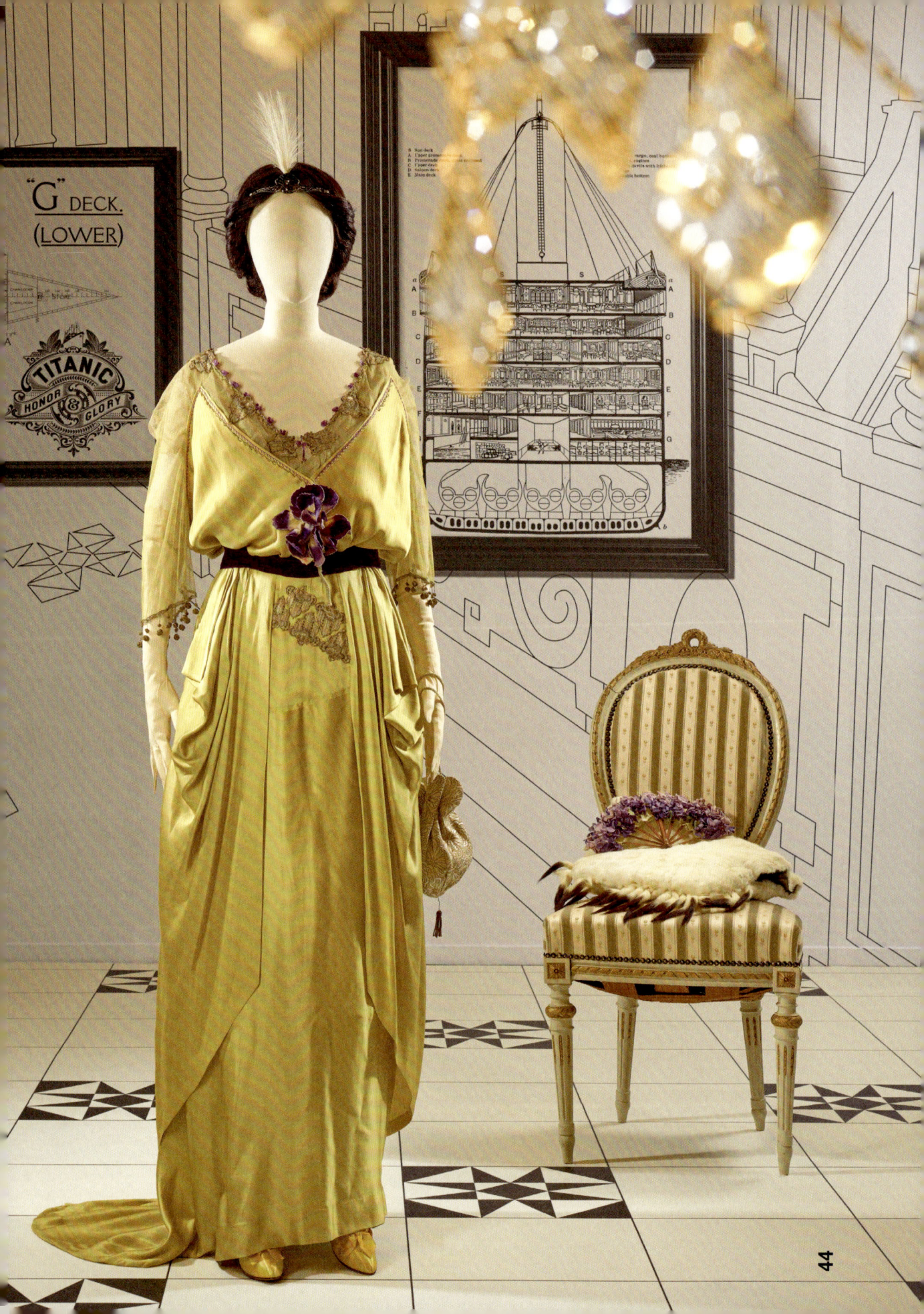

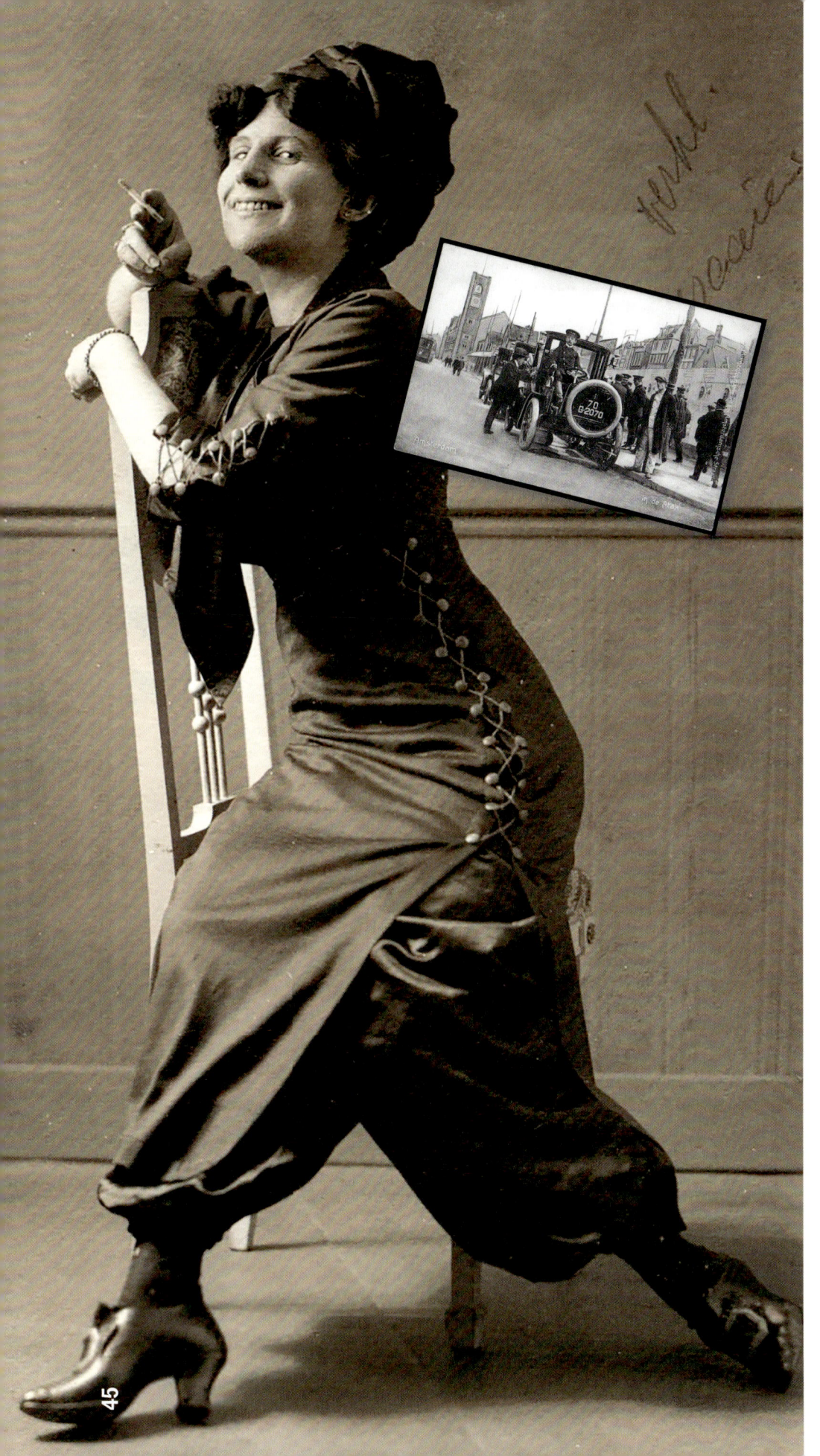

45

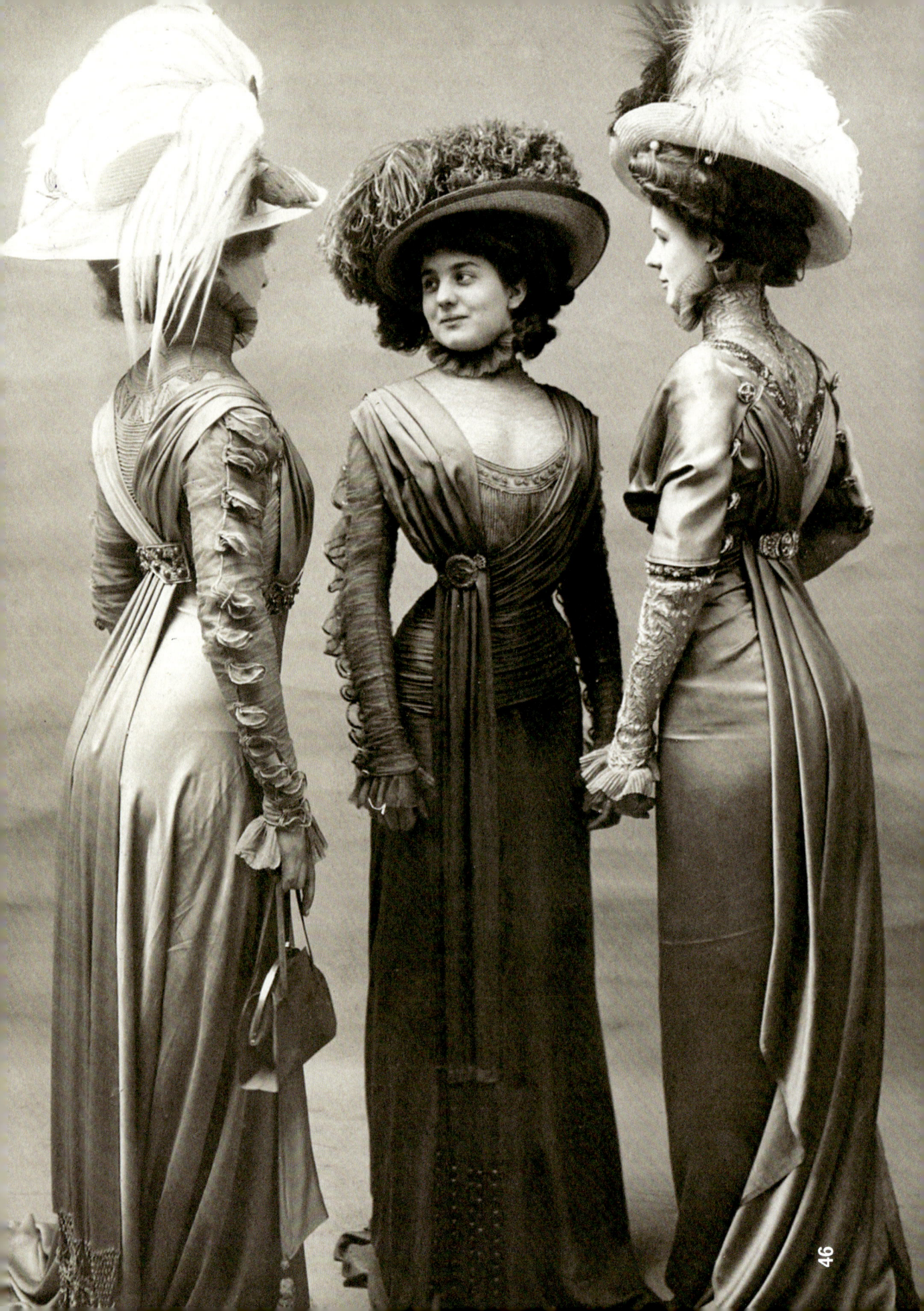

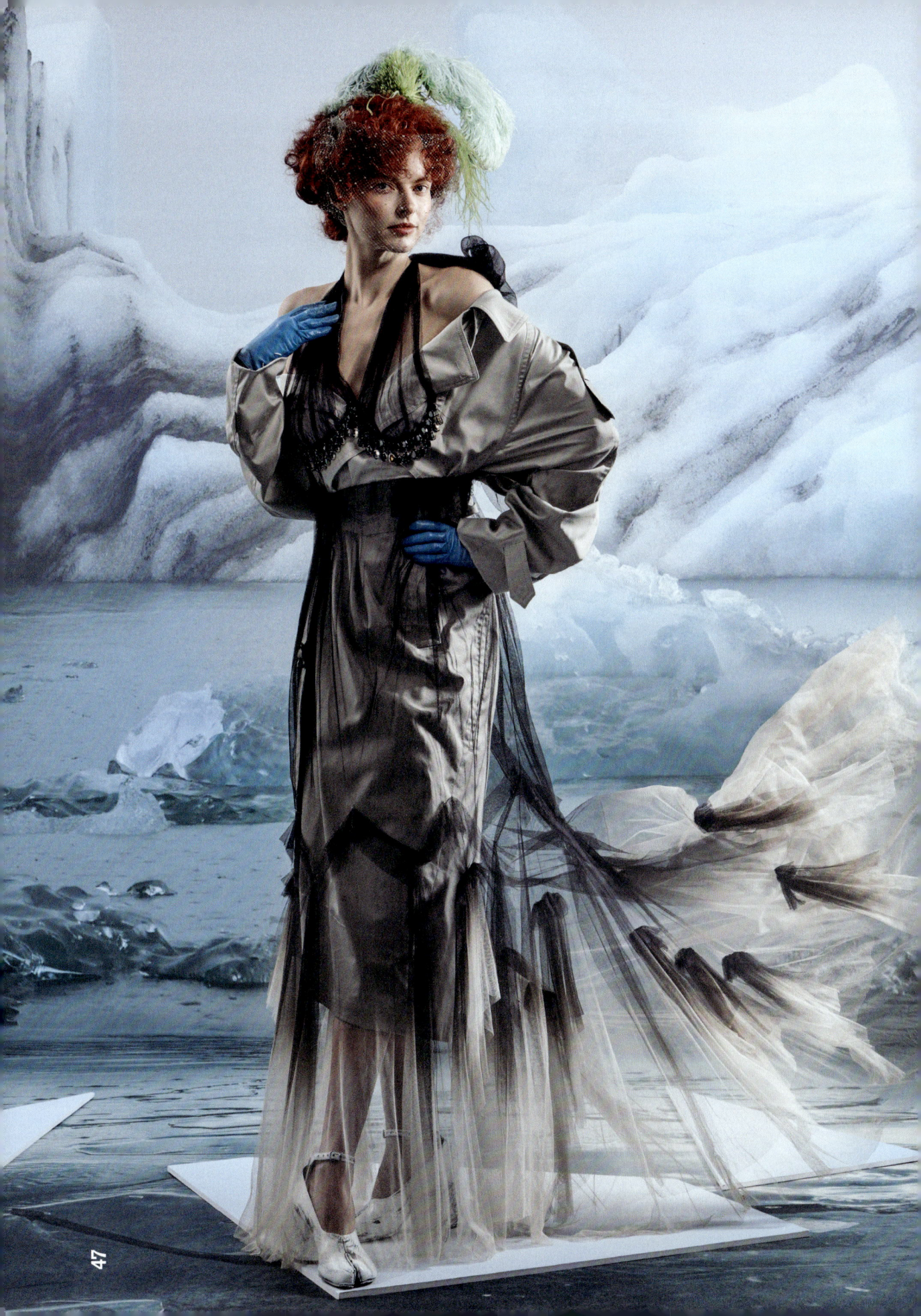

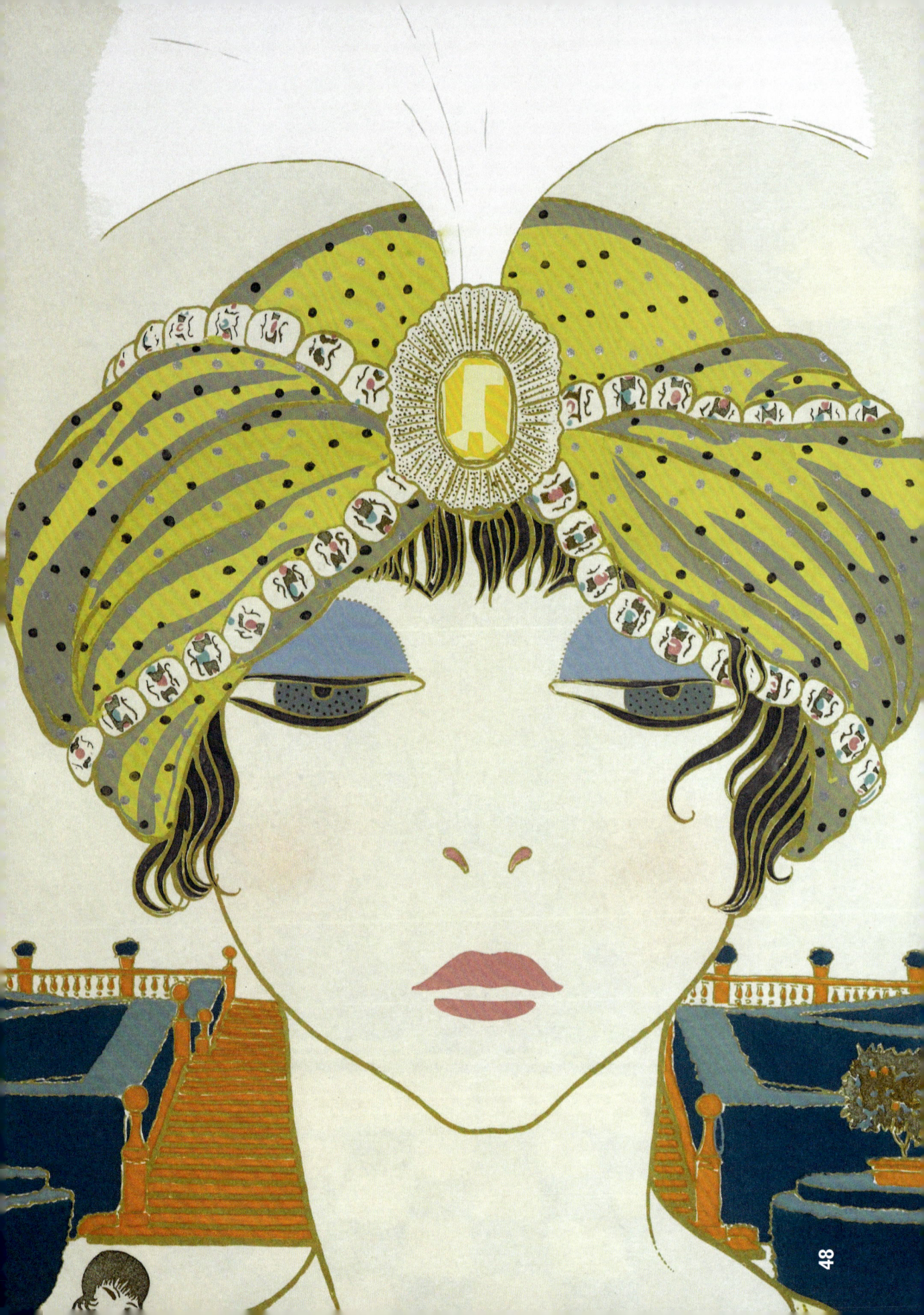

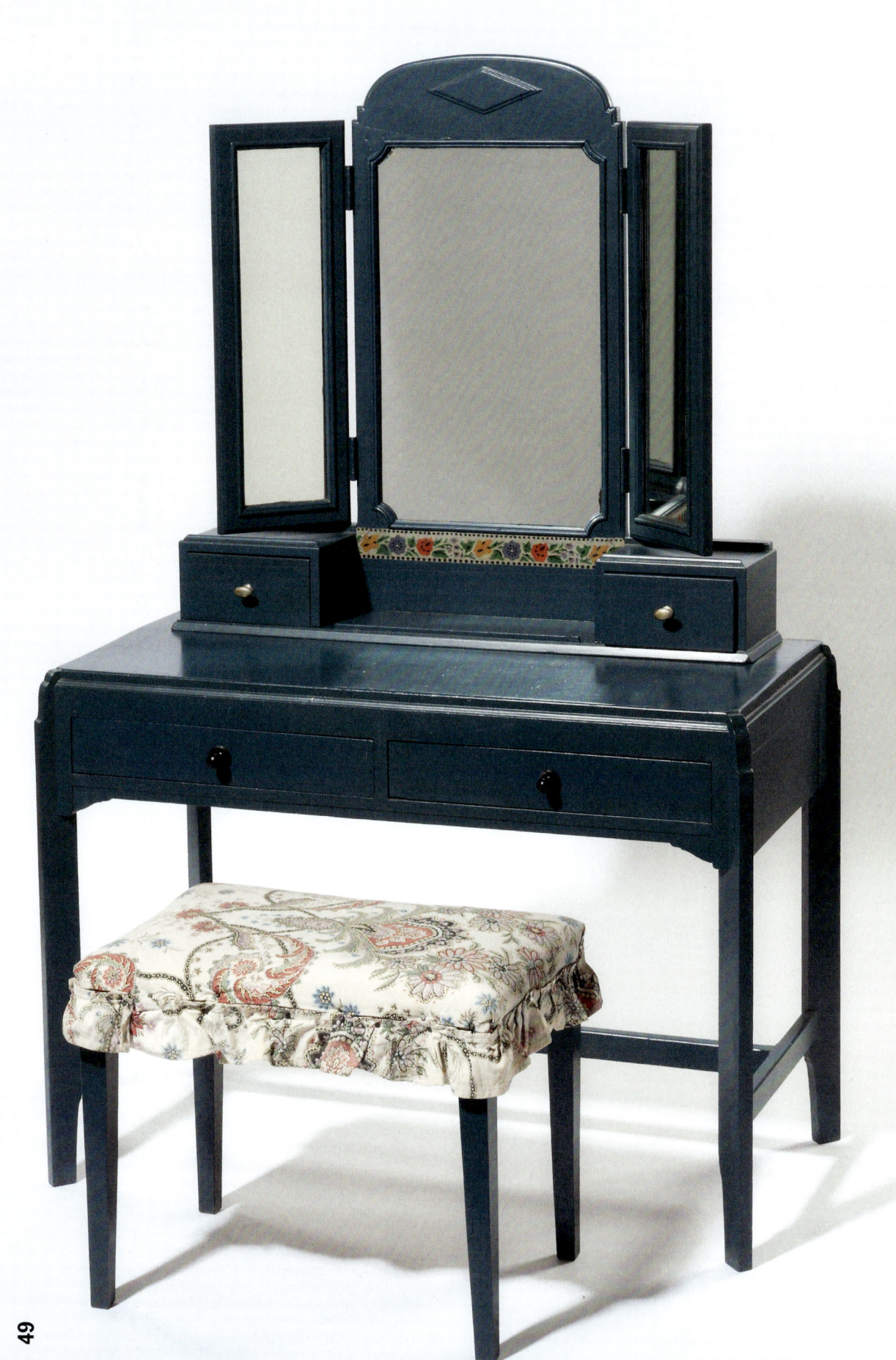

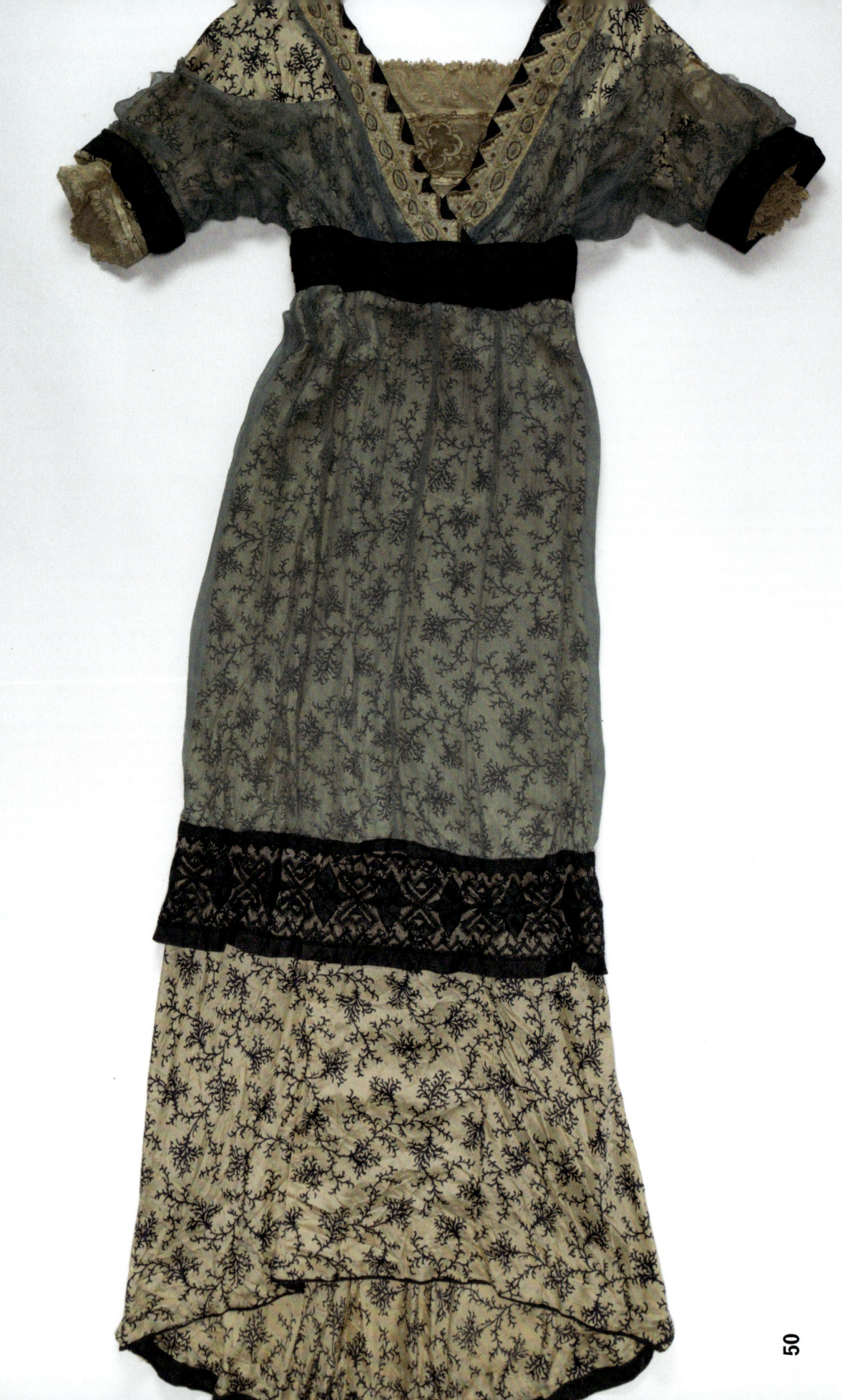

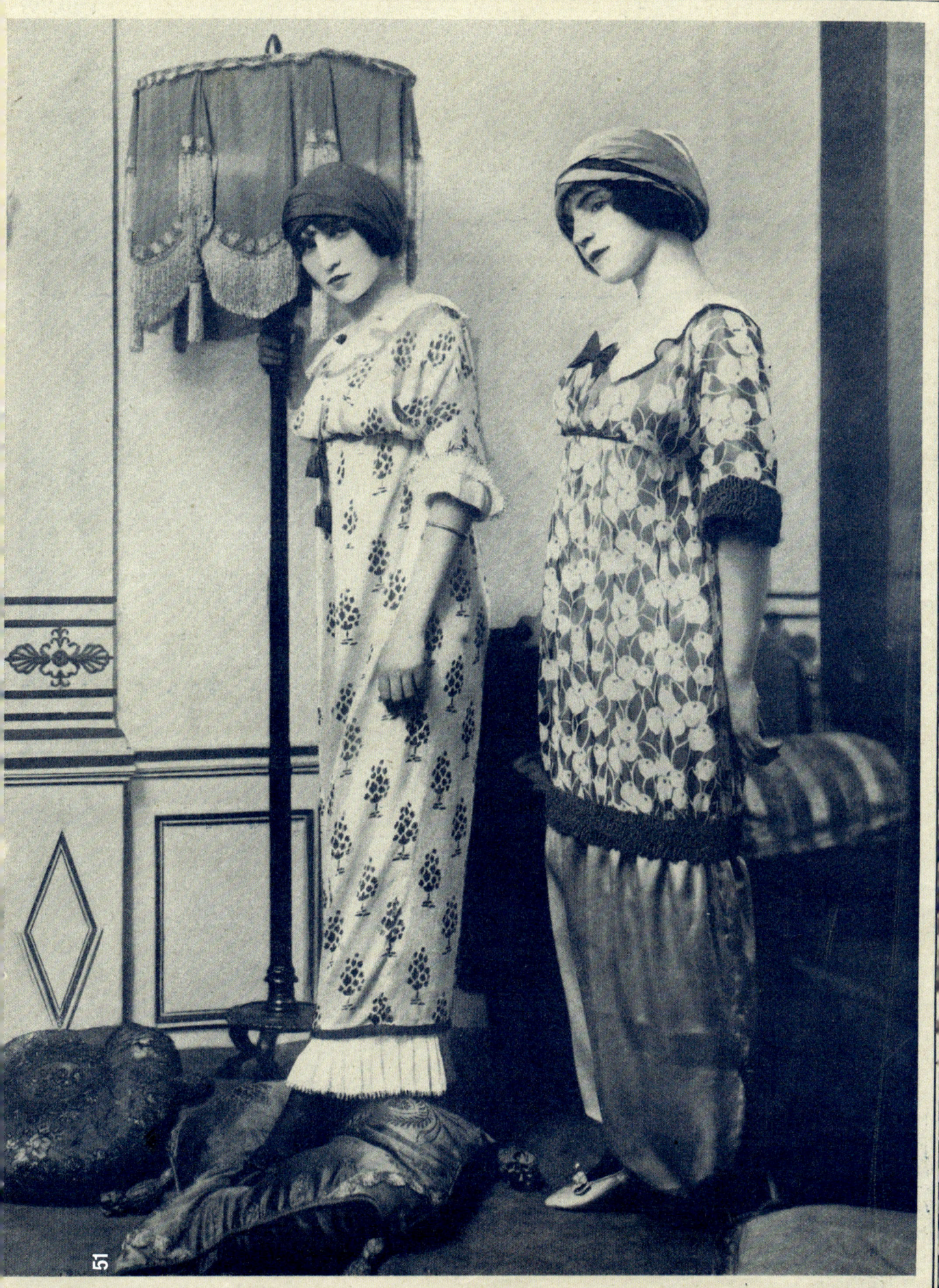

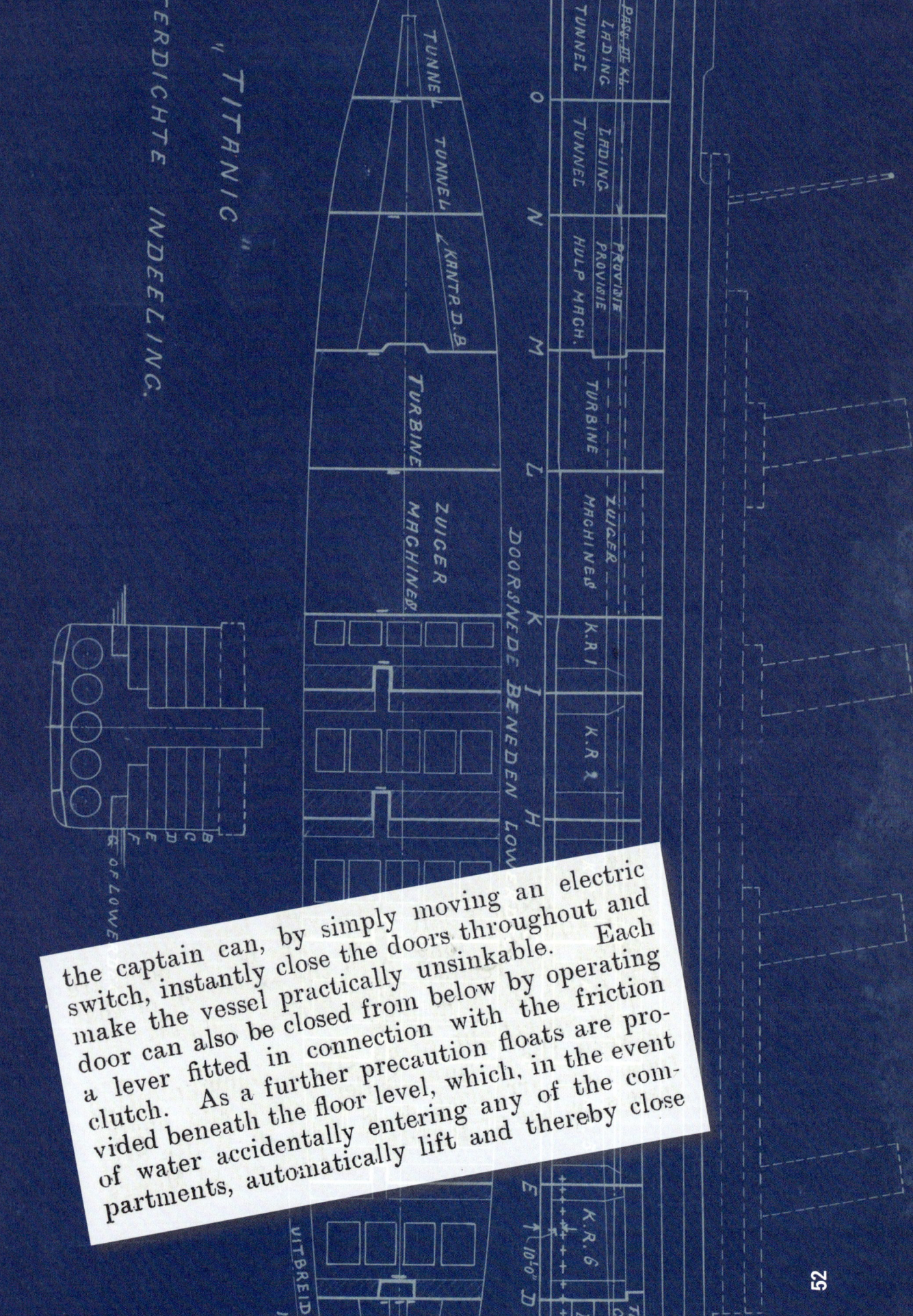

the captain can, by simply moving an electric switch, instantly close the doors throughout and make the vessel practically unsinkable. Each door can also be closed from below by operating a lever fitted in connection with the friction clutch. As a further precaution floats are provided beneath the floor level, which, in the event of water accidentally entering any of the compartments, automatically lift and thereby close

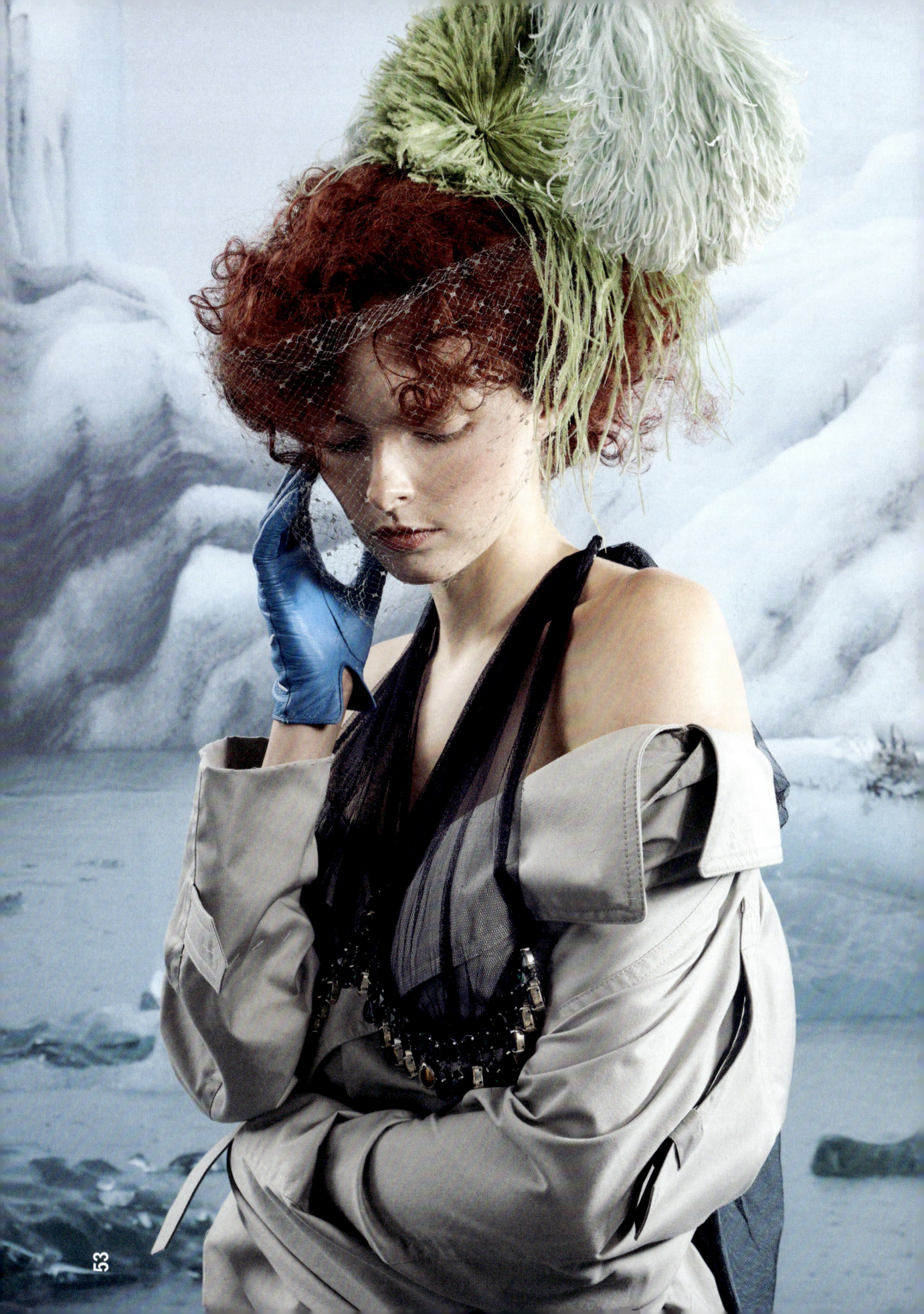

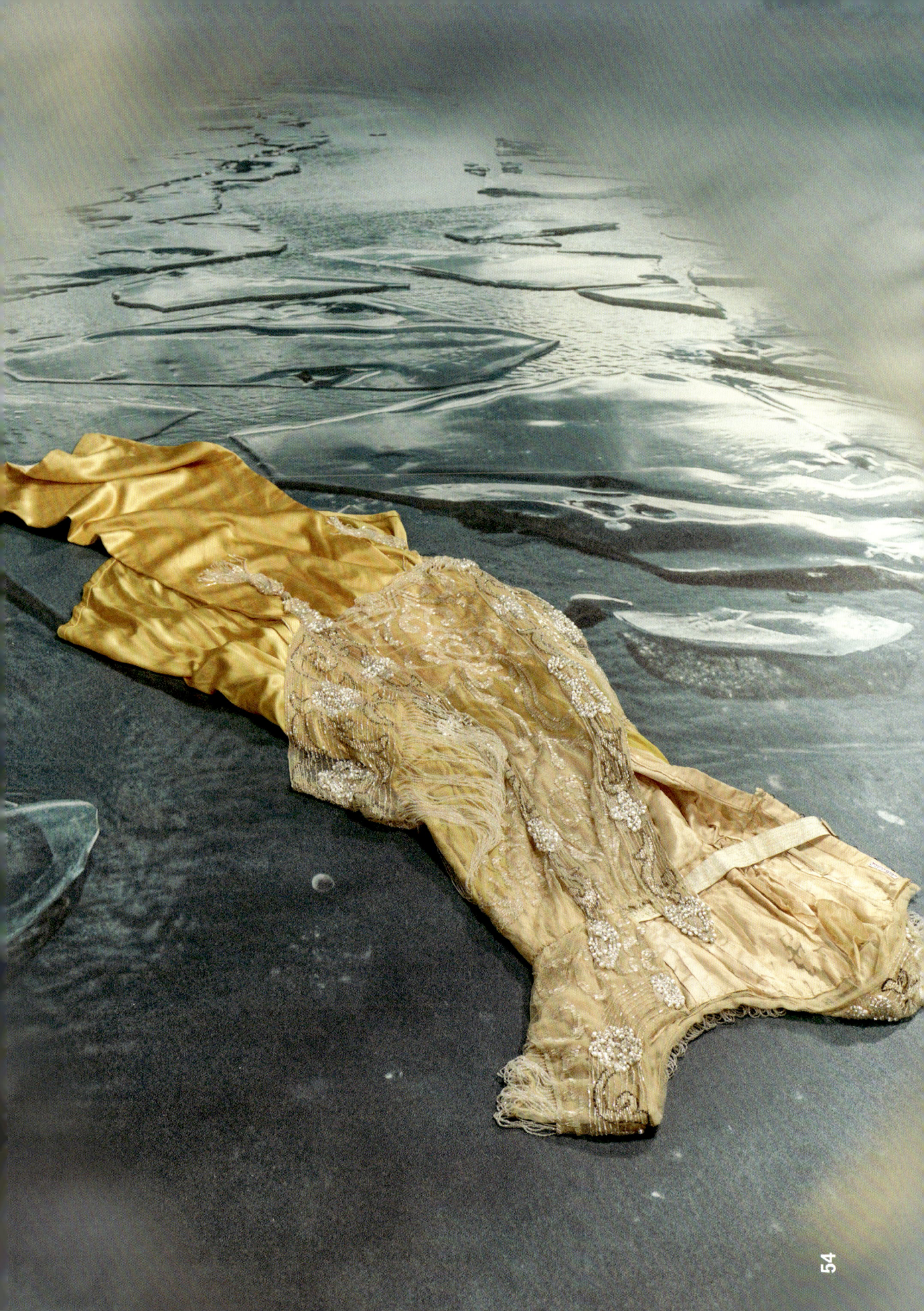

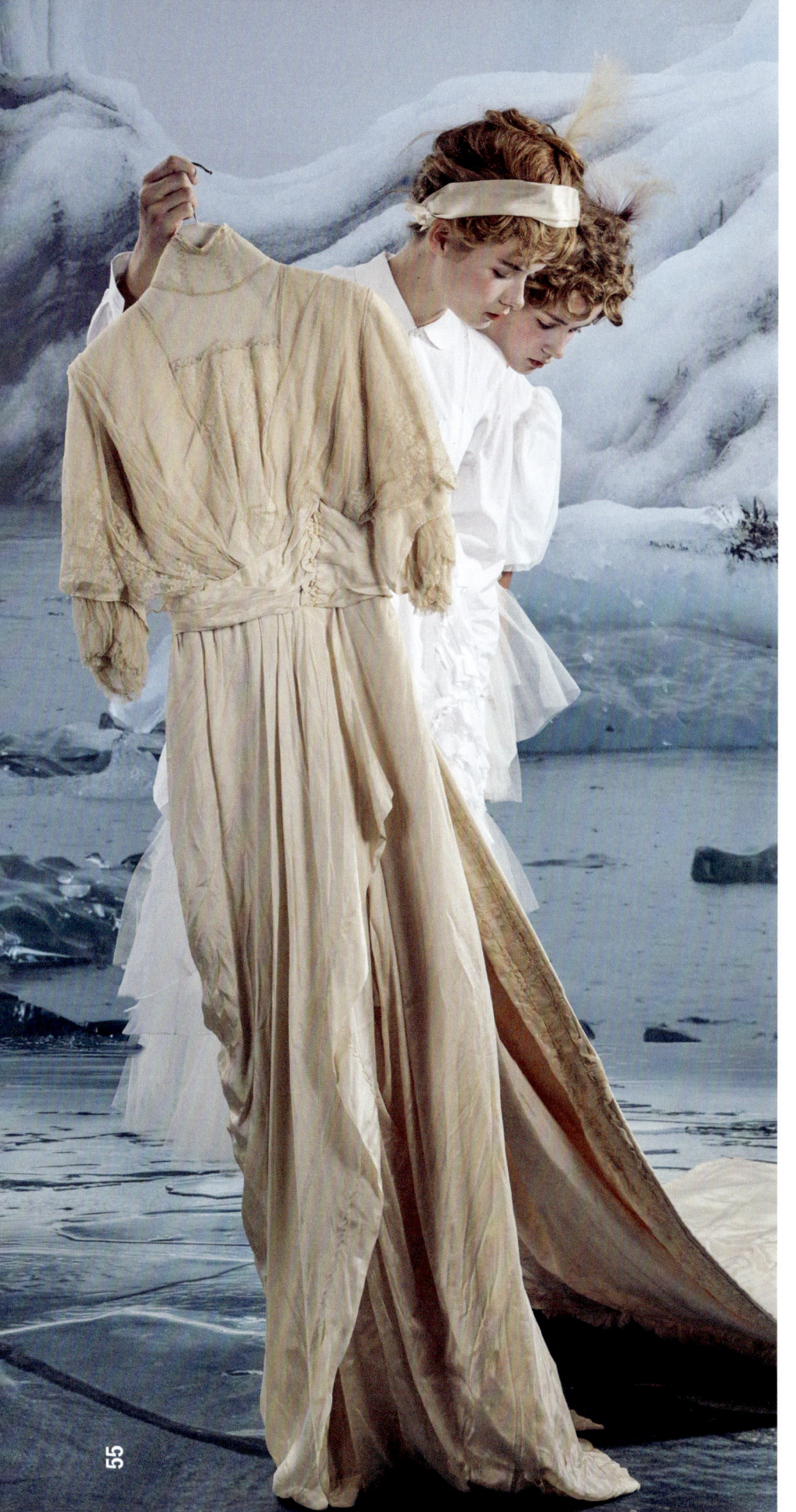

p. 46 Three models wearing the revolutionary 'naked' dresses ('genre directoire') in yellow, green and pink, by Margaine-Lacroix, Paris 1908. When they walked, the gowns revealed their legs up to the knee, causing a 'très grand sensation' at Longchamp.

p. 47, p. 53 John Galliano for Maison Margiela, Evening dress inspired by 1910s fashion and the trench coat, Artisanal Co-ED collection, spring/summer 2020, courtesy of Maison Margiela, Paris.

p. 48 Georges Lepape, stencil from *Les choses de Paul Poiret*, 1911.

p. 49 H.P. Mutters, The Hague, Dressing table and stool made for the Statendam (construction commenced in 1912), Maritime Museum Rotterdam.

p. 50 Maison Dosimont, Gown with tunic in the style of Paul Poiret, Namur, c. 1912-1913. Probably worn by Henrietta Catarina Elisabeth Volkiera van Teijlingen, Baroness Bentinck van Schoonheten (1871-1947).

p. 51 Paul Poiret, Two gowns in stencil-printed silk, in: *Les Modes*, 15 March 1911.

p. 52 Technical drawing of the Titanic, built by Harland and Wolff in Belfast: blueprint of watertight compartments.

p. 54 De Waele, Pale yellow silk evening gown with embroidered tulle tunic, Brussels, c. 1912, from the wardrobe of Countess Eugénie Hélène Ferdinanda van Bylandt (1882-1963).

p. 55 Wedding gown worn by Frederika Wilhelmina Reuchlin-Kolff (1890-1963), who married Dr. Otto Reuchlin Esq. (1882-1962) in Leeuwarden on 21 October 1913. Otto was a nephew/cousin of George Reuchlin, who died in the Titanic disaster in 1912.

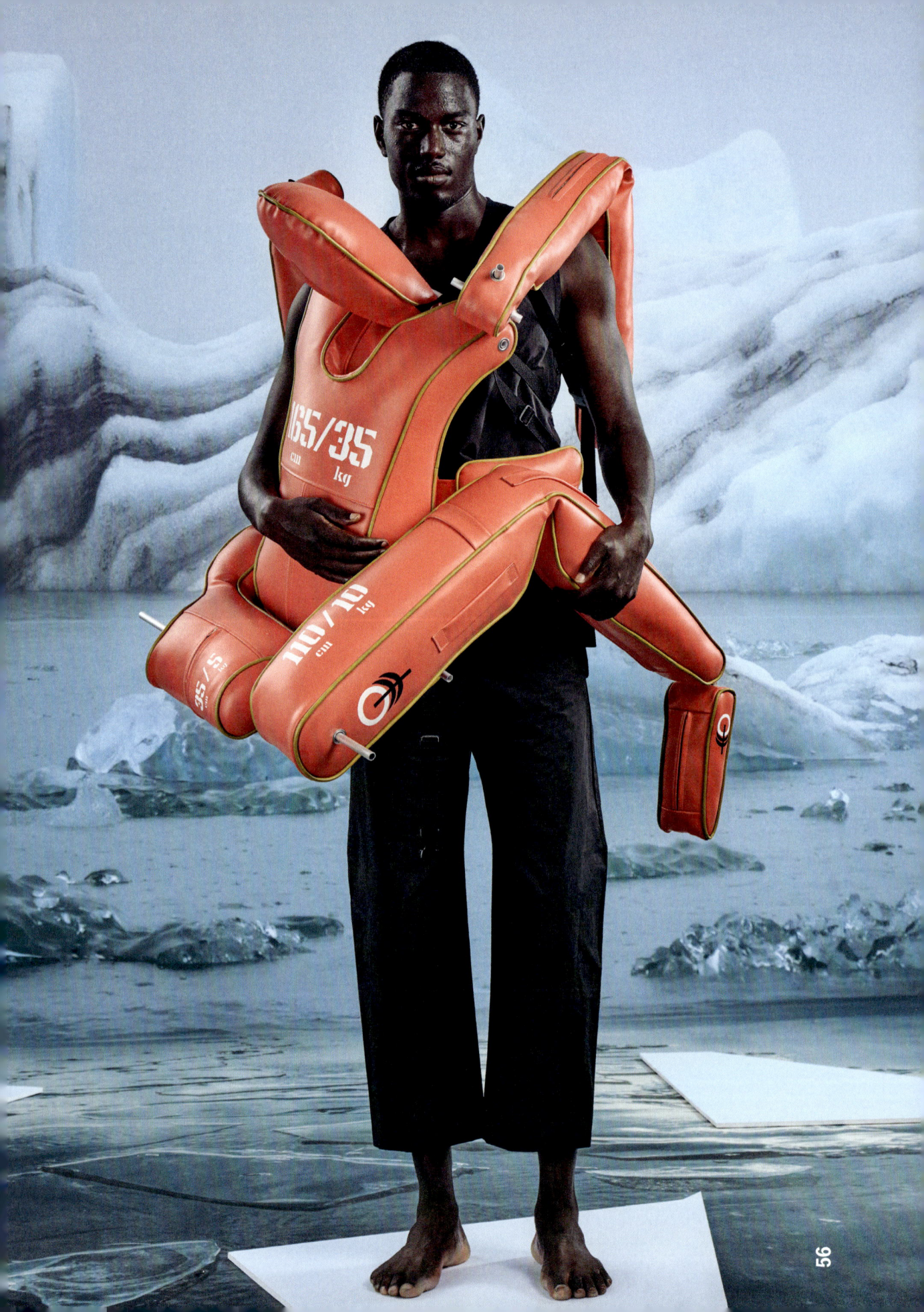

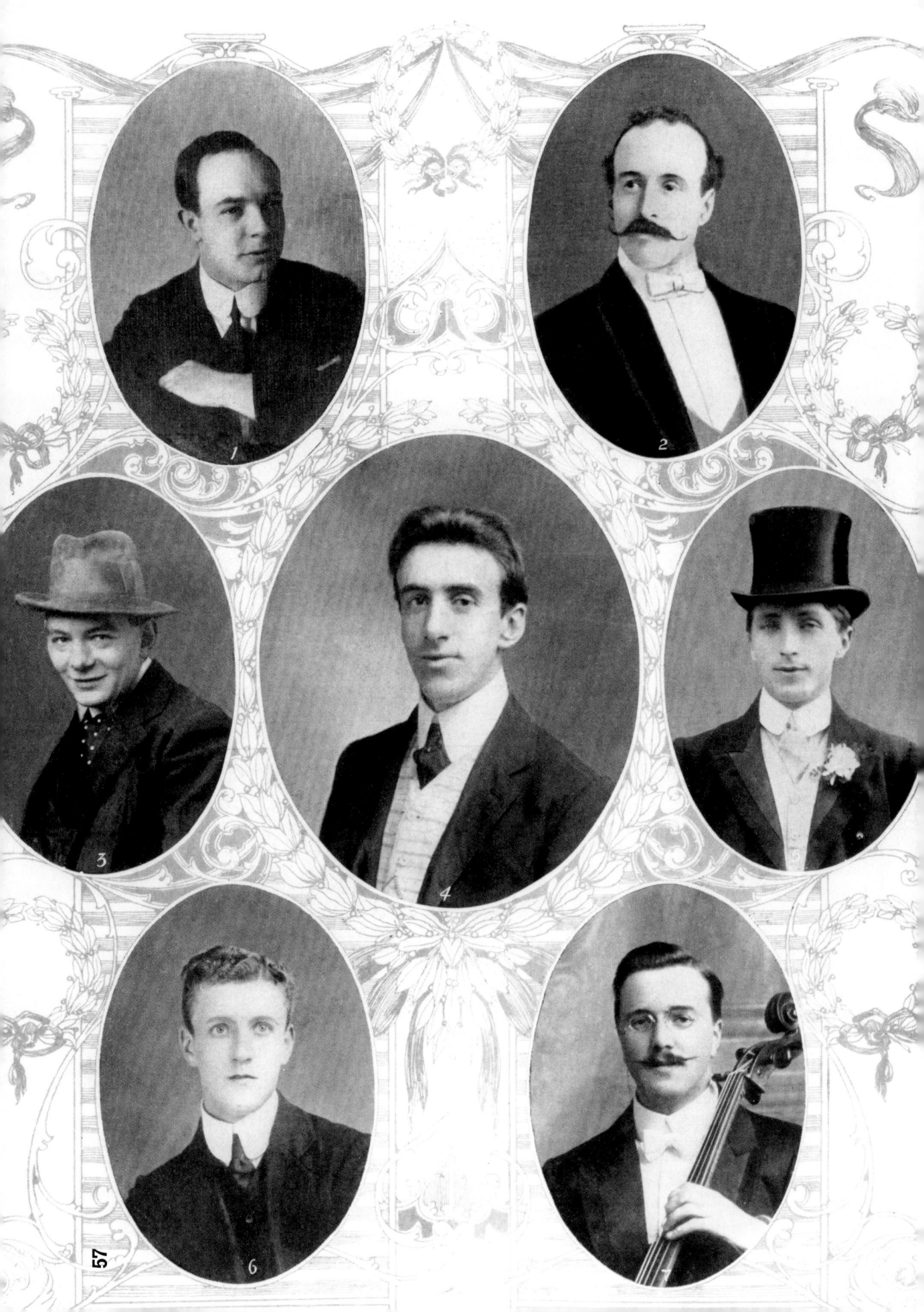

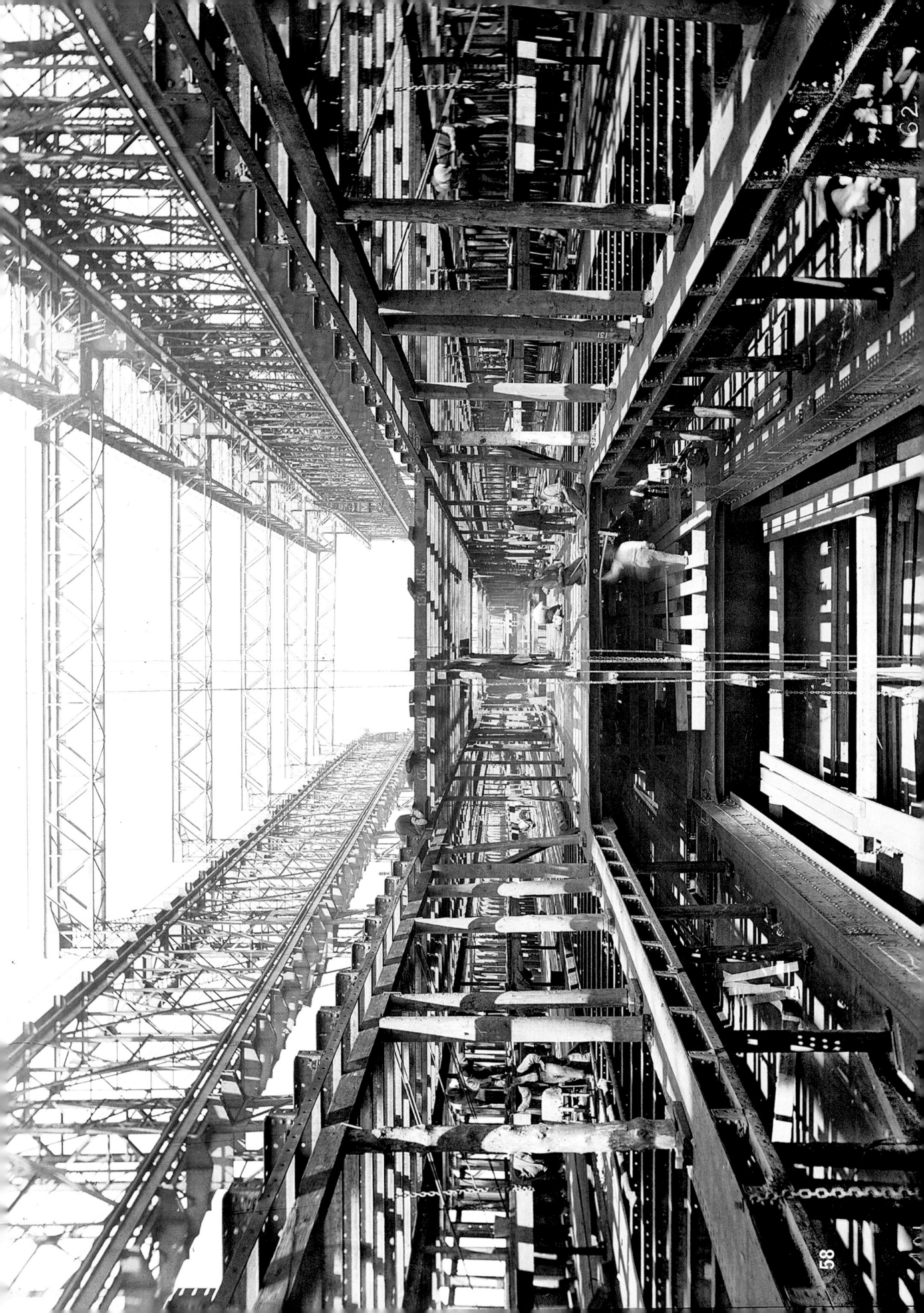

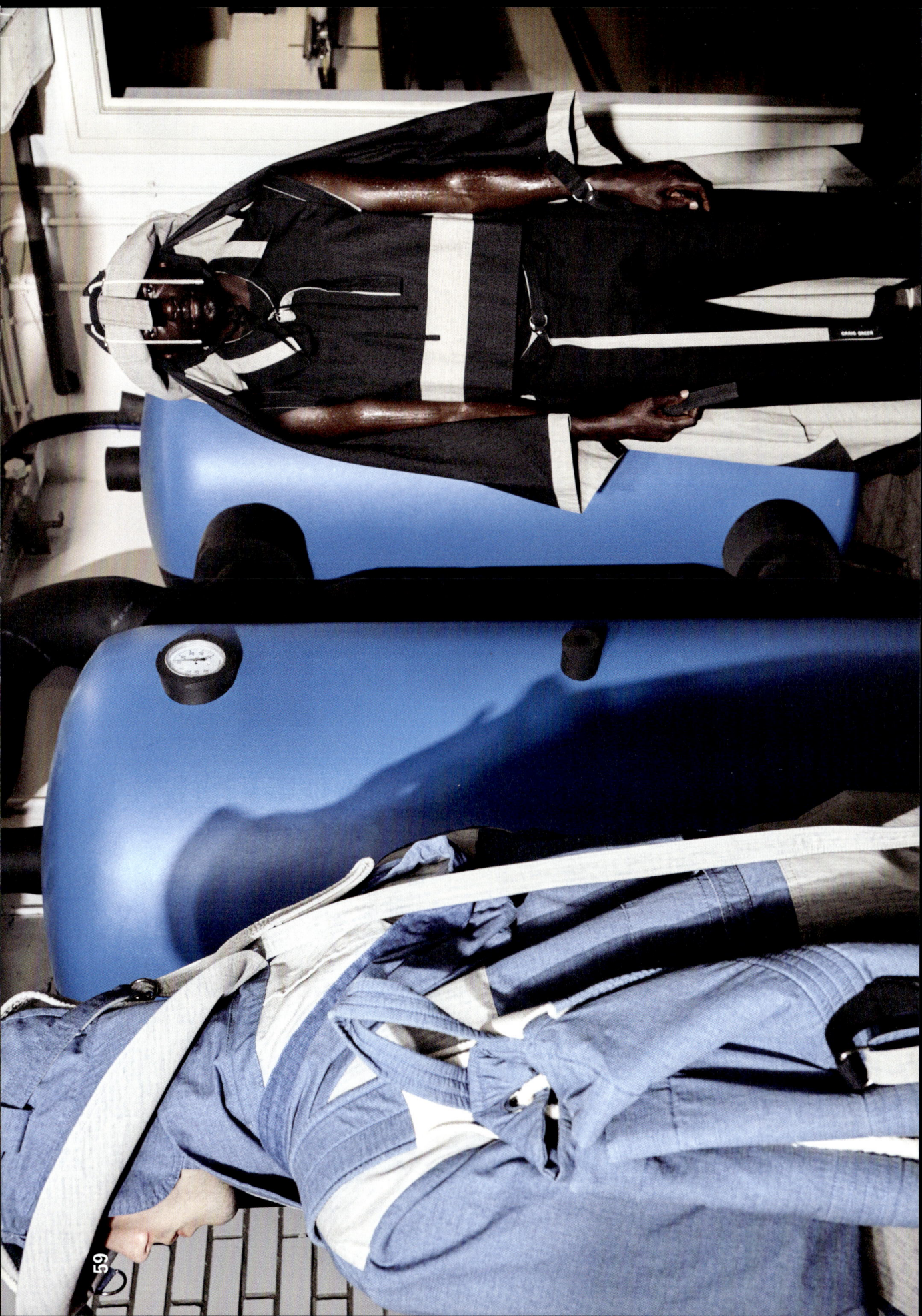

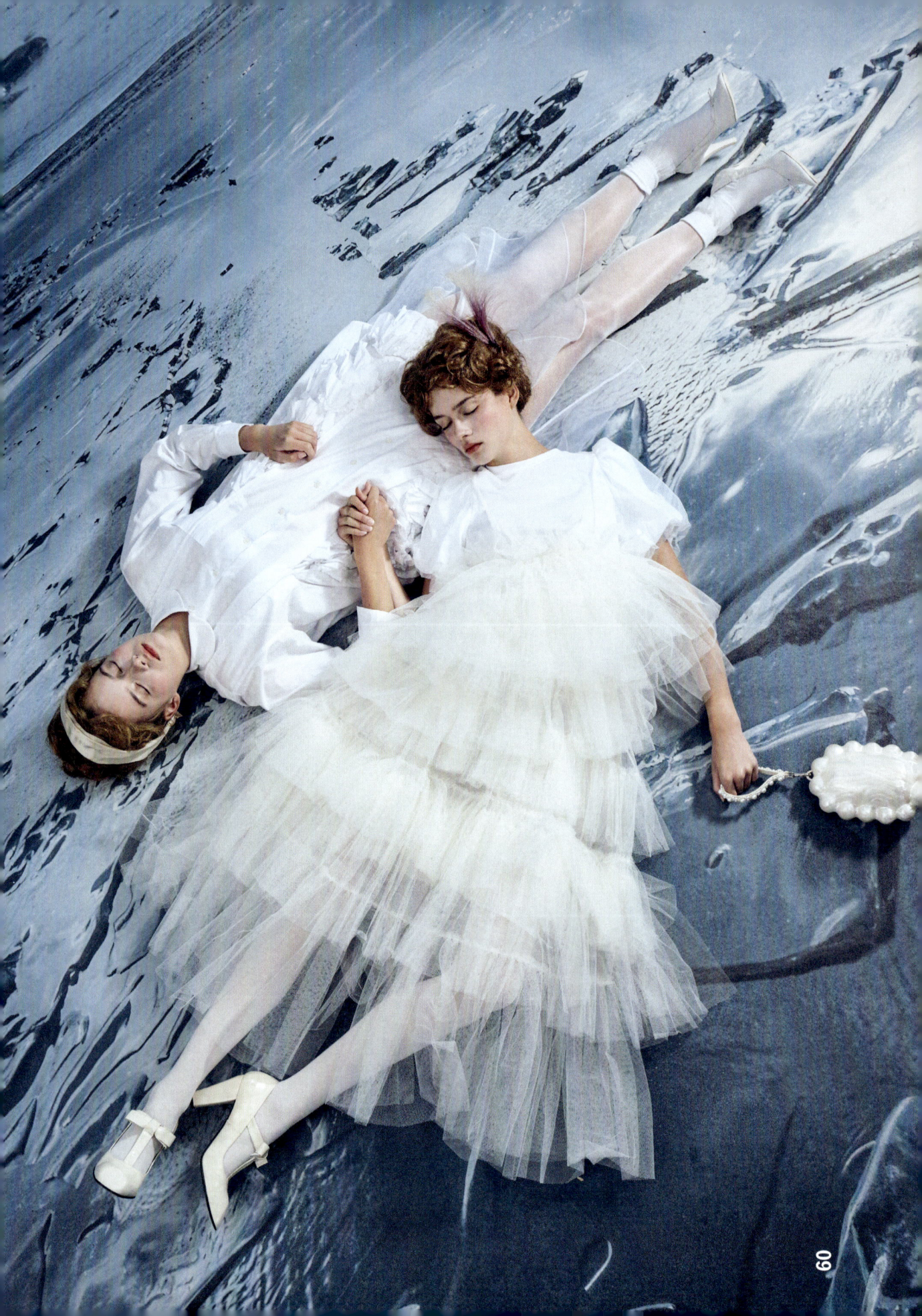

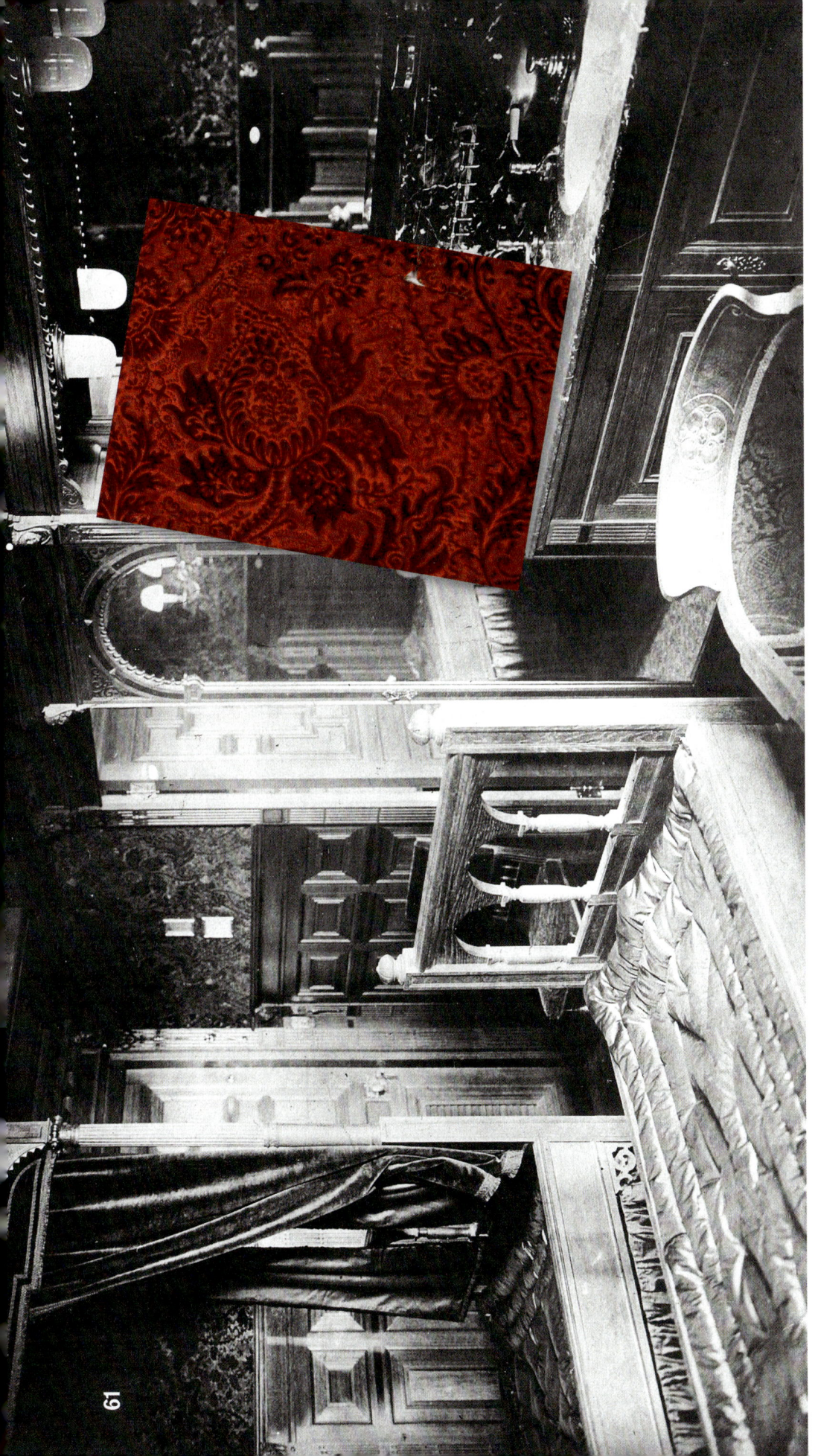

p. 56 Craig Green, Ensemble with sculpture, in collaboration with David Curtis-Ring, spring/summer 2024, courtesy of Craig Green, London.

p. 57 Musicians onboard the Titanic, 1912. Their repertoire included several musical styles: classical, hymns and also ragtime. They continued to play on deck as the Titanic went down.

p. 58 Photograph of the internal structure of 'Ship No: 401. Name: Titanic. Type: Passenger Ship. Tonnage: 46328. Launch: 31 May 1911. Delivery: 2 April 1912. Owner: Oceanic Steam Navigation Company (White Star Line)', at the Harland & Wolff shipyard, Belfast, 1910.

p. 59 Craig Green, two ensembles inspired by work clothes, spring/summer 2021, courtesy of Craig Green, London.

p. 60 Comme des Garcons, White cotton dress, spring/summer 2025; Simone Rocha, Top and skirt with silhouette resembling that of 1912-1914, spring/summer 2021, vintage; Simone Rocha, Pearl bag, spring/summer 2021.

p. 61 Interior of luxury first-class cabin on the Titanic, furnished in traditional Dutch style by H.P. Mutters, 1912.

p. 61 The Superbe printed velvet wall covering was supplied by the Hengelosche Trijpweverij, courtesy of Gert Banis.

Fashion of the 1910s:

A Pivotal Point in Fashion

Kunstmuseum Den Haag's fashion collection is based on the collection of the Nederlands Kostuummuseum (Dutch Costume Museum), which opened in The Hague in 1951. Collecting began in the 1950s, when the 1910s were not so very long ago. That is why the fashions of this decade are so prevalent in the collection, proportionally more than any other decade represented. The garments – elegant women's outfits, tailored suits for men, adorable kids' clothes – were worn mainly by the Dutch elite. They also include sport and outdoor clothing, in line with fashions from Paris and Britain, the great favourites of the time. None of the items in the collection would have looked out of place in the first-class section of the Titanic. The collection does not include many examples of the type of clothes worn by those in second class, the emerging bourgeoisie. And 'third-class' clothes are very few and far between. There are some individual items that could have been worn by those in third class – altered, repaired, worn – and some examples of Dutch traditional dress, which one can also imagine having been worn on board the Titanic. The photographs of European migrants taken on arrival at Ellis Island often feature people in traditional dress, and New York Public Library has a number of fine examples of women's regional costumes from Zeeland. (p. 109)

Kunstmuseum Den Haag has never before done such a deep dive into the 1910s era, despite the fact that it is such an interesting time, when so much was changing, so much was in motion. Women's fashion would never be the same again following the First World War. The silhouette of the belle époque was consigned to history once and for all in the 1910s, as a new age dawned. It is for this reason that, at some point in the past, Kunstmuseum Den Haag's fashion collection was divided into two periods – fashion from before 1914, and fashion from after 1914. For many years, each period had its own curator.[1] What changed so radically in the 1910s that it is regarded as a time of such important innovation in women's fashion? To understand this, we must first consider the fashion of the belle époque, around the turn of the twentieth century. French fashion set the tone for women's clothes and each new style was communicated through the growing body of fashion magazines. In the nineteenth century this medium had burgeoned into an industry producing countless magazines and prints, often with hand-tinted lithographs and engravings. In the early twentieth century, more and more fashion photography appeared in these publications, as in *Les Modes*, a magazine first published in 1901.[2] Most were images of models wearing the latest fashions, generally photographed indoors at a studio in Paris. Increasingly, photographs of fashionable society ladies also began to appear in fashion magazines, alongside fashionably dressed actresses and other celebrities. Designers also used photographs taken at the races in Longchamp, near Paris, where they had their models parade in their latest designs, the images ending up in fashion magazines. This was also the heyday of imitation and fashion espionage, made possible by new technology, which allowed the latest fashion news from Paris to be transmitted immediately to the United States of America by telegraph.[3]

Women's fashion was categorised by the time of day. Each part of the day had its own kind of fashion, so women would change several times during the course of a day. There were simple clothes for home, daywear, afternoon wear, lavish negligees with lots of lace and embroidery for nighttime, and for those who played sports there were modern outfits for hiking, horseriding, golf and tennis. This sport clothing for women was based largely on men's suits. The same applied to the increasingly popular modern walking costumes, which offered freedom of movement. Rose (Kate Winslet) wears such a costume when she boards the Titanic in the 1997 film. These walking costumes would be combined with a modern blouse, a garment that made its first appearance in the late nineteenth century. In the 1910s, the blouse became an increasingly important element of a woman's wardrobe, worn with a walking costume or skirt. This was an important modernisation of women's clothing, and a combination that many working women preferred to a dress for wear during the day. As well as high collars, 'Peter Pan' collars also came into fashion around 1909/1910, on both blouses and dresses.[4]

Madelief Hohé

Innovation in fashion in the 1910s actually started in 1908. The S-shaped silhouette that had previously defined fashion, achieved by wearing a fashionable corset, fell out of favour. A new style came in its place, featuring dresses that were straighter and had a higher waistline. Paul Poiret had Paul Iribe make drawings of his innovative creations, which were based on the empire style. (p.51) A different type of corset, straighter and more modern, would be worn with these dresses; some women did not wear a corset at all. In that same year, 1908, a notorious photograph was taken at the races in Longchamp depicting three models from the Paris fashion house Margaine-Lacroix wearing tight-fitting gowns, apparently without a corset or much else underneath. (p. 46) These garments became known among the public as 'naked dresses'. Jeanne Margaine-Lacroix called the gown, inspired by classical antiquity, *robe Tanagréenne* (Tanagra was a Greek nymph); she became even more famous for her *robe Sylphide* in the same style, possibly named for the romantic ballet *La Sylphide* of 1832.[5] 'Lingerie dresses' also became popular. Made of soft white cotton, they were so called because they were thought to resemble undergarments.[6]

The colours and decorative elements of fashion also changed. New styles of decoration and vibrant colours were introduced, rivalling the powdery colours and lace of the belle époque. This occurred in part thanks to the influence of *Les Ballets Russes* – seen in Paris for the first time in 1909 – and resulted in much more intense colours in the fashions of the day, including dark red, ochre, purple, emerald green and petrol blue, all of which can be found in the collection at Kunstmuseum Den Haag. Black remained a chic and elegant colour, by no means only worn during mourning, though often preferred by older women. The 1910s started with splendid gowns with heavy embroidery, glittering with gold and kilos of sequins. The dresses themselves became straighter, were more likely to have a short dolman sleeve, and were sometimes weighed down with beads and sequins. Lightweight silk (satin) fabrics were also popular. A lead weight would sometimes be sewn into the hem or train to prevent the skirt from flying up.[7] It was also, unfortunately, the age of silks that were given more body by adding metallic salts to make them heavier – known as weighted silks – which has proved disastrous for the conservation of the fabrics. (p. 120) Yet a surprisingly large number of dresses from the 1910s remain in good condition, and a recent project has helped identify the owners of more and more of these garments. This gives us interesting information on personal tastes and choices in Dutch wardrobes, and who could afford (in terms of money and status) to wear what in Dutch society at the time.

In *Titanic* we see Rose struggling with a corset, as her mother laces it up. It was this garment in particular, symbol of the constraints on women's independence and freedom of movement, that declined in popularity in the 1910s. This started with the protests of the reform movements, who campaigned for the reconsideration and improvement of women's clothing. This was an important international movement, and the Nederlandse Vereeniging voor Verbetering van Vrouwenkleeding (Dutch Association for the Improvement of Women's Clothing, established 1899) played an important role in the Netherlands. (p.110) Although there were differences of opinion as to how the new clothing should look, most were in agreement that the corset should be abandoned. In the 1910s, more and more day and evening dresses were designed to be worn without a corset. The influence of designers like Paul Poiret and Gabrielle 'Coco' Chanel is often cited in this context. In reality, many more designers and many other factors played a role. The above-mentioned, now relatively unknown French designer Jeanne Margaine-Lacroix regularly advertised her innovative corsets, designed to be worn with her modern dresses, like her straight, front-fastening *Sylphide* corset.[8] It differed from older types of corset in the sense that it was longer, emphasised the waist less and was more elastic. Margaine-Lacroix reinforced her dresses with sturdy internal bodices so that they could be worn without a corset. A woman could therefore modernise her wardrobe by opting for a different corset, wearing more revolutionary 'reform dresses' without a corset, or opting for an interim solution whereby stays were incorporated into the dress. Most dresses still had an internal waistband that kept the dress in place, to which a woven or printed label with the name of the designer would be sewn. Many dresses also had a cotton bodice lining, which also served as a foundation for the dress. More dresses consisted of one piece, rather than a separate bodice and skirt.

Under her dress, a woman would wear a chemise, open-crotched drawers, a corset with a camisole over it, one or more underskirts and stockings. These were usually machine-knit and made of luxury silk, in shades that matched the dress, although skin-coloured and black stockings were also popular (under daywear). As a result of the new, close-fitting fashions, women started to wear less underwear, which also became shorter and more lightweight. Shorter drawers, simpler bodices, even some without a corset. Around 1912/1913 the brassière (bra) started to gain in popularity as a new form of foundation garment under sleek modern dresses.[9] The new underwear was very different from the Victorian 'unmentionables' in chaste white cotton, and was now available in beautiful, attractive designs. This was even held up as 'a woman's universal right'.[10] As a result, young designers like Callot Soeurs started to include chic (coloured!) underwear in their collections, as eye-catching novelties. The one thing that did increase in size was the hat. This was still a time when no one would leave home without a hat, or some other form of head covering. (p.116) People were afraid that their hair would otherwise become 'horribly discoloured'. Make-up became more and more acceptable in the 1910s, having for decades been associated with actresses and prostitutes.

Influential designers of the time included Jeanne Paquin, Jeanne Lanvin, Paul Poiret, Callot Soeurs, Boué Soeurs, Chéruit, Jeanne Margaine-Lacroix, Lucile, Redfern, Brandt, Beer, Jenny, Douillett and Premet. Gabrielle 'Coco' Chanel opened a hat shop on rue Cambon in Paris in 1910, and later expanded her range to include sporty clothes, some of them made of jersey, a fabric that other couturiers also experimented with. Styles changed even more under the influence of trendsetting designer Paul Poiret, who introduced the most innovative silhouettes of the time. Poiret introduced the 'hobble skirt' in 1909, which fitted very tightly round the legs, making walking difficult. He loved 'Oriental' clothing, and brought kimono-style coats into fashion, as well as harem pants and his famous, extravagantly flared flared 'lamsphade tunic'. But were these fashions actually worn in the Netherlands? A series of photographs published in the Dutch magazine *Het Leven* in 1911 showed actress Sophie de Jong walking around Amsterdam wearing a 'jupe culotte'. (p.45) This caused quite a stir and even some disturbances, as a result of which it was concluded that this fashion was highly unconventional and certainly not suitable for everyday wear in the Netherlands. In 1911 the tunic became even more fashionable, and dresses were increasingly made in one piece, rather than in the form of a separate bodice and skirt. In 1912 dresses with a panier effect were in fashion, and in 1914 asymmetrical designs and draping at the hip were all the rage.[11]

In 1915, during the First World War (1914-1918), skirts became fuller, and also slightly shorter. By 1916 hemlines were around 15 cm above the ground, and in 1917 skirts became even shorter and fuller. They were dubbed 'war crinolines'.[12] This was the fashion when Christian Dior was a child, and it inspired the New Look silhouette which he introduced in 1947. There are plenty of examples of these new fashions in the collection at Kunstmuseum Den Haag, in the form of voluminous day dresses in fabrics that are much more lightweight than the dresses from before 1910. Since the dresses had become shorter, they were now also referred to more often as a 'dress' – a term previously used mainly for short children's dresses – rather than 'gown', used mainly for long dresses. At Kunstmuseum Den Haag we have therefore traditionally chosen the term 'gown' for pre-1914 garments, and 'dress' for those dating from after 1914. As a result of the war, some military elements were incorporated into the decoration on women's clothes.[13] In 1915 the waistline dropped. A fashion had also developed for covering the waist with a broad band of shirred fabric, creating a wide waistband, for both daywear and evening wear.

Colours were somewhere in the mid-range of classic pastel shades, though vibrant modern colours were also used. Those who favoured an alternative style would also opt for alternative fabrics, like the Liberty silks sold by Metz & Co in Amsterdam and The Hague, with appropriate motifs, decorations and colours. As a result, the collection clearly shows who was following Paris fashion, and who was more inclined towards an alternative style. By the end of the First World War, the fashionable silhouette was shorter than ever, presaging the short skirts of the roaring twenties. The walking costume was commonplace by now, as were a whole range of blouse and skirt combinations. Corsets fell out of fashion and were replaced by step-ins and other less constricting foundation garments, combined with 'chemises' and 'combinations'. Fashion adapted to modern life. It was now more common for women to work (in some cases because of the war) and to exercise, which meant clothing had to meet other requirements. Modern dances like the tango and foxtrot also required dresses that allowed freedom of movement. The world was ready for a new age, the roaring twenties, when designer Gabrielle 'Coco' Chanel, the personification of the 'garçonne', would play a key role.

Men's fashions changed less dramatically in the 1910s. It was vital for a man to look good and fashionable. 'If a man does not dress well in society, he cannot be a success', it was said.[14] A man's wardrobe was also divided into clothes for different occasions throughout the day. Those who followed fashion looked to London, which had become famous for its tailoring in the nineteenth century, developing countless techniques for creating the perfectly tailored suit. During the day, while at work, a man would wear a tailored suit in a fine wool fabric. A suit traditionally consisted of long trousers, a waistcoat and a jacket. The waistcoat might be in the same fabric, or in a different fabric, for those who wished to add their own striking detail. This was one of the few ways, apart from socks, ties and other accessories, for a man to add a personal touch to his wardrobe. In the Netherlands, the frock coat went out of fashion in the 1910s. 'Dead as a Dodo', *The Cutter* magazine declared in 1921. The bespoke suit with a short jacket became increasingly popular as an alternative. For official occasions during the day, a man would wear a 'morning suit', consisting of a morning coat and grey striped trousers. A black dress suit, with a satin stripe down the outer seam of the trousers, was common as evening wear. The dinner suit, with silk lapels and a shorter jacket (known as a tuxedo) did not become popular for formal occasions until the 1920s.[15] Then of course there were also sporty outfits, like the Norfolk suit, made of coarser tweed than a normal wool suit. Driving was also regarded as a sport, and 'dusters' and fur coats were available for drivers. A gentleman would wear a top hat when out in the evening, while during the day the bowler hat was popular among fashion-conscious men. A gentleman only wore a cap for sporting activities, but they were common among the majority of the poorer male population. The trench coat, part of the standard military issue and suitable for the trenches, also came into fashion as a result of the war.

Some elements of children's attire resembled adult fashions, though they were designed specially for children, and were not simply copies of what their parents wore. Sailor suits and Norfolk suits – both with short trousers – were popular for boys. The latter were made in pastel colours, with large buttons and a belt. Girls wore flowery silk or cotton dresses. On special occasions, they would wear a white dress, showing that they were able to wear clothes that were difficult to keep clean, displaying the luxury of clean clothes and an extensive wardrobe.[16] Fur coats – real or fake – were popular, as were coats with matching hats and lavish embroidery or broderie anglaise. A number of items of children's clothing in Kunstmuseum Den Haag's collection worn by children whose parents had less to spend contrast starkly with this opulence. They have been repeatedly altered, and look as if they were worn every day. Wealth and fine clothes were not accessible to all.

67

1 The first curator of the Nederlands Kostuummuseum (now the fashion and costume department of Kunstmusem Den Haag) was Mary C. de Jong, and Ietse Meij, who joined the museum in 1966 and became curator of the collection in 1986. As a result of the way the collection was divided into two time periods, Ietse Meij focused mainly on fashion from after 1914, while Mary de Jong was concerned largely with the period before 1914. After Mary de Jong retired in 1989, Ietse Meij became curator of the entire collection. In 2003 she was succeeded in this role by Madelief Hohé. Madelief Hohé, Ietse Meij: 'Vier decennia werkzaam in Mode en Kostuum, een inspirerend levenswerk. Een gesprek met de oud-conservator Mode van het Gemeentemuseum Den Haag', in *Kostuum, Jaarboek van de Nederlandse Kostuumvereniging 2003*, Zwolle 2003.

2 See issues of *Les Modes*, from the Kunstmuseum Den Haag collection, kept at the special collections department of the Royal Library in The Hague. See also: M.A. Ghering-van Ierlant, *Vrouwenmode in Prent. Modeprenten 1780-1930*, Amsterdam 2007, p. 167.

3 Heard at a conference in Paris on '*Fashion, Dress, and Society in Europe during World War I*', February 2014, to which this publication is a follow-up: Maude Bass-Krueger, Sophie Kurkdjian, *French Fashion Women & The First World War*, New York 2020.

4 Alan Mansfield, Phillis Cunnington, *Handbook of English Costume in the 20ᵗʰ century 1900-1950*, London 1973, pp. 19, 21.

5 Daniel Milford-Cottam, *Edwardian Fashion*, Oxford 2014, p. 34.

6 Mansfield and Cunnington 1973, p. 25; Milford 2014, p. 25.

7 Mansfield and Cunnington 1973, p. 36.

8 For example, advertisement in *Les Modes*, March 1911: 'Margaine-Lacroix, 19 Boulevard Haussmann, Créatrice de la Robe Sylphide et de la Robe Tanagréenne, Corset Sylphide-fourreau, indispensable sous les robes collantes [close-fitting dresses]'.

9 See also Tirza Westland, 'Uitdagend en uiterst modieus. Een studie naar twee 'gewaagde' japonnen in het Kunstmuseum Den Haag' in: *Kostuum*, Zwolle 2024, pp. 132-143; Mansfield and Cunnington 1973, p. 57.

10 According to Mrs Eric Pritchard, who published *The Cult of Chiffon* in 1902. Milford-Cottam 2014, p. 15.

11 Mansfield and Cunnington 1973, pp. 59-61.

12 Mansfield and Cunnington 1973, p. 61.

13 Mansfield and Cunnington 1973, p. 57.

14 Milford-Cottam 2014, p. 39.

15 Mansfield and Cunnington 1973, p. 264.

16 Milford-Cottam 2014, p. 25.

A first-class wardrobe

Madelief Hohé

What did a fashionable wardrobe of the 1910s look like? That of the wealthy Den Beer Poortugael-Rijnbendes in Kunstmuseum Den Haag's collection gives us a good idea.[1] The majority of it came from the estate of Mrs Maria Clara Magdalena Rijnbende (1879-1966), known to friends and family as 'Mary'. She married lawyer and prosecutor, and later banker, Mr Louis den Beer Poortugael Esq. (1865-1939) in The Hague on 16 February 1899. Several garments that belonged to Mr Den Beer Poortugael are in the museum's collection, including bespoke items from the Brothers Domhoff of The Hague, purveyors to the royal court, and from London tailors.[2] Mrs Den Beer Poortugael's wardrobe includes her white wedding gown from 1899, plus thirty fashionable items of day and evening wear, mainly from the period 1900-1940. A number of accessories have also survived, along with several négligés. They include a silk and lace négligé from the Maurice Soeurs fashion house in Brussels, very similar to the lace-trimmed peignoir that Kate Winslet (Rose in *Titanic*) wears when her fiancé, Caledon 'Cal' Hockley, hangs 'The Heart of the Ocean' around her neck. A similar peignoir from another wardrobe in the museum's collection, which belonged to Mary's contemporary Baroness Ada van Hardenbroek van Lockhorst (1889-1971), bears an even stronger resemblance to the négligé in *Titanic*. (p.27) A yellow gown, also from her wardrobe, by Gustav Beer, is also very similar to the yellow gown worn by the character Rose on the deck of the Titanic. (p. 17) But of course, the reverse is in fact true. Costume designer Deborah Lynn Scott studied the fashions of the period so well that her designs for the *Titanic* are exceptionally accurate.

Mrs Den Beer Poortugael closely followed changes in fashion. In the 1910s there was still a major difference between the dresses she wore during the day and those she wore in the evening. More and more sporty clothing was introduced to her wardrobe, including tennis outfits, knitted jumpers and sporty cardigans, novelties for women at the time that had been adopted from men's fashion. She also wore soft modern underwear, entirely in line with the new age, a time when the corset was gradually disappearing. Her wardrobe of the 1910s also contains several creations by Paris couture houses Maison Gustav Beer and Maison Brandt. Mary's wardrobe also included an expensive fur coat, with a broad collar trimmed with dark ermine tails.[3] (p.90) White ermine had been used for royal cloaks for centuries. She bought the coat secondhand around 1918 from a Russian refugee who had fled the Russian Revolution in 1917.

The Den Beer Poortugaels led an international life, moving between The Hague, Paris, London and other glamorous places. Their fashion tastes were classic and voguish, following the trends in Paris and Britain, and they bought their clothes there or in The Hague. Mrs Den Beer Poortugael had clothes made at the leading fashion houses Schüler & Cie (1900) and J.B. Lessur (1903), both on Lange Voorhout in The Hague, which sold Parisian fashions under licence to their Dutch clients. Both of these fashion houses had ties with Hirsch & Cie in Amsterdam, which opened in the Netherlands in 1882.[4] In 1912, the year when the Titanic would sink, the Amsterdam fashion house opened its grand new premises on Leidseplein, designed to be an opulent palace of fashion.[5]

The Den Beer Poortugaels' wardrobe would not have looked out of place among the first-class passengers on the Titanic, with which, however, they had no direct connection. Or did they? The family archive includes newspaper articles from April and May 1912 describing the Titanic disaster. They were kept by Louis den Beer Poortugael's father Jacobus Cornelis den Beer Poortugael Esq. (1832-1913), a former general and member of the Council of State.[6] Notes written on the newspapers indicate that Jacobus den Beer Poortugael was angry at Captain Smith's role in the disaster. He noted on *De Nieuwe Courant* of 1 May 1912: 'Captain Smith left the Titanic before some others were rescued, and was not therefore at his post when his ship went down.'

See notes pg. 69

An American wardrobe

Fabienne Hom

Sometimes, a museum is fortunate enough to acquire a wardrobe that not only paints a picture of an era, but also of the owner's personal tastes. This is the case with the wardrobe that belonged to Virginia Pearce Delgado-Orth (1891-1985) that was donated to Kunstmuseum Den Haag from her estate in 1987.[7] She was an American, born on 23 September 1891 in Washington D.C., United States. After the death of her husband Frederick Pearce Delgado (1877-1921) in 1921, she remarried. Her second husband was a Dutchman, Jean Ulric Marie de Kuyper (1893-1972), and they moved to the Netherlands.[8] The finest daywear and evening wear in Virginia's wardrobe dates from her time in America, in the 1910s. (p. 126)

These are pleasant garments that represent an 'American' taste that is rather saccharine by European standards. One striking day dress from 1915-1917 is made of pale pink linen. Floral motifs in cream cotton have been applied to the collar and other details. The belt is fastened by two distinctive mother-of-pearl buttons. Another dress from Virginia's wardrobe is made of cream voile with woven stripes, and has a red and blue floral motif. The front consists of a V-shaped centre panel in cream dotted tulle; it has additional pink satin features, including a small rosette. Virginia also had an expensive black silk evening coat dating from 1915-1922. The lining, and also the cuffs and collar, are made of white ermine, in which the tails are still visible. (p.90) The collection also includes two white cotton nightgowns, two summer dresses, one blouse, one evening coat, two scarves, three sets of underwear, three separate pairs of drawers and one underskirt. The initials VJS are on several items. V is for Virginia, J. for Johnston, and S for Stoughton, her mother's maiden names. Virginia Pearce Delgado-Orth's clothes show that she was one of the wealthier Americans of her day. Had she travelled on the Titanic, she would certainly have been in first class.

1 On this wardrobe, see also Ietse Meij, *Haute Couture & Prêt-à-porter*, Zwolle 1998, pp. 82-83; Madelief Hohé and Trudie Rosa de Carvalho, *Haagse Hofmode*, exh.cat. (Gemeentemuseum Den Haag) Zwolle 2007, pp. 66-67.

2 Kunstmuseum Den Haag, inv.nos. K 201-1996 to K 207-1966.

3 In 1925, this coat was valued at 3000 guilders, as part of Mary den Beer Poortugael's entire fur collection, which included silver fox, sea otter, astrakhan and chinchilla. Den Beer Poortugael family archive, National Archives, The Hague, inv.no. 0869-01-81. Thanks to Fleur Blom, trainee curator, who in 2024 performed research in the archive for this exhibition.

4 Madelief Hohé (ed.), *Ode aan de Nederlandse Mode*, exh.cat. (Gemeentemuseum Den Haag) Zwolle 2015, pp. 87-90.

5 Photographer Jacob Merkelbach had had his studio on the top floor of Hirsch's premises on Leidseplein since 1913. He photographed the Dutch beau monde and Hirsch models. See also Anneke van Veen, *Fotostudio Merkelbach* 1913-1969, Amsterdam 2013.

6 Jacobus Catharinus Cornelis den Beer Poortugael (1832-1913), National Archives, The Hague, inv.no. 0869-0175. Thanks to Fleur Blom (see note 5).

7 The gift came from Victor Bouter (1928-2004) of Voorburg; we do not know what his relationship was to Virginia Pearce Delgado-Orth or how the items came to be in his possession. Bouter was from a family of painters. His father was Cornelis W. Bouter (1888-1966), a Dutch painter who produced mainly cityscapes and landscapes. Victor's uncle (his father's brother) was Pieter Adrianus Bouter (1887-1968), better known as Piet Bouter. He too was a painter, who also specialised in landscapes. Victor Bouter also painted cityscapes, architecture and architectural fantasies. Information via https://research.rkd.nl accessed in July 2025.

8 In the 1930s Virginia worked for the Holland-America Line, publicising the Netherlands in America, both onboard ships travelling between the two countries (in first class), and among her acquaintance in America. Virginia also wrote articles on American literature for the Dutch newspaper *Het Vaderland: staat- en letterkundig nieuwsblad*, and she attempted to organise an American contemporary art exhibition in the Netherlands, including at Gemeentemuseum Den Haag. The archives of Kunstmuseum Den Haag include several documents relating to and photographs of Virginia, gifted by Mrs A.C. Rühl, who is also mentioned in Virginia's death notice in the *De Telegraaf* newspaper, 26 July 1985. The archives of the Roosevelt Institute for American Studies in Middelburg also have information on Virginia; visited in June 2025.

Lucile and the Titanic

Lucile, a pioneering female British fashion designer, is also widely known for her association with the Titanic. For many years, only those with an interest in the Titanic knew her name, but that all changed when the film *Titanic* was released in 1997.[1] The fashion house Maison Lucile was established by Lady Duff Gordon, née Lucy Christiana Sutherland (1863-1935), in 1893. It was not only the first fashion house to hold a catwalk show, it was also the first to offer a special range for debutantes, and the first to provide a complete look. It was the maker of 'personal dresses' and 'Gowns of Emotion', and the first couture house to collaborate with a large department store, and to expand to other countries.[2] Lucile opened a fashion house in New York in 1910, in Paris in 1911 and in Chicago in 1915.[3] Her designs were enthusiastically received both in Paris and in America. However, the expansion meant that Lucile had to travel more frequently, and that was how she came to be on board the Titanic on 15 April 1912.[4]

'The first days of the crossing were uneventful. Like everyone else I was entranced with the beauty of the liner. I had never dreamt of travelling in such luxury. My pretty little cabin, with its electric heater and pink curtains, delighted me so, that it was a pleasure to go to bed. Everything aboard this lovely ship reassured me, from the captain, with his kindly bearded face and genial manner, and his twenty-five years of experience as a White Star commander, to my merry, Irish stewardess, with her soft brogue and tales of the timid ladies she had attended during hundreds of Atlantic crossings. The time passed happily enough.[5] I remember that last meal on Titanic very well. We had a big vase of beautiful daffodils on the table, which were as fresh as if they had just been picked. Everyone was very gay, and at a neighbouring table people were making bets on the probable time of this record breaking run. Various opinions were put forward, but none dreamed that Titanic would make her harbour that night.'[6]

'I had been in bed for about an hour and the lights were all out, when I was awakened by a funny, rumbling noise. It was like nothing I had ever heard before. It seemed as if some giant hand had been playing bowls, rolling the great balls along. Then the boat stopped, and immediately there was the frightful noise of escaping steam [...].[7] Presently it stopped and there came an infinitely more frightening silence. The engines had stopped. Something in the cessation of this busy, homely sound filled me with panic.'[8]

Having become famous for her 'Tea-gowns' (loose dresses designed to be worn at home), Lucile designed for the nobility, the nouveau riche, for actresses, dancers and socialites.[9] Some even say that she created the first 'It Girl'.[10] One of those It Girls was French socialite Daisy Fellowes née Marguerite Séverine Philippine Decazes de Glücksberg (1890-1962), heir to the Singer sewing machine fortune. She had a talent for dressing well and setting trends, and thus became fashion editor at Harper's Bazaar Paris from 1933 to 1935. She was regarded as one of the most beautiful women of her day, and fashion designer Karl Lagerfeld once called her 'the chicest woman I have ever seen'.[11] But she was also provocative and attention-seeking. The dresses by Lucile in her collection are highly revealing, consisting of just a few layers of chiffon held together with a silk cord.

Less notorious but just as stylish, Charlotte Drake Martinez Cardeza (1854-1939) also travelled on the Titanic, with several Lucile gowns in her luggage. Like Lucile, she survived the disaster. She became famous when, after the sinking of the Titanic, she submitted a 20-page(!) claim to the White Star Line for a total of $177,352.75. On page 6 of the claim we read: 'Rose Gown, Lucile $350, and White satin petticoat, lace and flowers, Lucile London, $200'.[12] Mrs Cardeza, who was travelling with her adult son, his servant and her own maid, had with her a total of 17 large 'streamer trunks'; 2 large leather bags; 3 suitcases; 1 jewellery box and 3 crates of luggage.[13]

These dresses by Lucile ended up on the ocean floor along with the Titanic, but Mrs Cardeza and Lucile survived. Lucile continued her career as a designer until the mid-1920s. Her work was soon forgotten, but she has gone down in fashion history as a true fashion visionary and innovator, while to others her name is forever linked to that of the Titanic.

[1] The character Lucile, Lady Duff Gordon, was played by Rosalind Ayres (b. 1946).

[2] Lady Duff Gordon, *Discretions & Indiscretions, by Lady Duff Gordon*, London 1932, pp. 42 and 71. In her memoirs Lucile wrote of the 'personal dresses', 'I studied the type of each one and designed a gown for her which I thought would harmonize with her individuality, and they were all immensely intrigued of rediscovering themselves in my eyes. [...] Everyone who heard of me wanted to have one of my "personal dresses" [...].' She first got to know her client well, considered her good and bad sides, what should be accentuated, what should be played down, and by the end of the consultation Lucile knew what style would best suit her client.
As regards her Gowns of Emotion: As well as coming up with the idea of the fashion show, Lucile also devised a concept she called 'Gowns of Emotion'. She was appalled that, during the fashion show, her creations were announced as 'dress number 1' or 'pink silk dress'. She therefore adopted the habit of giving her dresses names that emphasised the character of the design. Examples include: *Happiness, Give Me Your Heart, The Sighing Sound of Lips Unsatisfied, When Passion's Thrall is O'er, The Harvest of Sin, The Shadow of Scandal,* and *Why Do You Hesitate?.* She drew her inspiration from literature and history, but some names were inspired by the character and taste of her clients. In 1905 Maison Lucile became Lucile Ltd., giving the company more freedom to expand to other countries.
In America Lucile entered into partnership with the Sears, Roebuck and Co. department store chain, committing to designing a line of ready-to-wear dresses; the partnership lasted only a year.

[3] *Designing the IT Girl: Lucile and her Style*, cat. (The Museum at FIT) New York 2005, p. 12.

[4] *Designing the IT Girl*, p. 12.

[5] Lady Duff Gordon 1932, pp. 148-149.

[6] Lady Duff Gordon 1932, p. 150.

[7] Lady Duff Gordon 1932, p. 151.

[8] Lady Duff Gordon 1932, p. 152.

[9] Lady Duff Gordon 1932. A Tea-gown was a loose-fitting comfortable dress worn by ladies during informal gatherings or parties, at afternoon tea or dinner at home. The dresses were often made of light, thin fabrics like chiffon and had few or no stays.

[10] *Designing the IT Girl* 2005, p. 9. Meaning of It Girl: a charming young woman with sex appeal who attracts a huge amount of media attention without actually doing anything of note.
Via: It-girl – Wikipedia Accessed on 17-7-2025.

[11] Via: Daisy Fellowes Biography, Fashion Icon Story, Catwalk Yourself by Bronte Naylor-Jones. Accessed on 11-7-2025.

[12] Via: Titanic Survivors: One Ship, Two Different Worlds, DocsTeach Accessed on 11-7-2025.

[13] Via: Titanic Survivors: One Ship, Two Different Worlds, DocsTeach Accessed on 11-7-2025.

Marije Blaasse

Perfumes with class: Fragrant echoes of the Titanic

A century ago, class differences were not only visible in the way people looked, but could also be detected by smell, and the Titanic was no exception. First-class passengers had access to chic smoking rooms, they often had their own lavatory and sometimes even a bath tub, or they could use the Turkish bath on board. They were also given complementary bars of the lemon-scented *Vinolia Otto Toilet Soap*, advertised alongside images of the miraculous 'unsinkable' ocean liner.[1]

The luxury cabins were deliberately positioned so that their occupants would hear as little noise as possible from the engines, and would also be spared the 'distinctly nauseating smell' of the engine room.[2] The second- and third-class passengers simply had to tolerate the odours, and would also have to use shared sanitary facilities. Although everything possible was done to keep the different classes and the associated odours separate, smells cannot always be contained behind notional barriers. On deck, everyone – whatever their background – would smell the vapours from the engine room and the bilge water below deck via the ventilation system.[3] Even the smell of the fatal iceberg reached people in different parts of the ship just before the collision. Despite being an experienced traveller, survivor Elizabeth W. Shutes grew nervous at the ominous smell (and she was not the only one): 'The air had so strange an odour, as if it came from a clammy cave'.[4]

One of the other first-class passengers surrounded himself with much more pleasant aromas, by virtue of his profession. Adolphe Saalfeld (1865-1926) was a chemist, entrepreneur and founder of a perfume company in Manchester. He had a satchel with him containing some sixty scent samples to promote his wares in New York, in the hope of breaking into a new market. After the first collision, Saalfeld left the smoking room and went to his cabin, then rushed to a lifeboat.[5] He wrote an account of his experiences:

'I saw a few men and women go into a boat and I followed and when lowered, pushed off and rowed some distance, fearing...Titanic sinking... As we drifted away gradually, saw Titanic sink lower and lower and finally her lights went out, and others in my boat said they saw her disappear. Our boat was nearly two miles away but pitiful cries could be plainly heard' [...].[6]

Although he suffered no physical injury, Saalfeld was a broken man plagued by survivor's guilt. So many women and children had not made it, as critics pointed out to him. Almost a century later (over seventy years after Saalfeld's death), his luggage turned out to be less damaged than he was. When the leather roll with vials of perfume was found near the wreck in 2000, the handwritten labels with the names of the essential oils of plants (known as 'otto') were still legible: *Floral Otto of Lily of the Valley*, *Floral Otto W* and *Thyme Red Otto*. There was still rose, bergamot (a citrus fruit) and lavender in the vials. These natural fragrances were popular among the wealthier members of the bourgeoisie at that time, though they were in fact fairly traditional. Around 1900 middle-class tastes shifted towards synthetic fragrances, their popularity reaching a high point in circa 1920.[7] Perfume magnate François Coty made his famous *L'Origan*, containing a molecule, 'coumarin', that smelled of hay, as early as 1905.[8] And Coco Chanel would have turned up her nose at Saalfeld's innocent floral fragrances, so redolent of bourgeois tradition. Her iconic Chanel No. 5 featured synthetic aldehydes (chemical compounds), whose metallic 'arctic' freshness counterbalanced the smell of warm, animal excretions like musk and civet.[9]

The most extraordinary thing about the find was the fact that the fragile glass bottles were still intact despite the enormous water pressures to which they had been subjected. Archaeologist and Titanic expert Bill Sauder was deeply moved:

'The one thing I will remember about Titanic artefacts until the day I die, is when the [...] perfume vials came up. When you recover things from the Titanic

it's wet, it's rusty and it's rotten. And the smell that comes off of it [...] is perfectly fetid [...]. And then all of a sudden somebody opens up this satchel [...] out comes the fragrance of heaven [...] So instead of being surrounded by all of these dead things [pauses, visibly affected, and starts to cry] for those few minutes the ship was alive again'.[10]

The 'late arrival' of Saalfeld's perfumes probably gave them more of an impact than they would ever have had otherwise.

[1] Encyclopedia Titanica a, over Vinolia otto toilet soap, op https://www.encyclopedia-titanica.org/vinolia-otto-toilet-soap.html. De achterkleinzoon van Thomas Eggleston Burrows – de uitvinder van de eerste geurende Vinolia zeep – vond in een archief een recept waaruit blijkt dat de eerste variant niet naar citroen maar naar iris en pepermunt rook: https://www.humblebeeandme.com/the-original-vinolia-soap-notes/. Geraadpleegd op 05.06.2025.

[2] Cathalijne Boland, *Reuchlins reis – De Holland-Amerika Lijn en de landverhuizers*, Amsterdam 2025, p. 57.

[3] Boland 2025, p. 29.

[4] Archibald Gracie, *The Truth about the Titanic*, New York 1913, p. 251.

[5] Encyclopedia Titanica b, over Adolphe Saalfeld, op https://www.encyclopedia-titanica.org/titanic-survivor/adolphe-saalfeld.html. Geraadpleegd op 05.06.2025.

[6] Encyclopedia Titanica b.

[7] Caro Verbeek, *Ruiken aan de tijd – de olfactorische dimensie van het futurisme 1909-1942*, Amsterdam 2020 (proefschrift verdedigd aan de Vrije Universiteit Amsterdam), p. 215.

[8] Idem, p. 216.

[9] Idem, p. 215.

[10] Bill Sauder in de documentaire *Titanic: The Final Word with James Cameron*, uitgezonden op National Geographic in 2012, transcript op https://www.imdb.com/title/tt2132504/characters/nm07766555.

Caro Verbeek

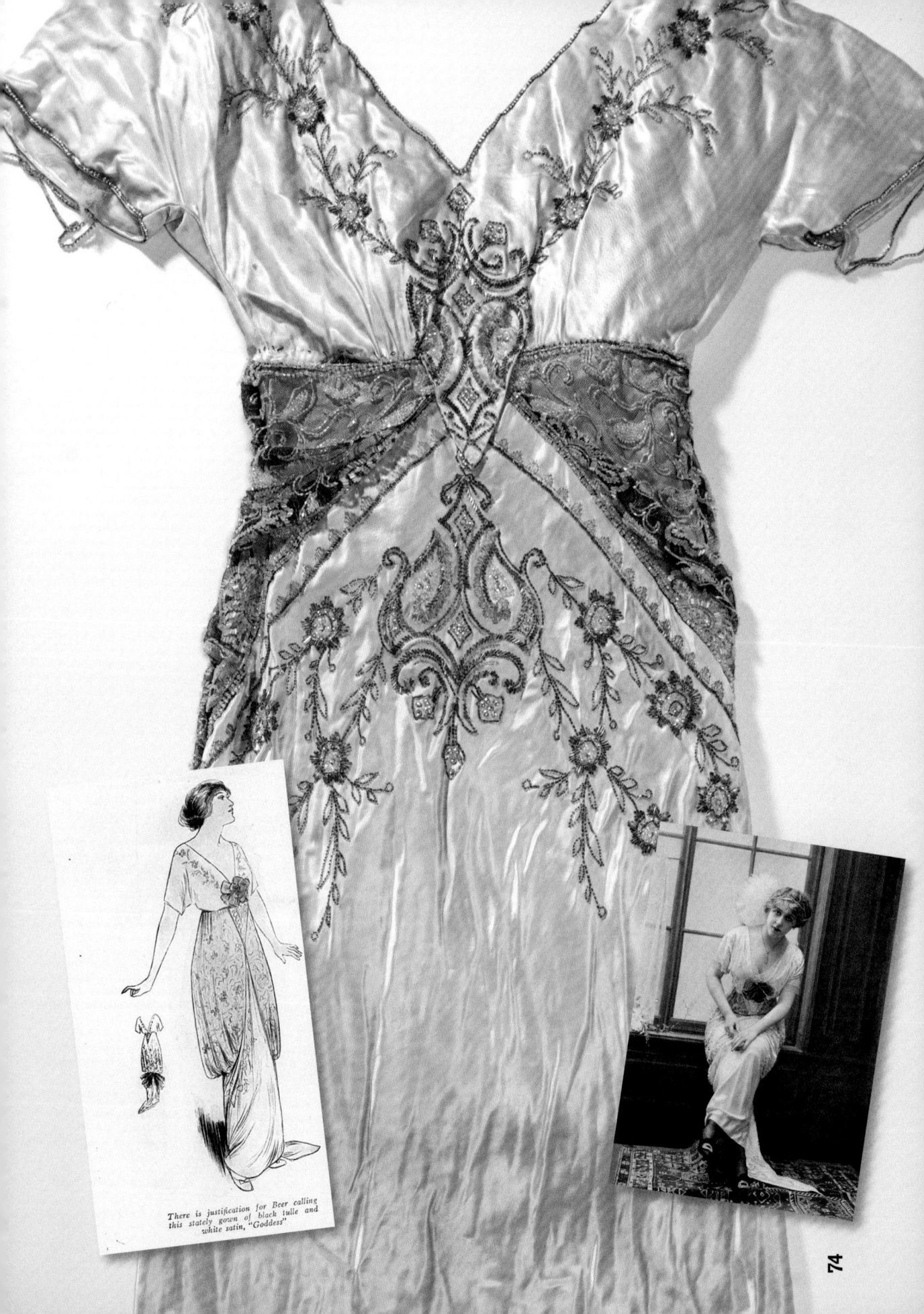

There is justification for Beer calling this stately gown of black tulle and white satin, "Goddess"

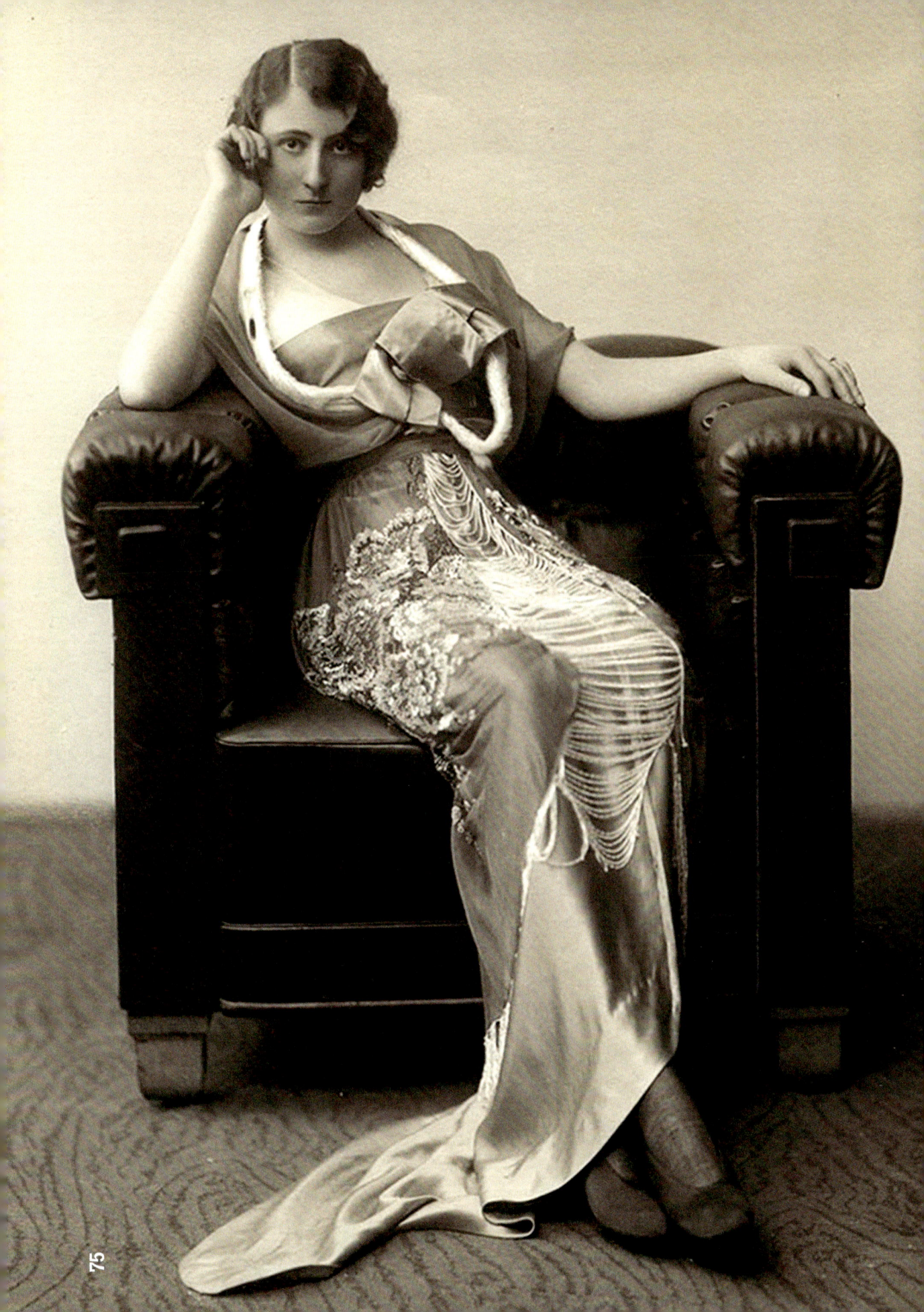

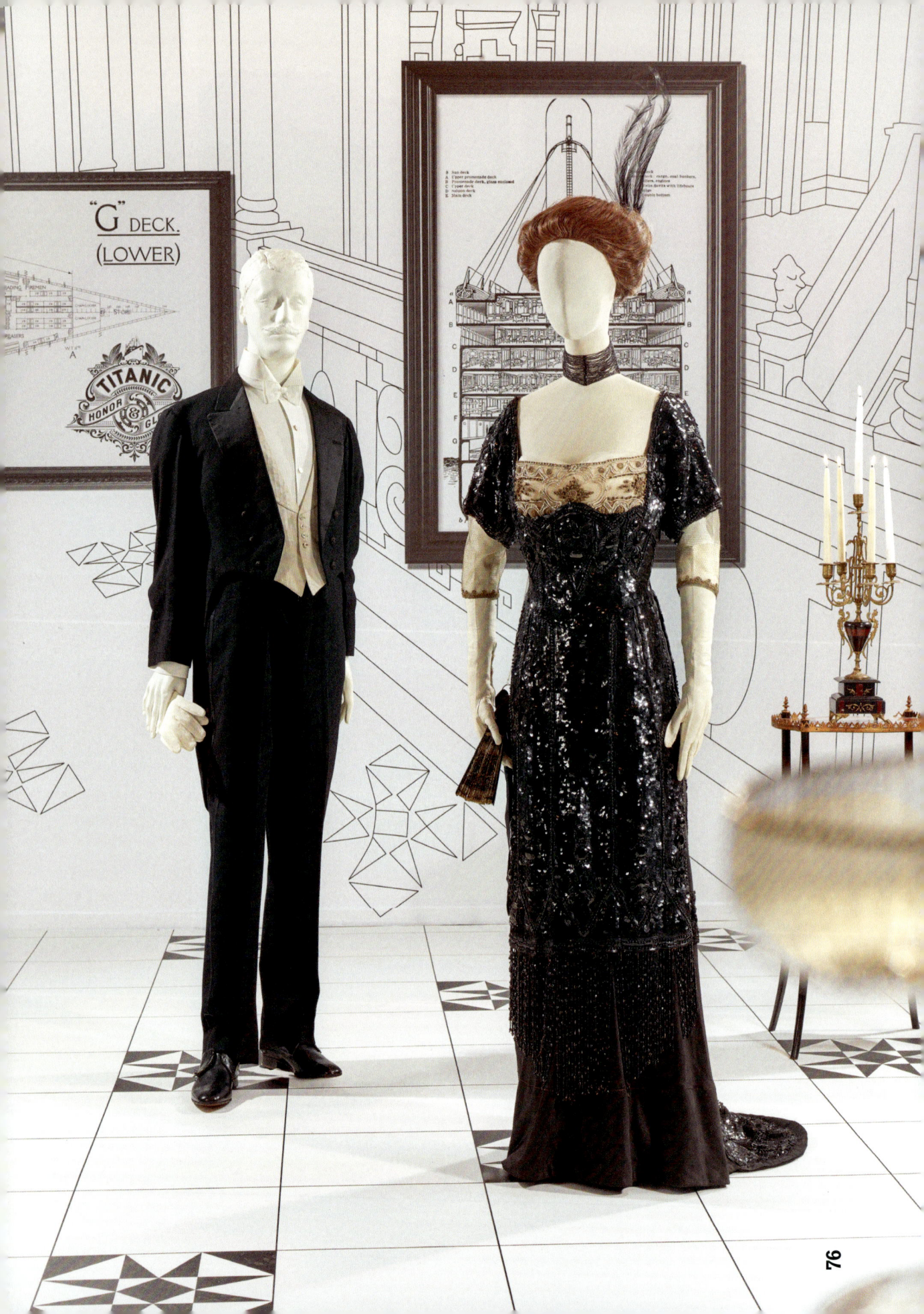

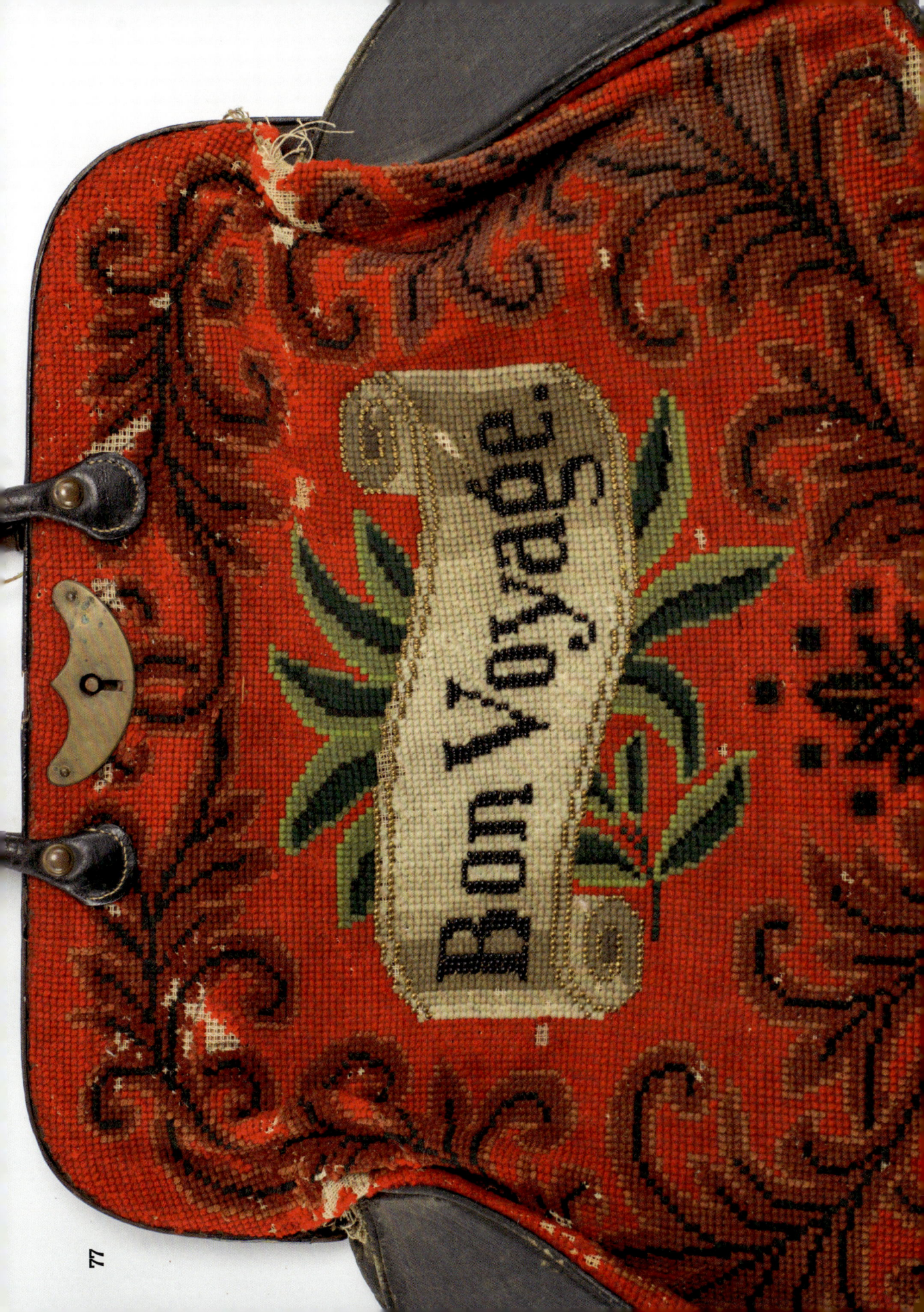

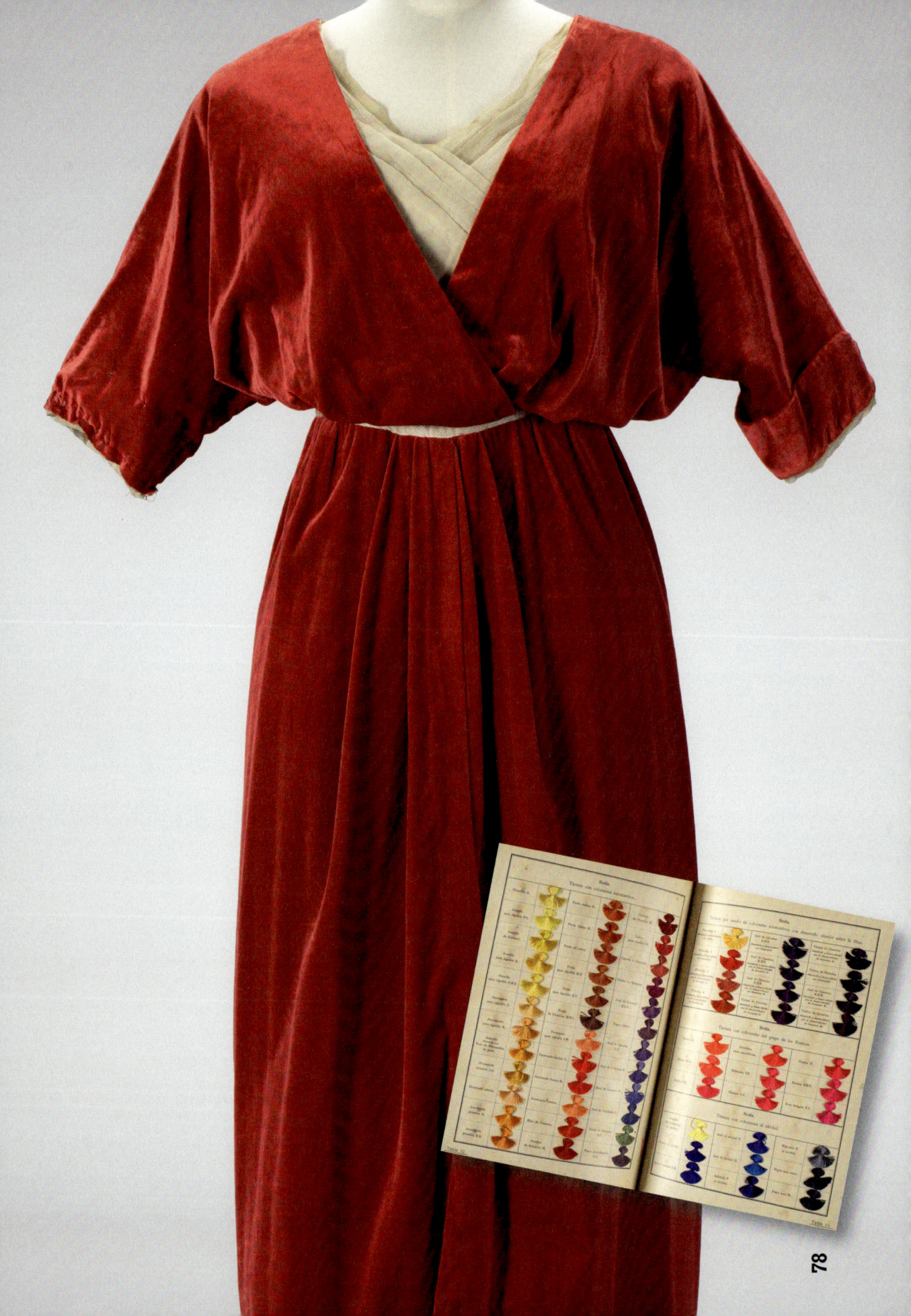

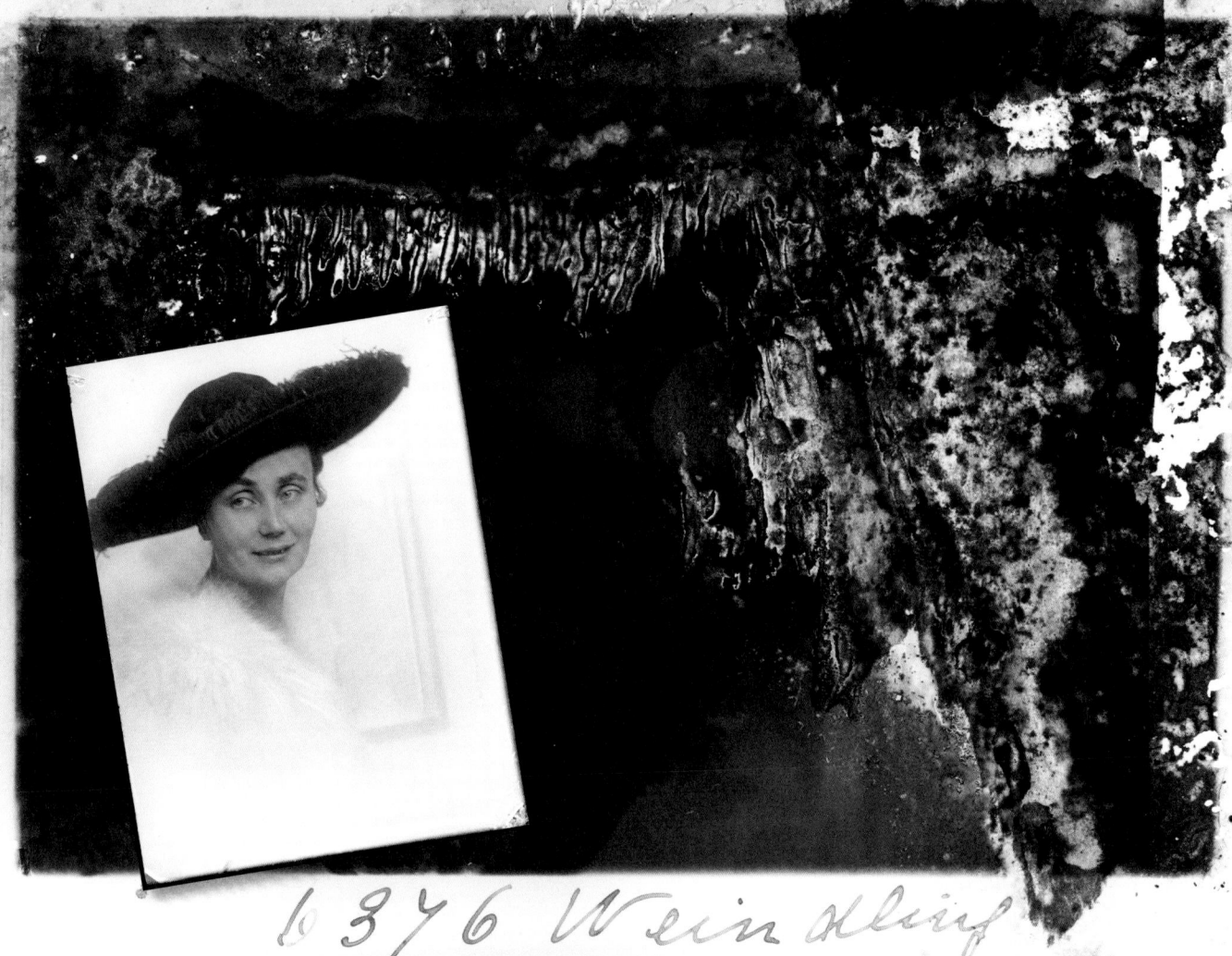

6376 Weindling

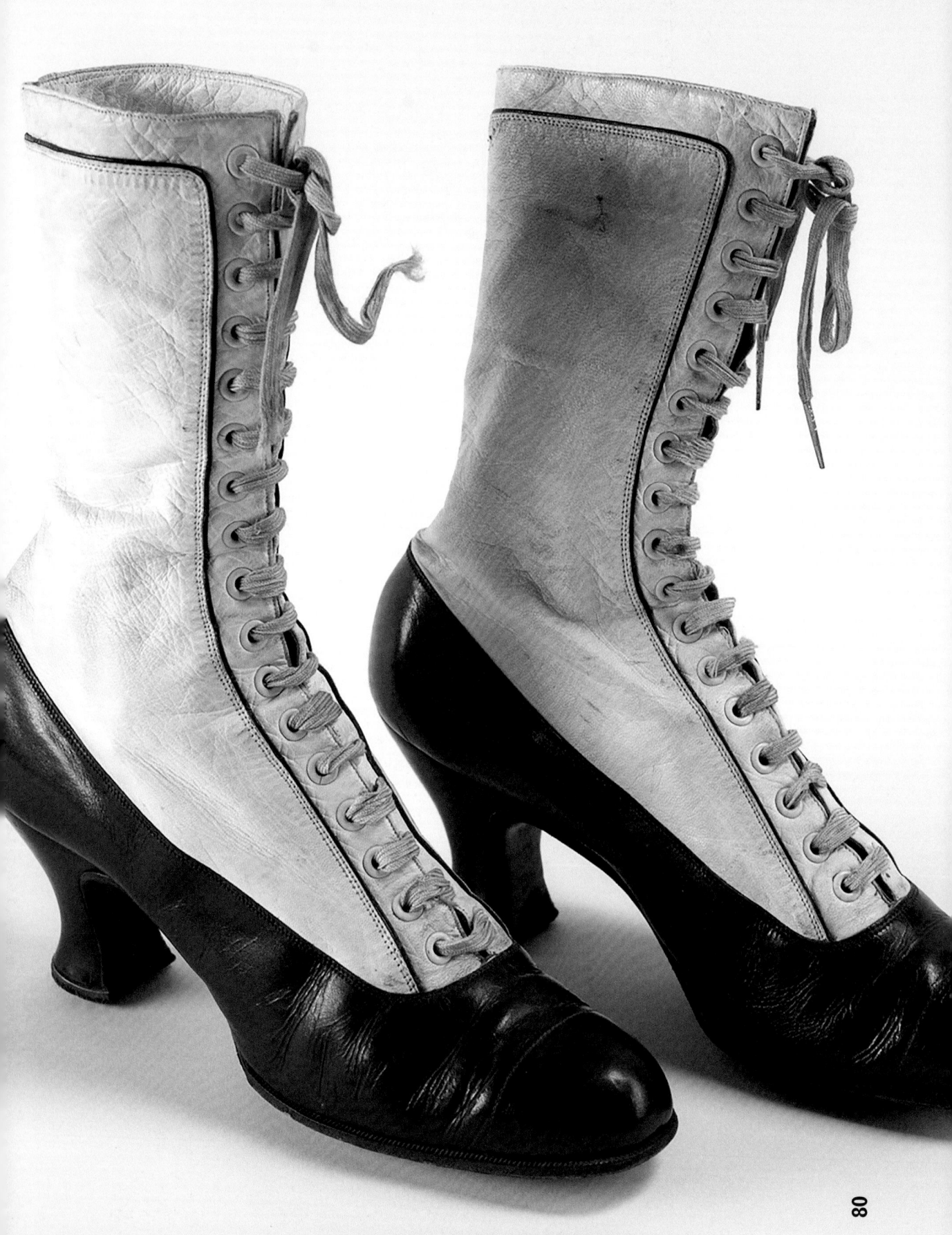

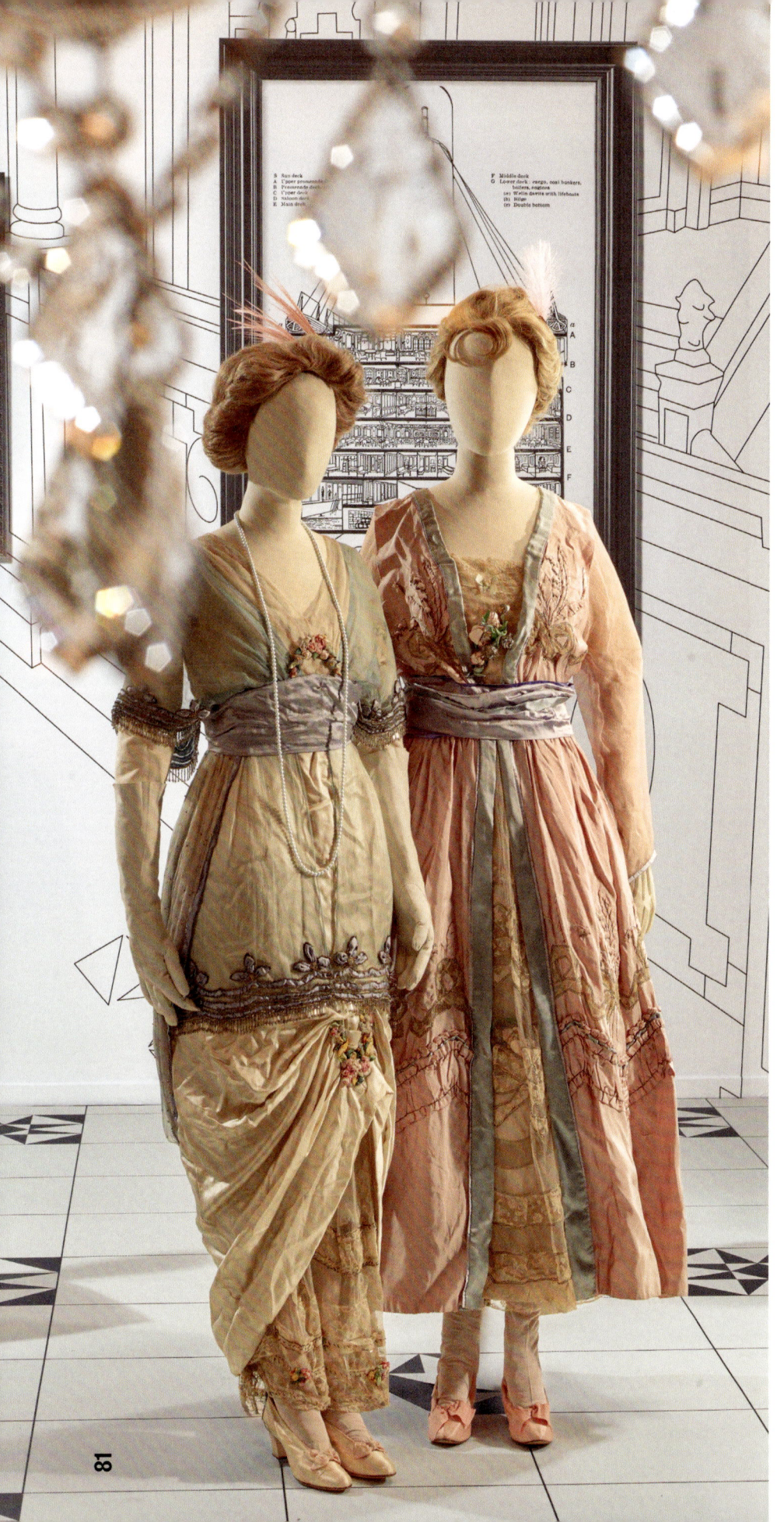

p. 74 Jérôme / Gustav Beer, *Déesse* gown in cream silk satin with silver and white beaded embroidery, Paris, c. 1912; illustrated in *Vogue* and *La Mode Illustrée* in 1912 and in *Les Modes* in 1913. Gallica BnF.

p. 75 Model from Paris wearing an evening gown at the fashion show for the opening of the new Hirsch 'fashion palace' on Leidseplein in Amsterdam, 1912.

p. 76 Mme Wiegandt-Riccard, Black tulle evening gown, covered in celluloid sequins, glass beads, jet beads, gold thread and passementerie, Geneva, c. 1909-1910, possibly worn by Maria Henriëtte Röell-Rutgers van Rozenburg (1872-1923); J. Campbell, Latham & Co., Dress suit, wool, silk, London, 1914, worn by Eugène Johannes.

p. 77 Travel bag with 'Bon voyage' in wool cross stitch, key, c. 1880-1910.

p. 78 Hirsch & Cie, Gown in red silk velvet and silk crepe, Amsterdam, 1914, worn by Mrs A.H. Hondius-Crone; described as follows when donated to museum: 'Hirsch, 1914, old rose velvet + bronze-yellow belt.'

p. 78 Synthetic dye book showing the use of acid dyes over silk and their possible combinations, *Badische Anilin & Soda Fabric*, 1902: 310-311. Courtesy of Cesar Rodriguez Salinas.

p. 79 Studio of J. Merkelbach, photograph of Regina Klara Weindling wearing a fur coat, hat and muff, 1920.

p. 79 Studio of J. Merkelbach (photographer on top floor of Hirsch building, Amsterdam): Ms Konings, dressed by Hirsch & Cie, 1917.

p. 80 Two-tone leather laced boots, c. 1910-1917.

p. 81 Lucile, Evening gown in lilac silk, Paris, c. 1911; Lucile, *Happiness* evening dress, c. 1915, courtesy of Lewis Orchard.

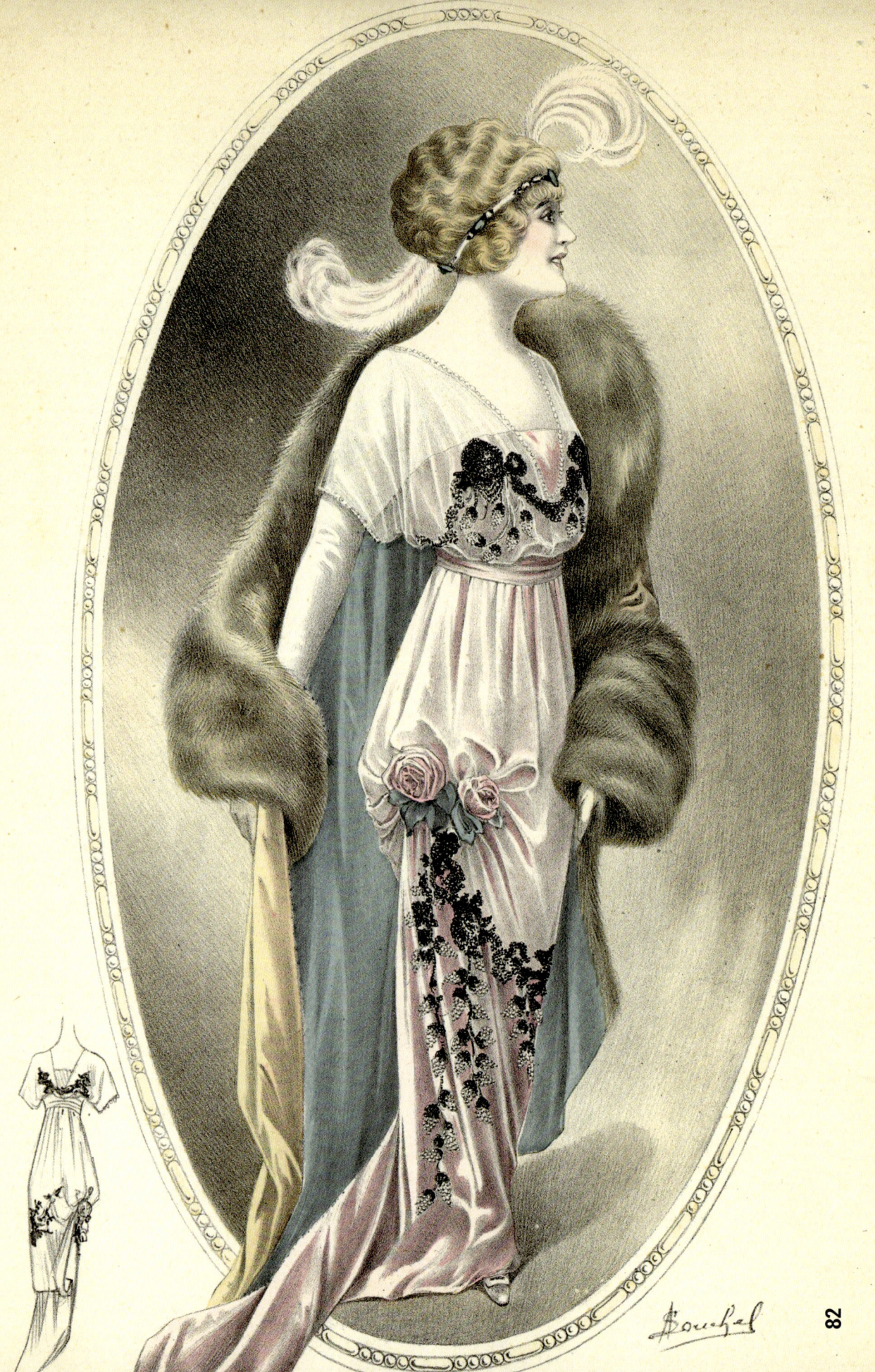

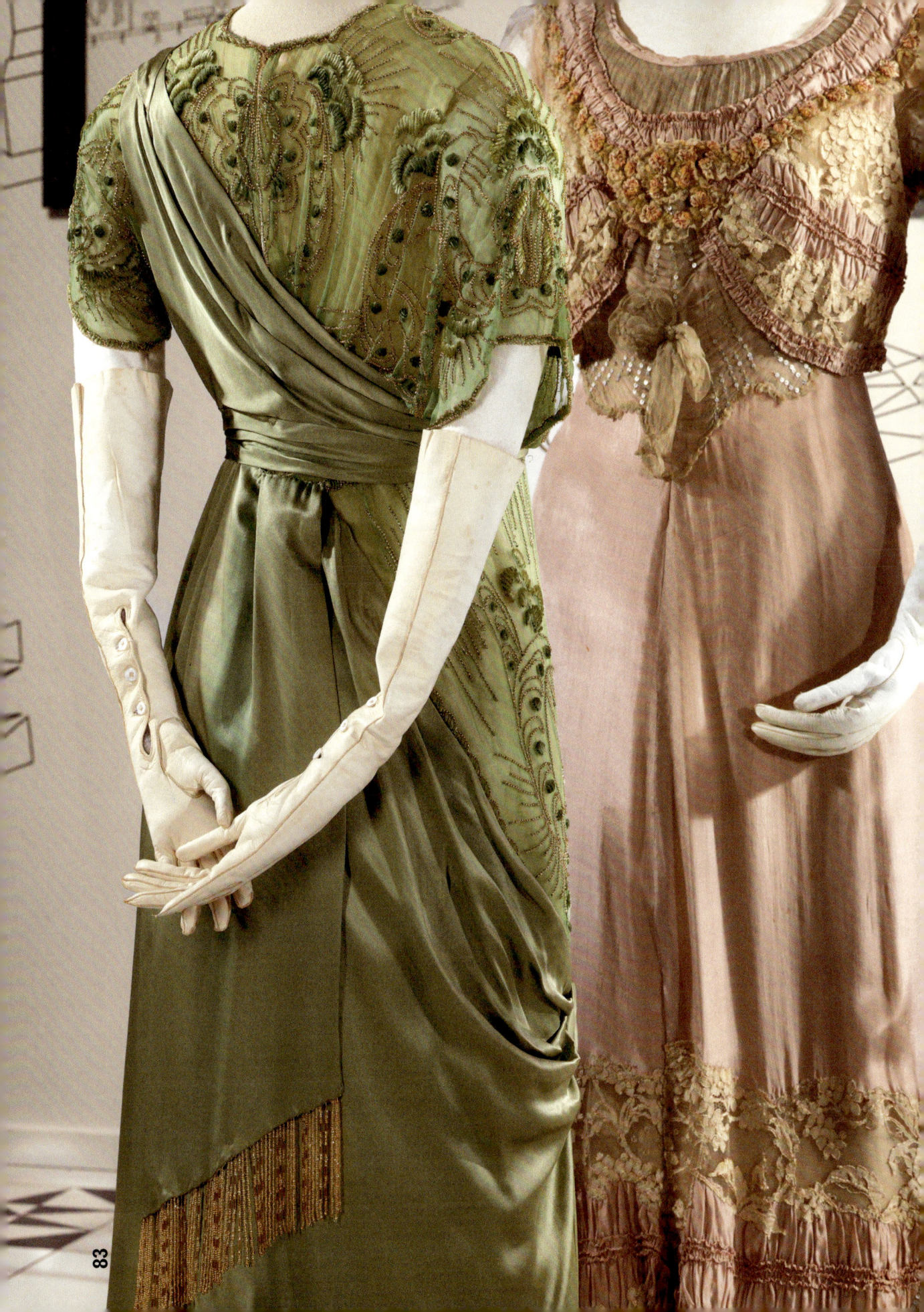

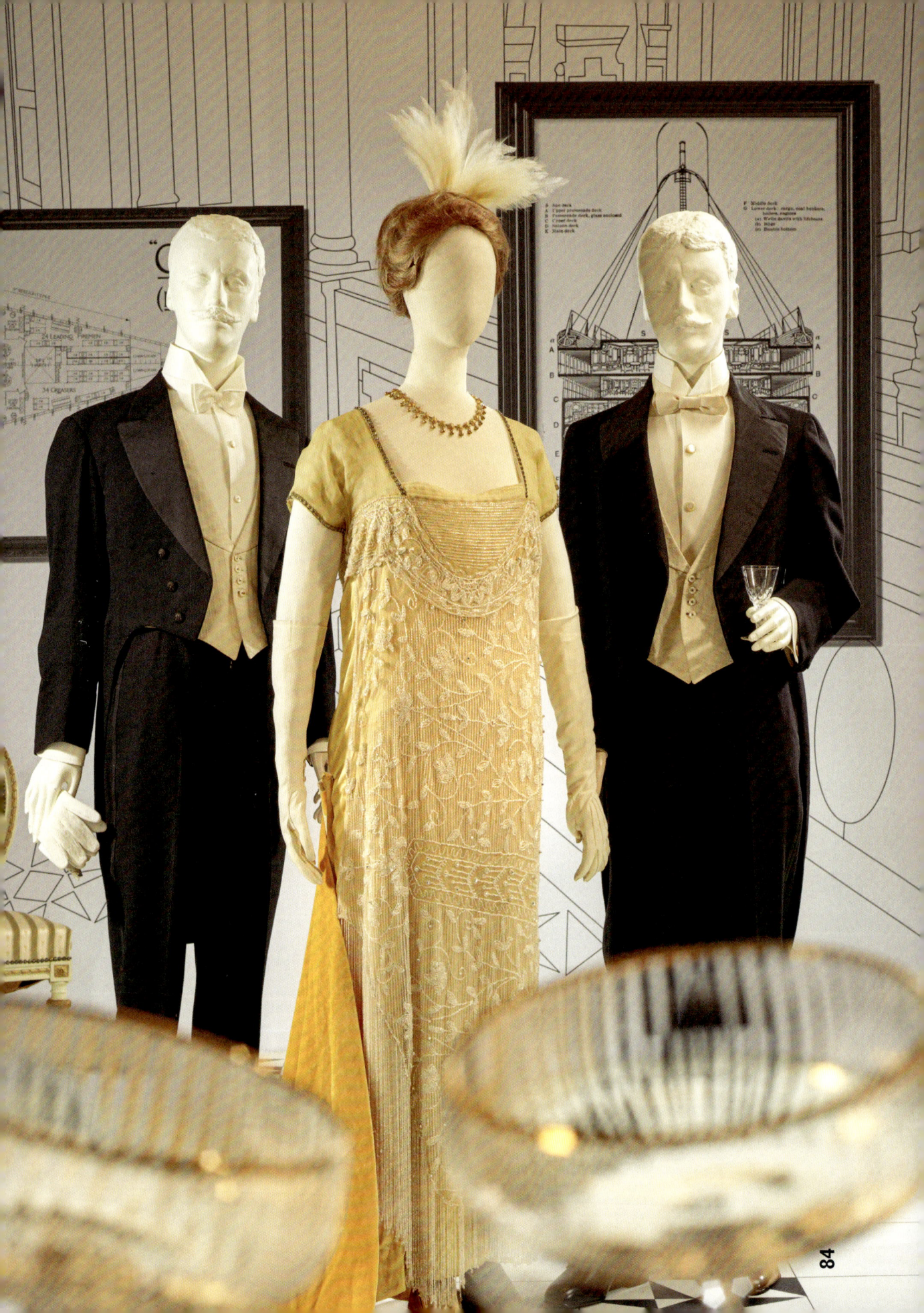

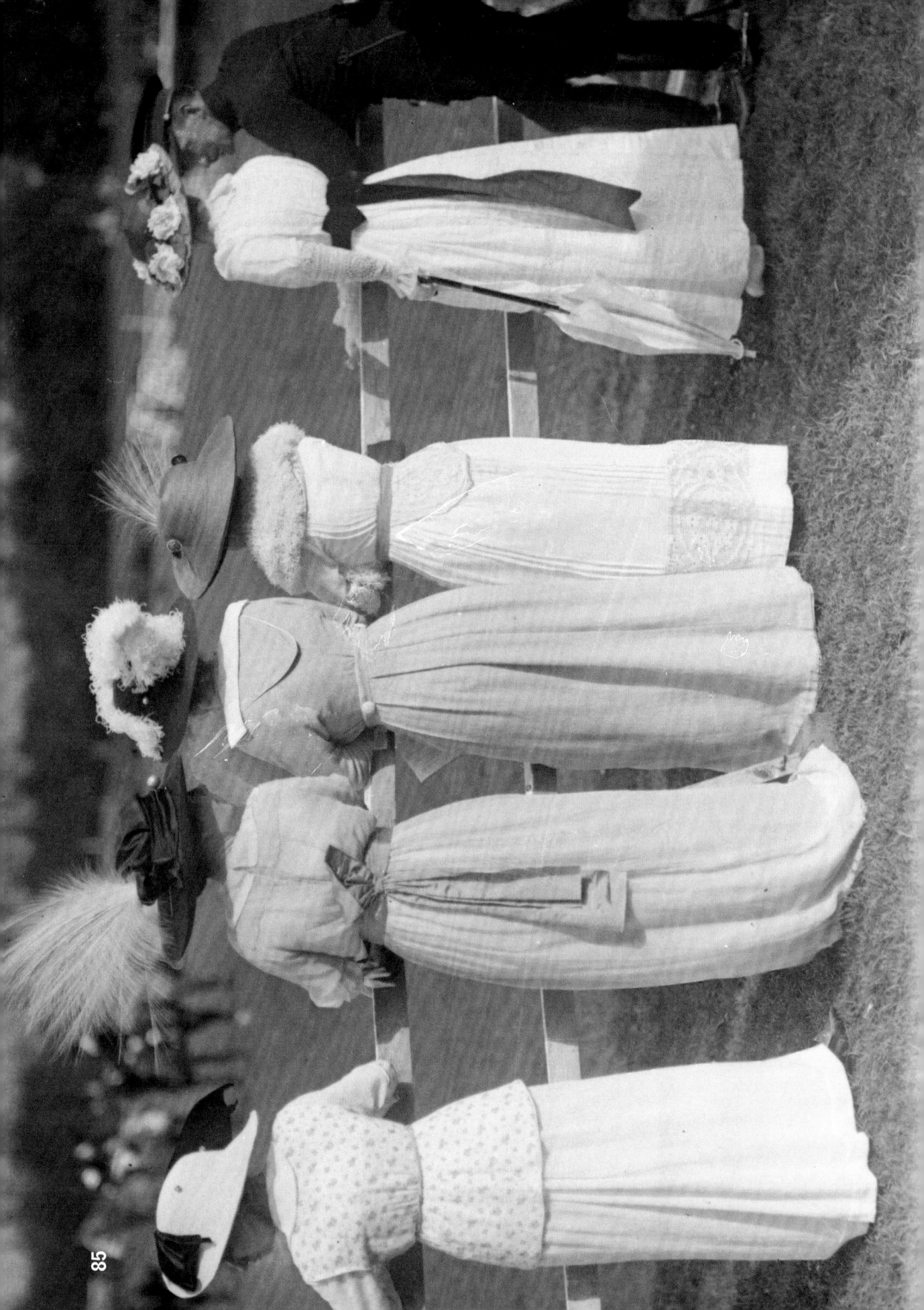

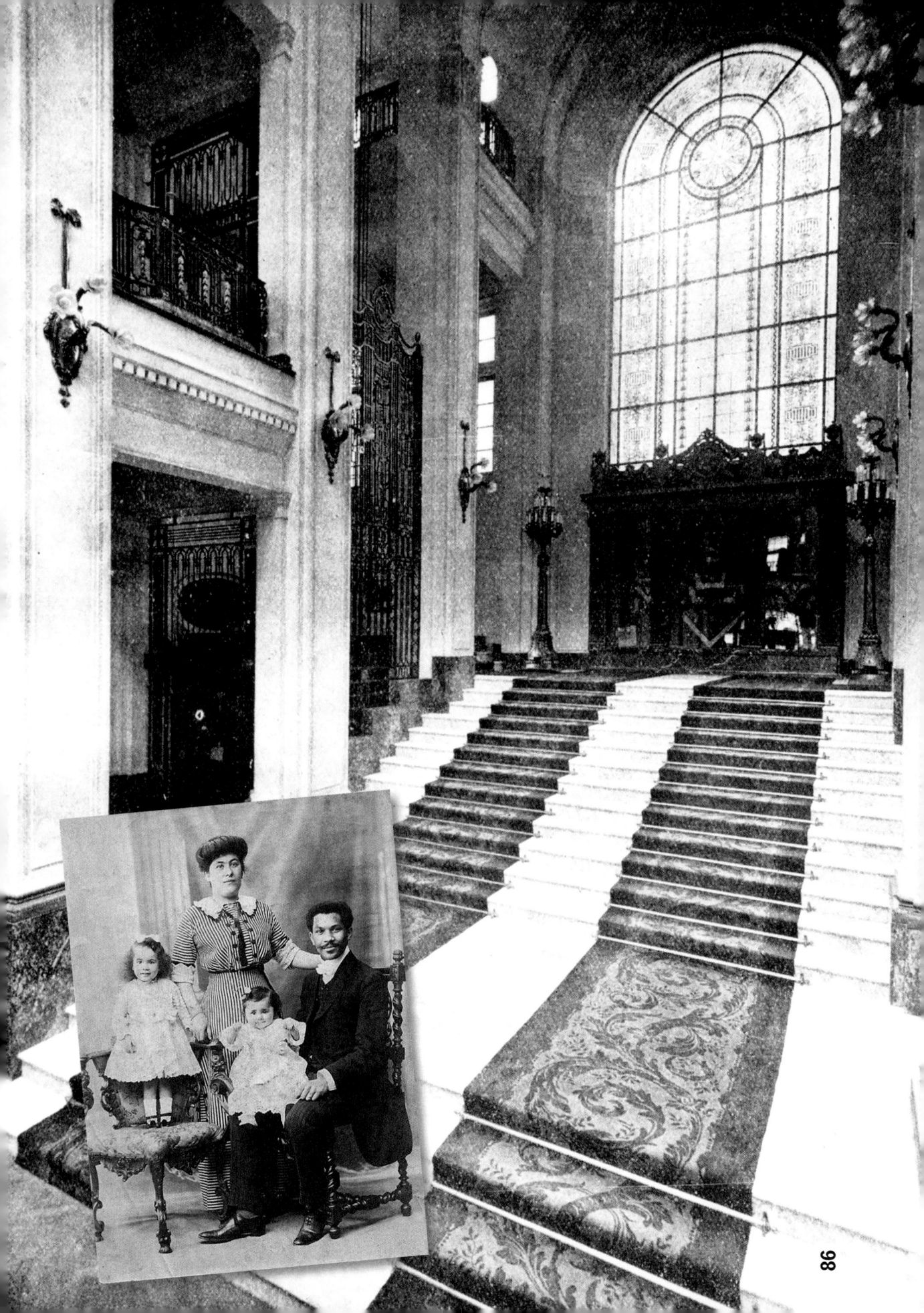

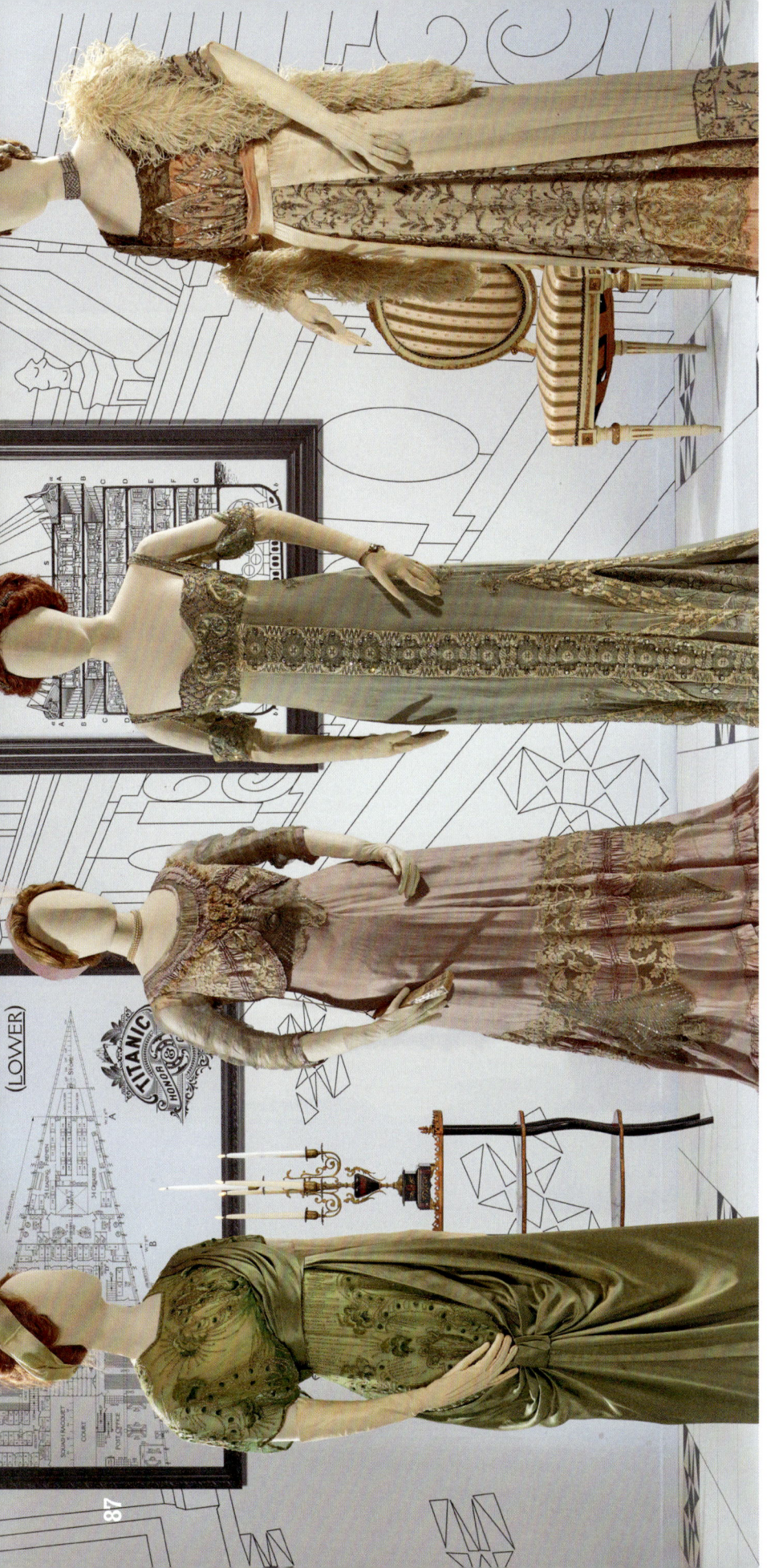

p. 82 A. Souchel, Fashion plate of a ballgown by Martial et Armand in: *La Femme Chic*, 1913.

p. 83 Maison Freyling, Evening gown in green silk satin and voile embroidered with gold-coloured glass beads and green chenille, Brussels, c. 1912-1913; Lilac pongee silk gown trimmed with lace on tulle, ruches and sequins, c. 1908.

p. 84 Two black wool dress suits: J. Campbell, Latham & Co., London, 1914, worn by Eugène Johannes, and Davies & Son, London, 1910, worn by Baron van Heeckeren; L. Beer-Corbel, Evening gown (kept in box with inscription reading: 'c. 1913/1914 maman, robe bal de cour') in light yellow satin and dark yellow velvet and rhinestones, Brussels, c. 1913-1914.

p. 85 Fashionably dressed visitors at a horse show on Museumplein in Amsterdam, 1914.

p. 86 Staircase at the Hirsch & Co. premises (built 1912) on Leidseplein, Amsterdam, 1915.

p. 86: As far as is known, Joseph Philippe Laroche (1886-1912) was the only Black passenger onboard the Titanic. He was born in Haiti and studied in France. He and his French wife Juliette Lafargue and their two daughters Simonne and Julie were travelling second-class to New York on their way back to Haiti, as they had suffered discrimination in France. Joseph lost his life in the disaster, and his family returned to France.

p. 87 Two evening gowns (see p. 83); Evening gown in light-green silk crepe georgette over a base of grey satin, lavishly decorated with bands of rhinestones and sequins, c. 1911-1912, probably worn without a corset or underskirt by Baroness Ada van Hardenbroek van Lockhorst (1889-1971); Maison Lessur & Cie, Evening gown in cream silk satin and salmon pink velvet embroidered with tube beads and sequins on silk voile, The Hague, c. 1910-1913, worn by Maria Clara Magdalena den Beer Poortugael- Rijnbende (1879-1966).

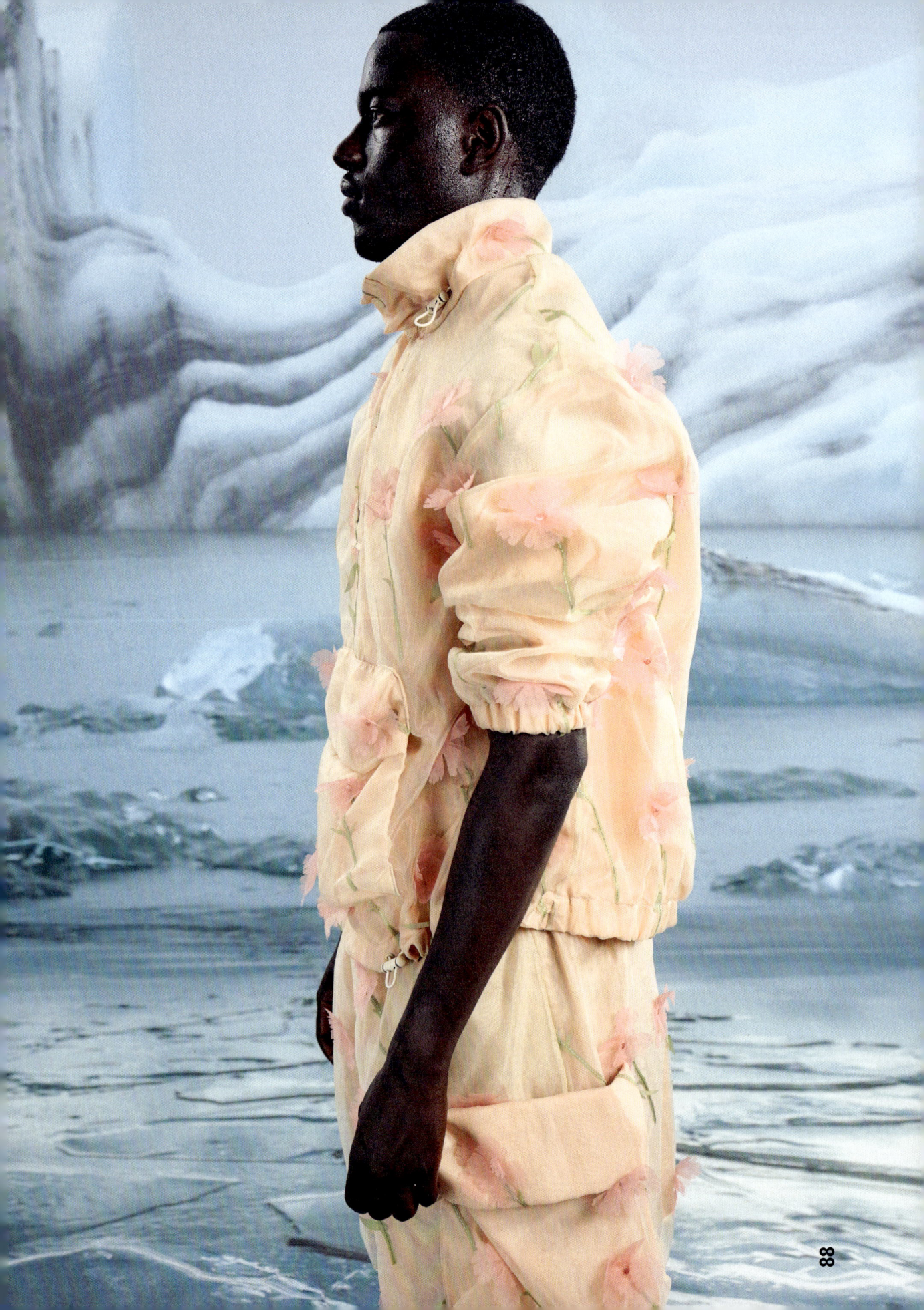

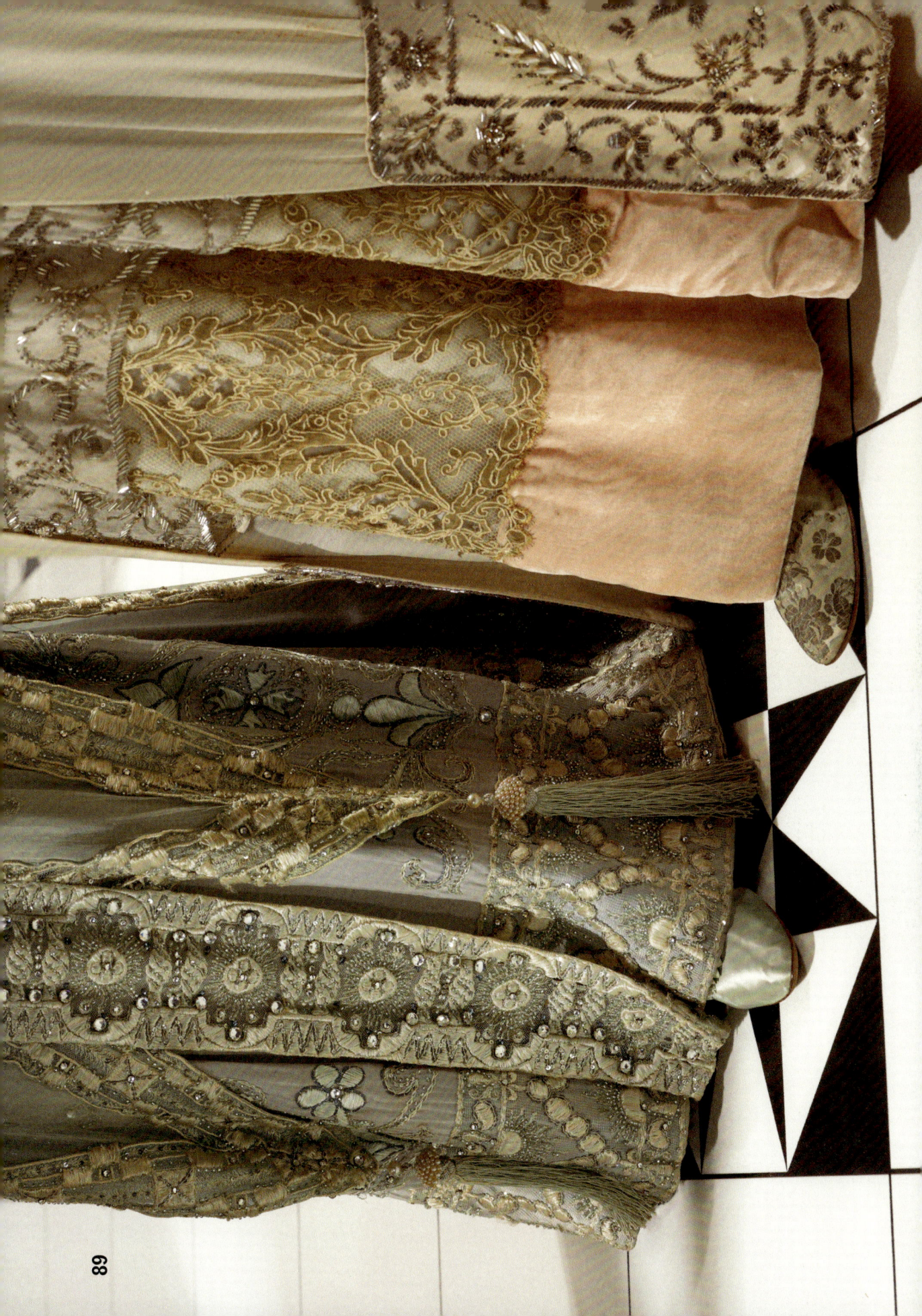

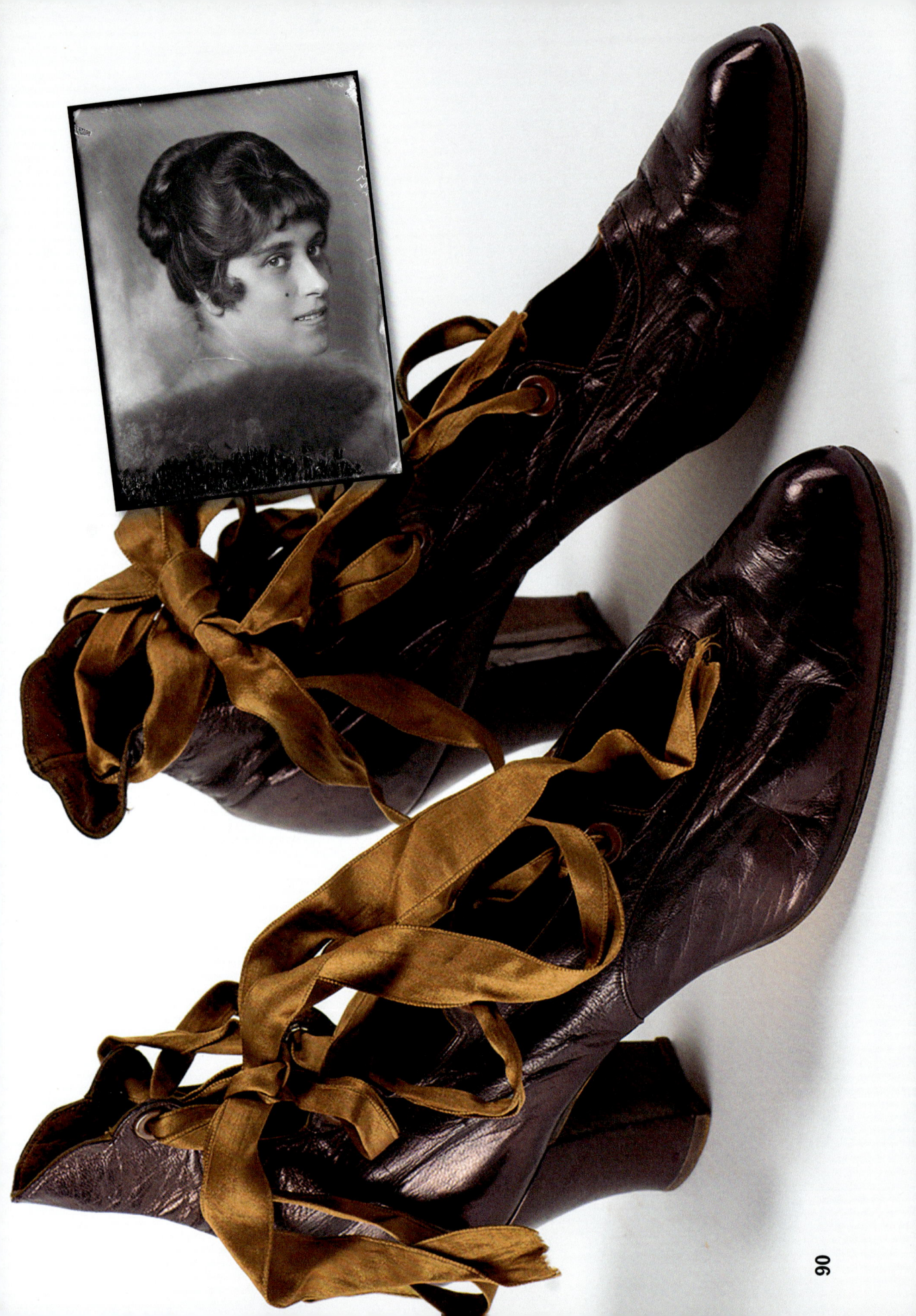

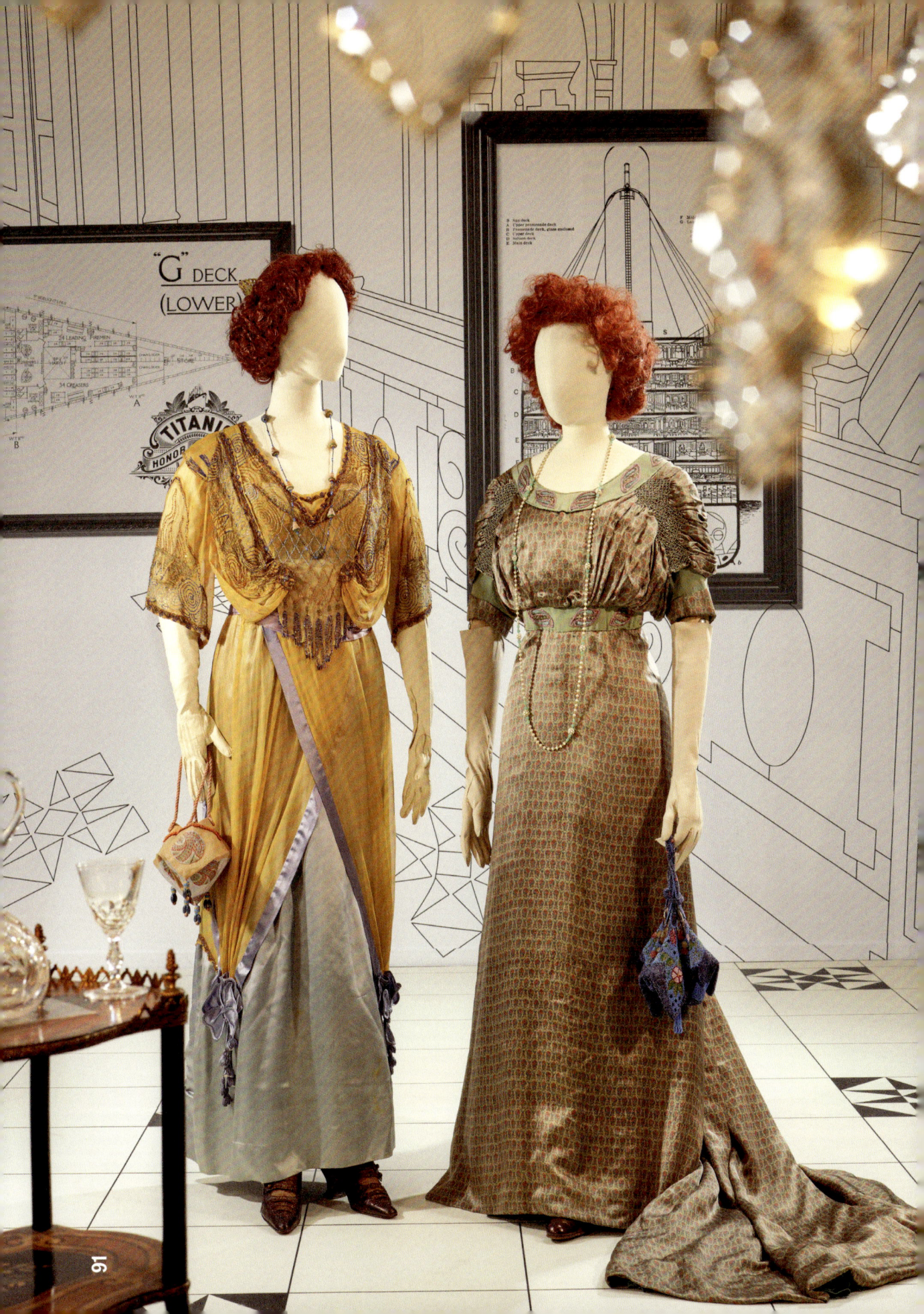

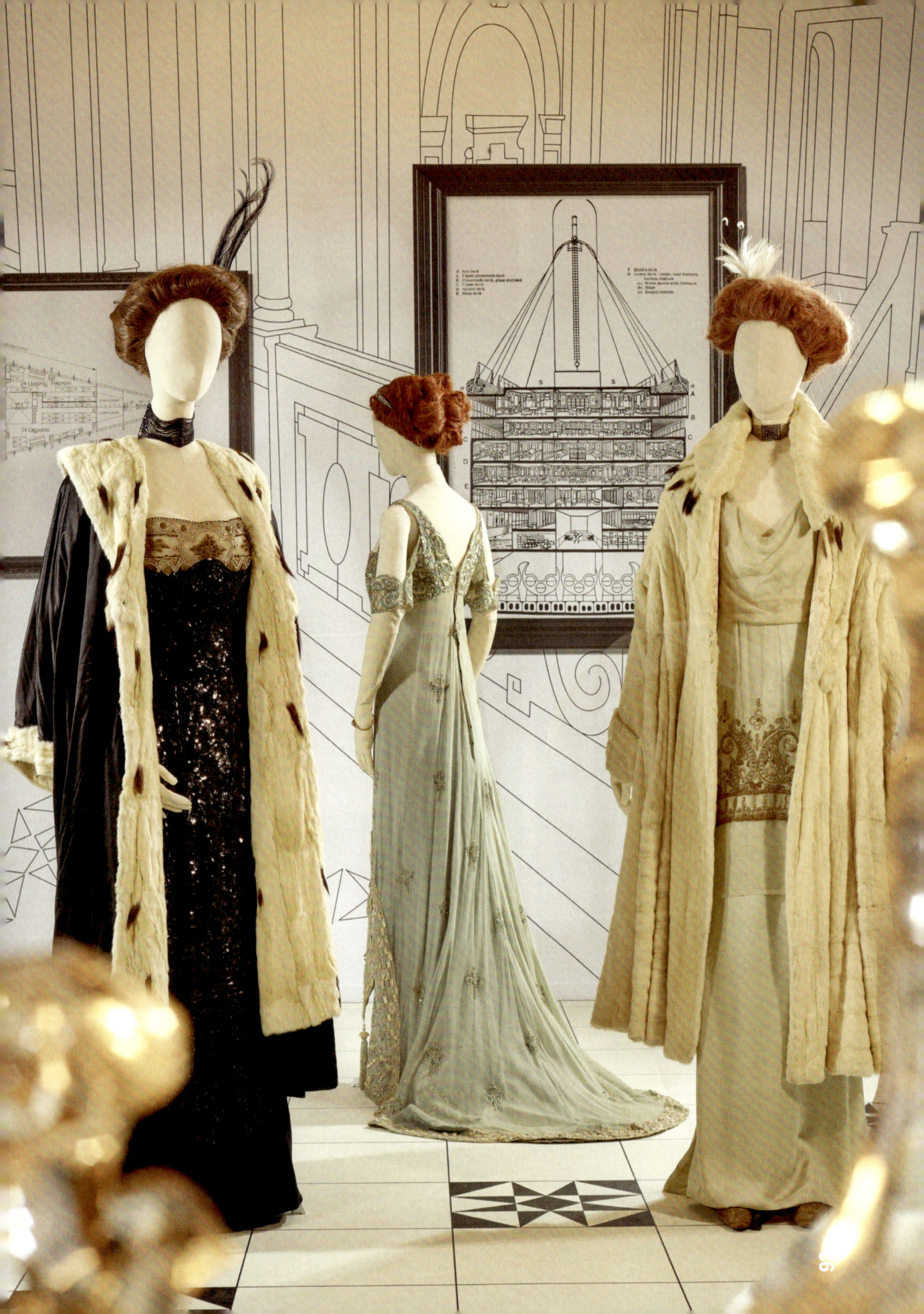

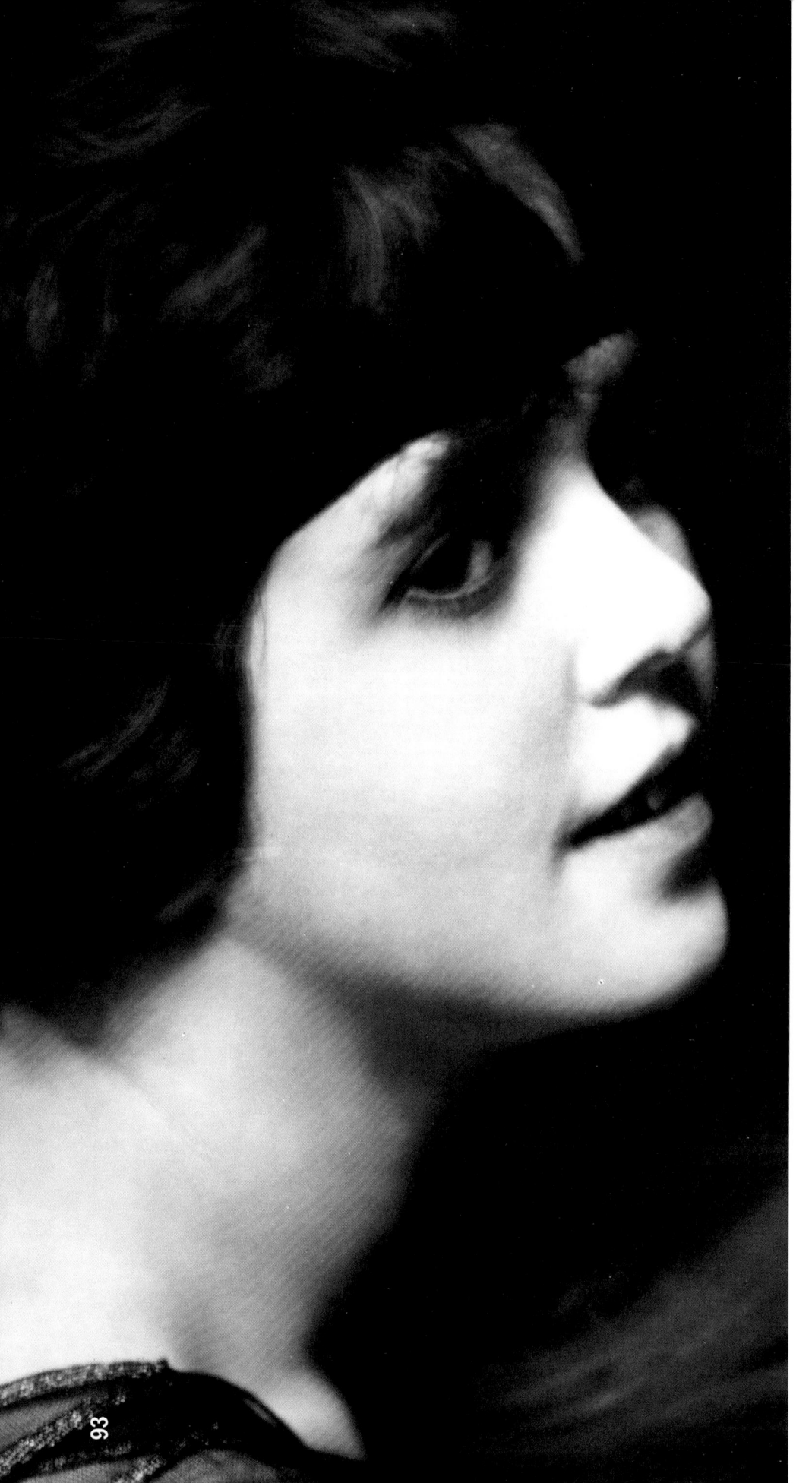

93

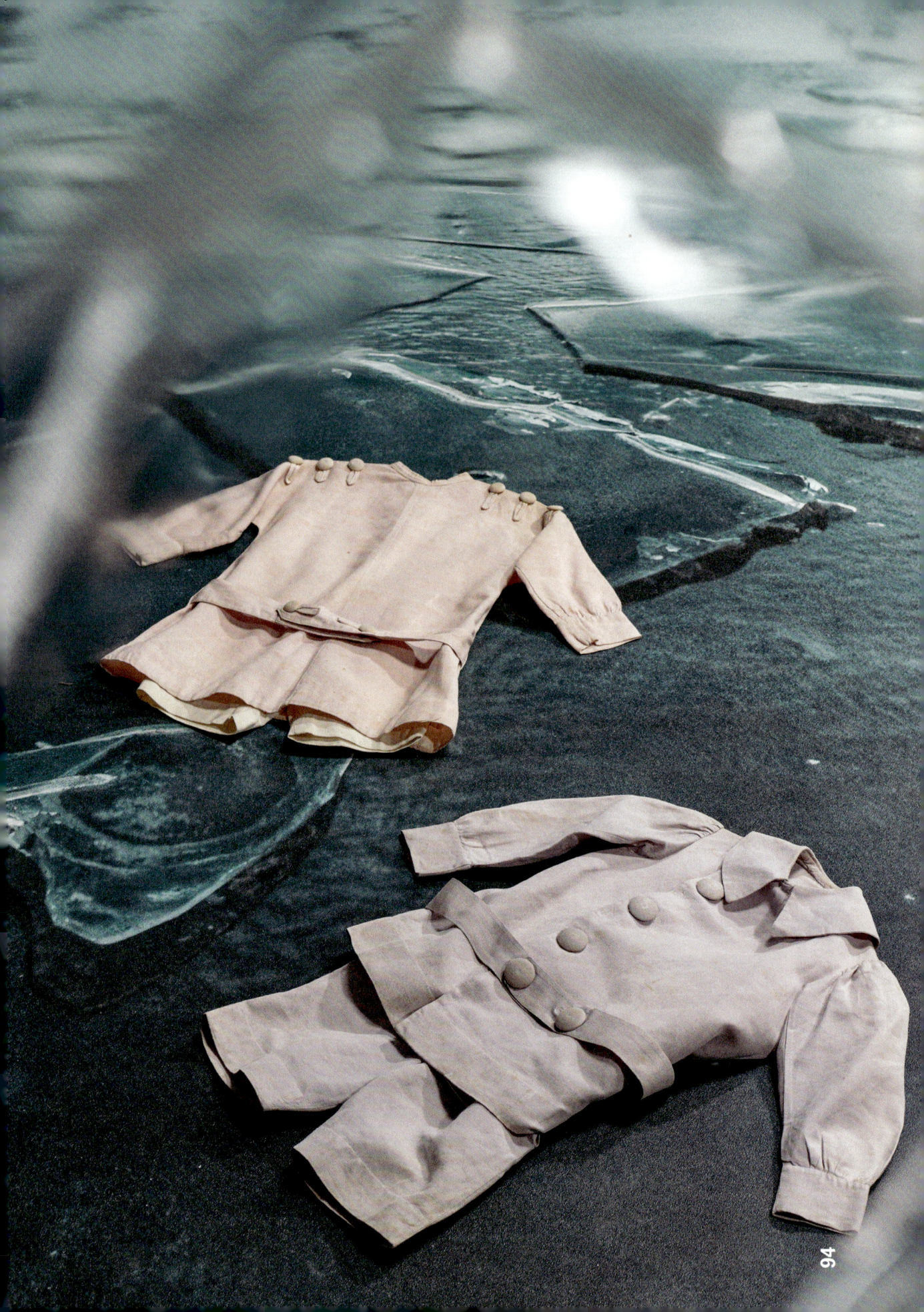

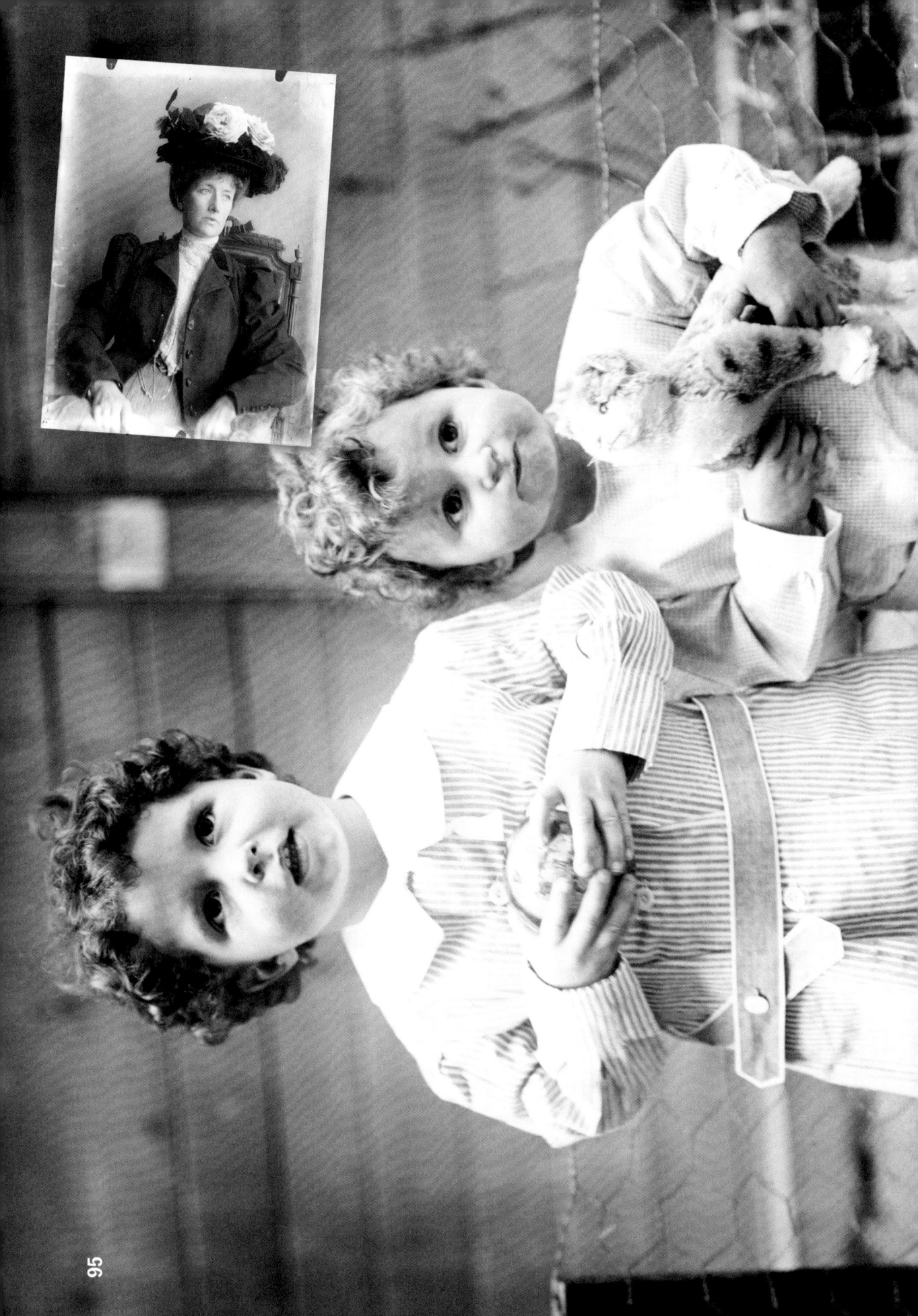

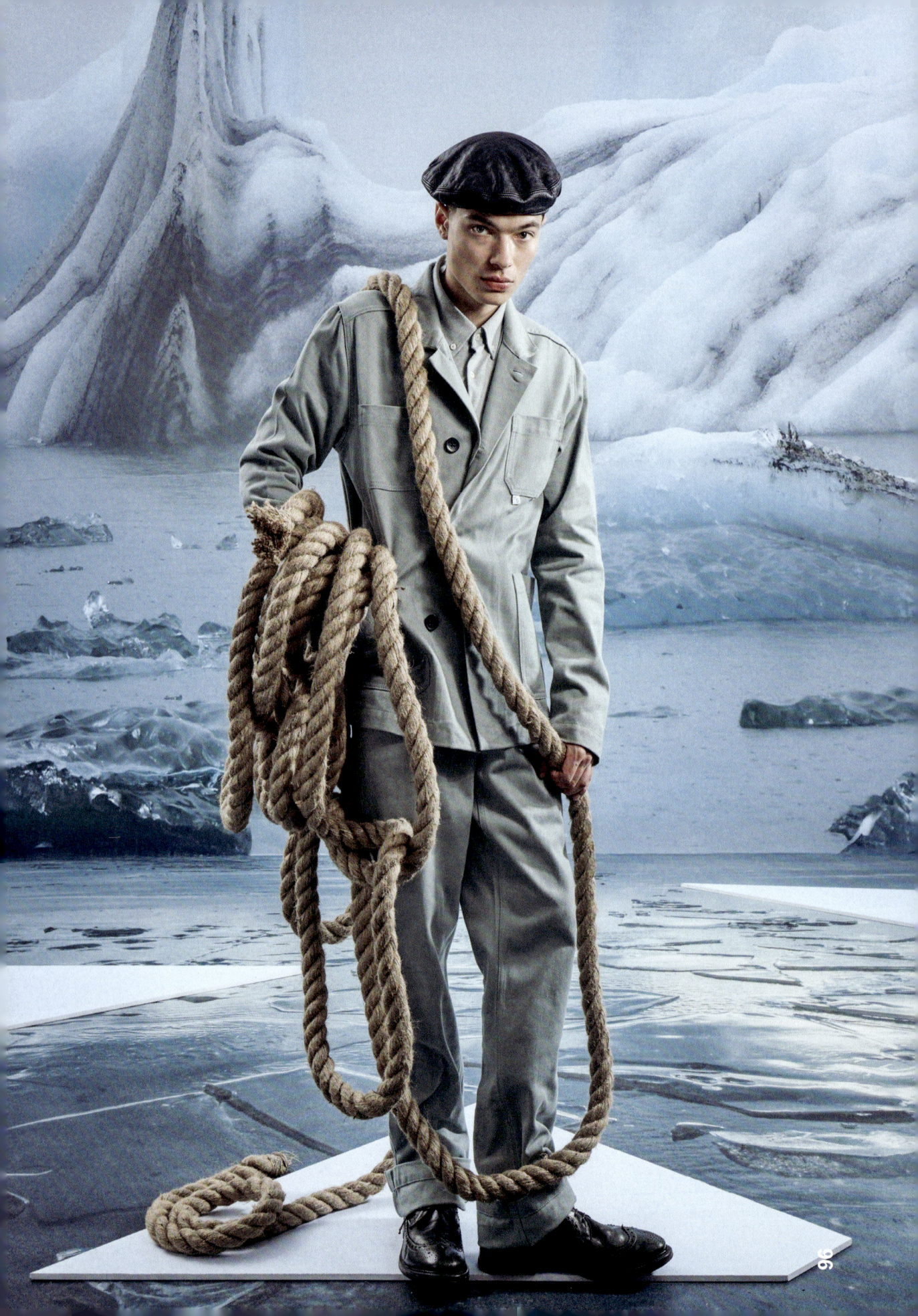

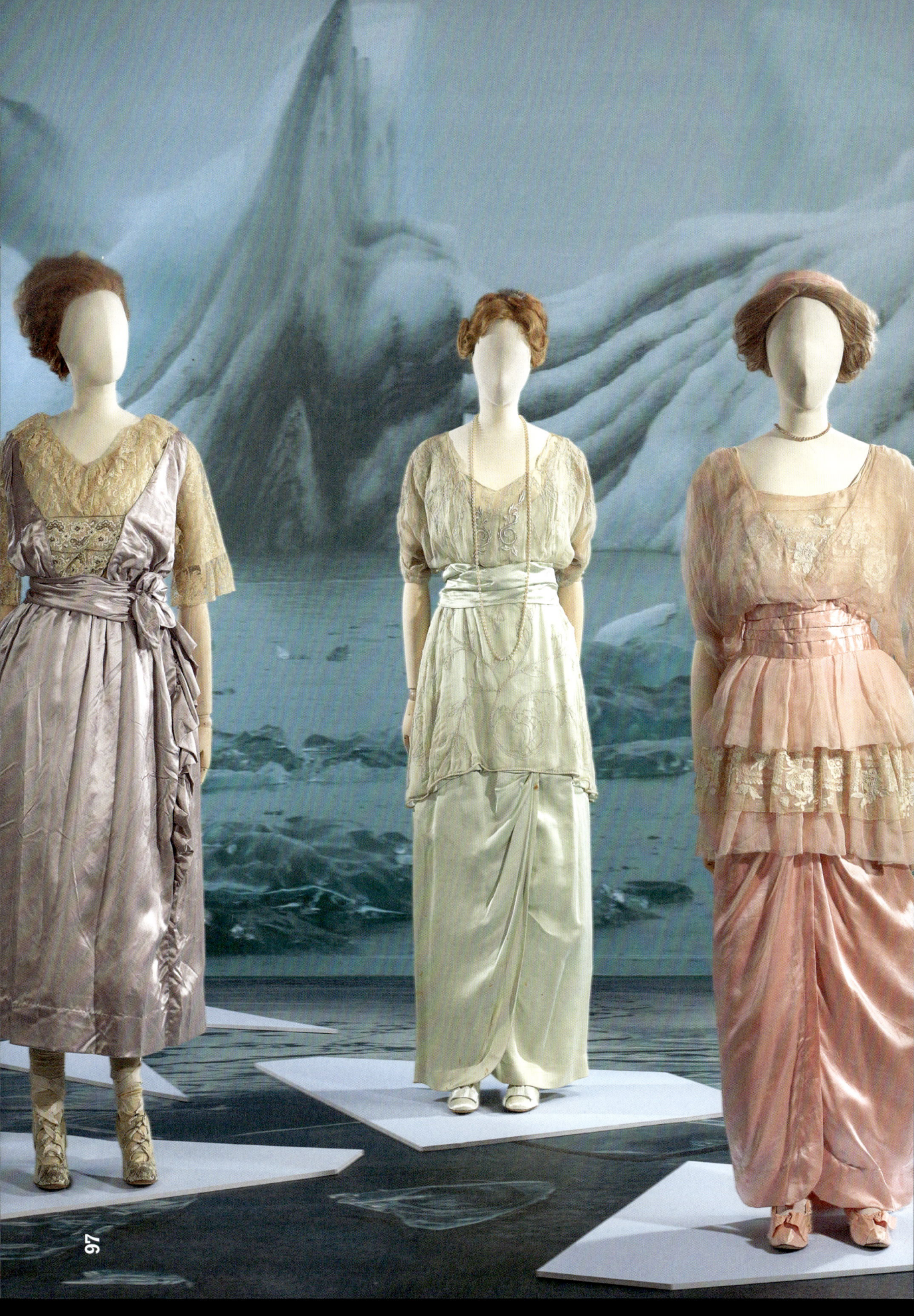

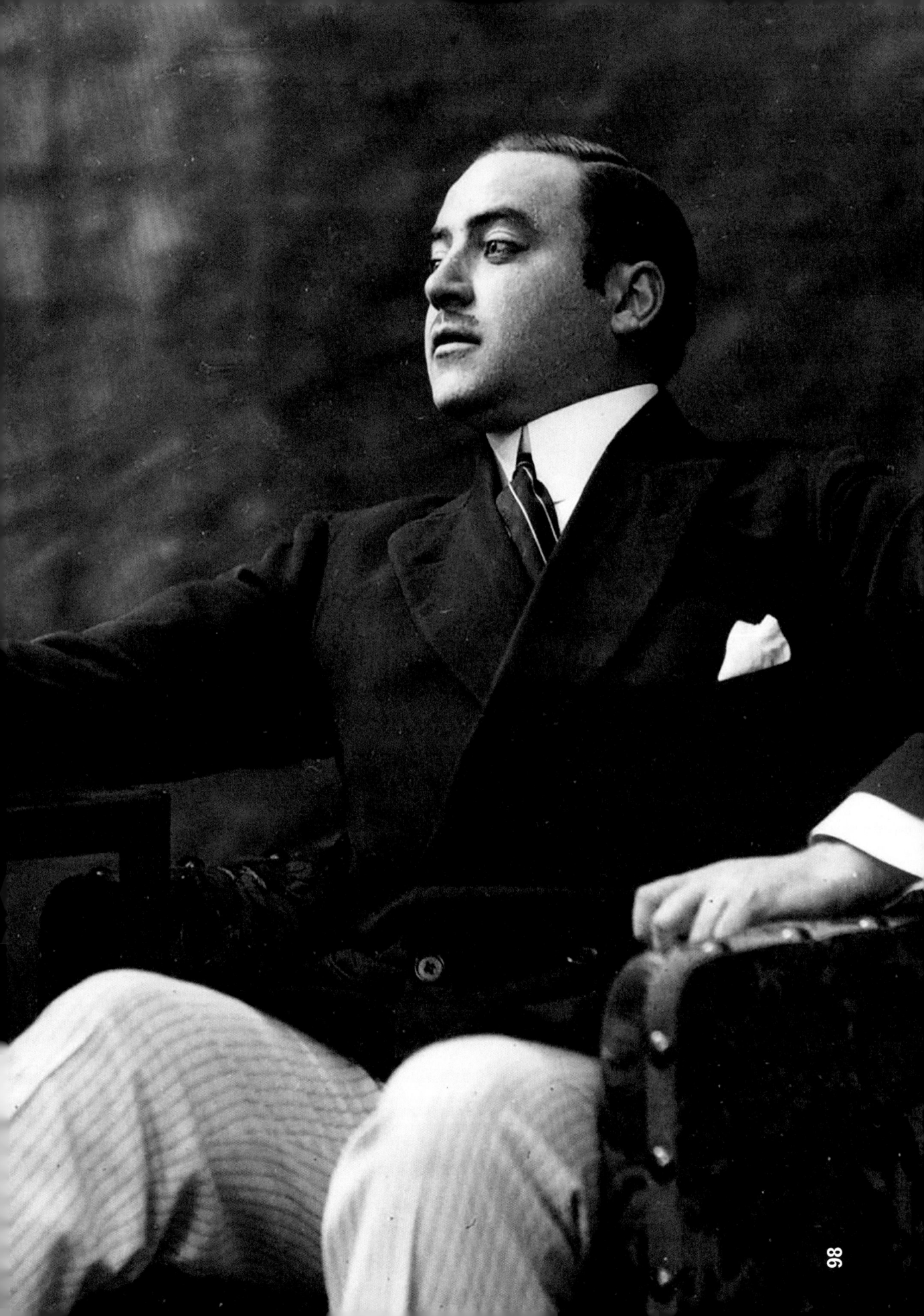

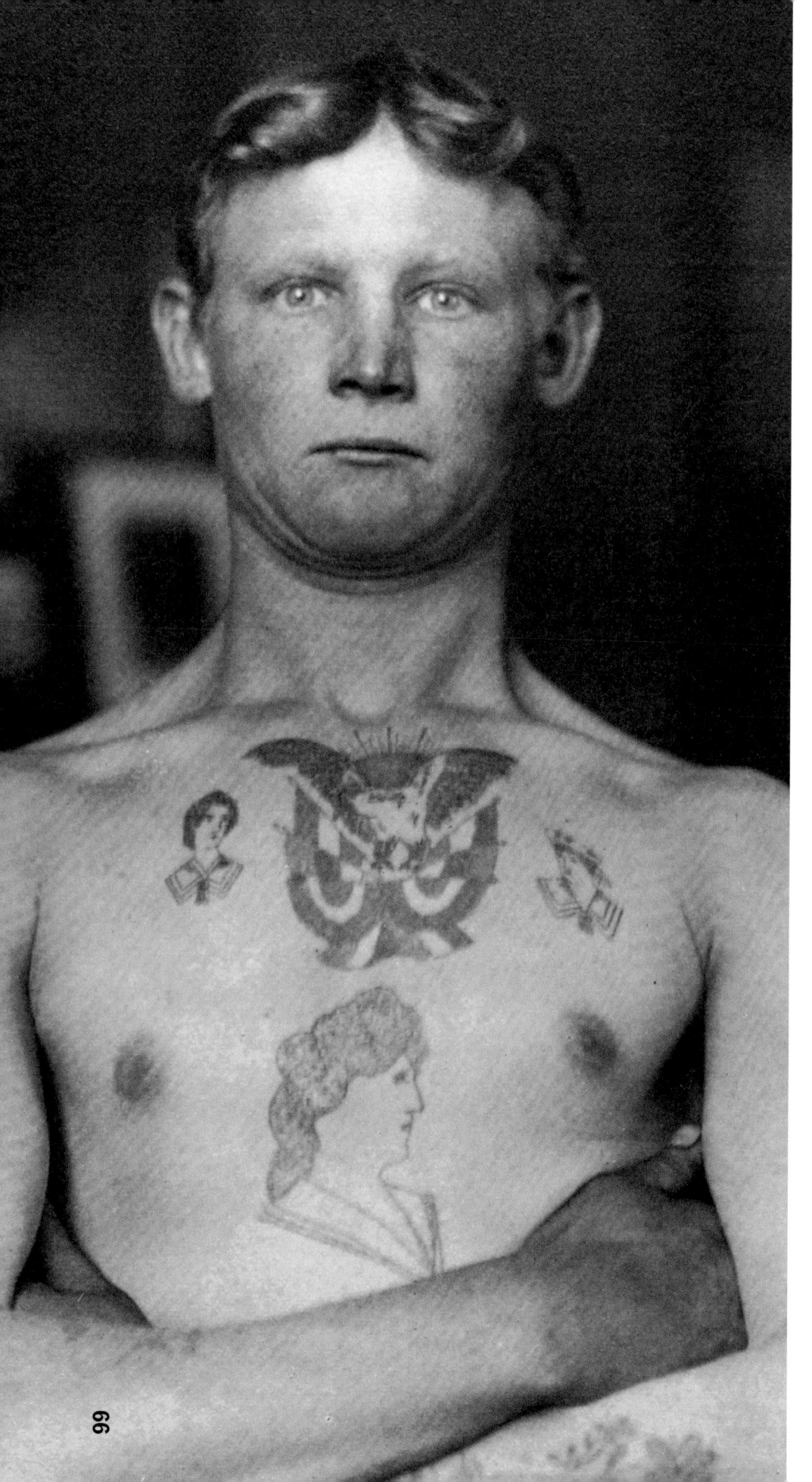

p. 94 Norfolk-style boy's suits belonging to two brothers from the De Beaufort family, pink and lilac linen, c. 1910-1918.

p. 95 Michel Marcel Navratil (1908-2001) and Edmond Roger Navratil (1910-1953), survivors of the Titanic, photographed after the disaster. Their father (who did not survive) had kidnapped them in Nice and was taking them to America. The boys were reunited with their mother on 16 May 1912.

p. 95 Portrait by photographer Jan Zeegers of his wife Eugénie Zeegers-Kuinders, wearing a tailored suit, 1908.

p. 96 Bonne Suit, Suit in limestone-coloured cotton inspired by work clothing, Amsterdam, spring/summer 2025.

p. 97 Lilac satin gown with cream lace, c. 1918-1920; Mejuffrouw Haag, Turquoise silk satin and mousseline gown with embroidery, Amsterdam, c. 1913-1914, worn by Mrs A.H. Hondius-Crone; Loelgen & Kriegel, Gown with hobble skirt in pink satin and tulle, Düsseldorf, c. 1913-1914, worn by Hildegard Kock-Wiedemeijer (1883-1971).

p. 98 Studio of J. Merkelbach, photograph of actor Louis Theodoor van Drielen Gimberg (1880-1959), in day suit, 1913.

p. 99 German stowaway photographed at Ellis Island, New York, deported back to Europe in May 1911.

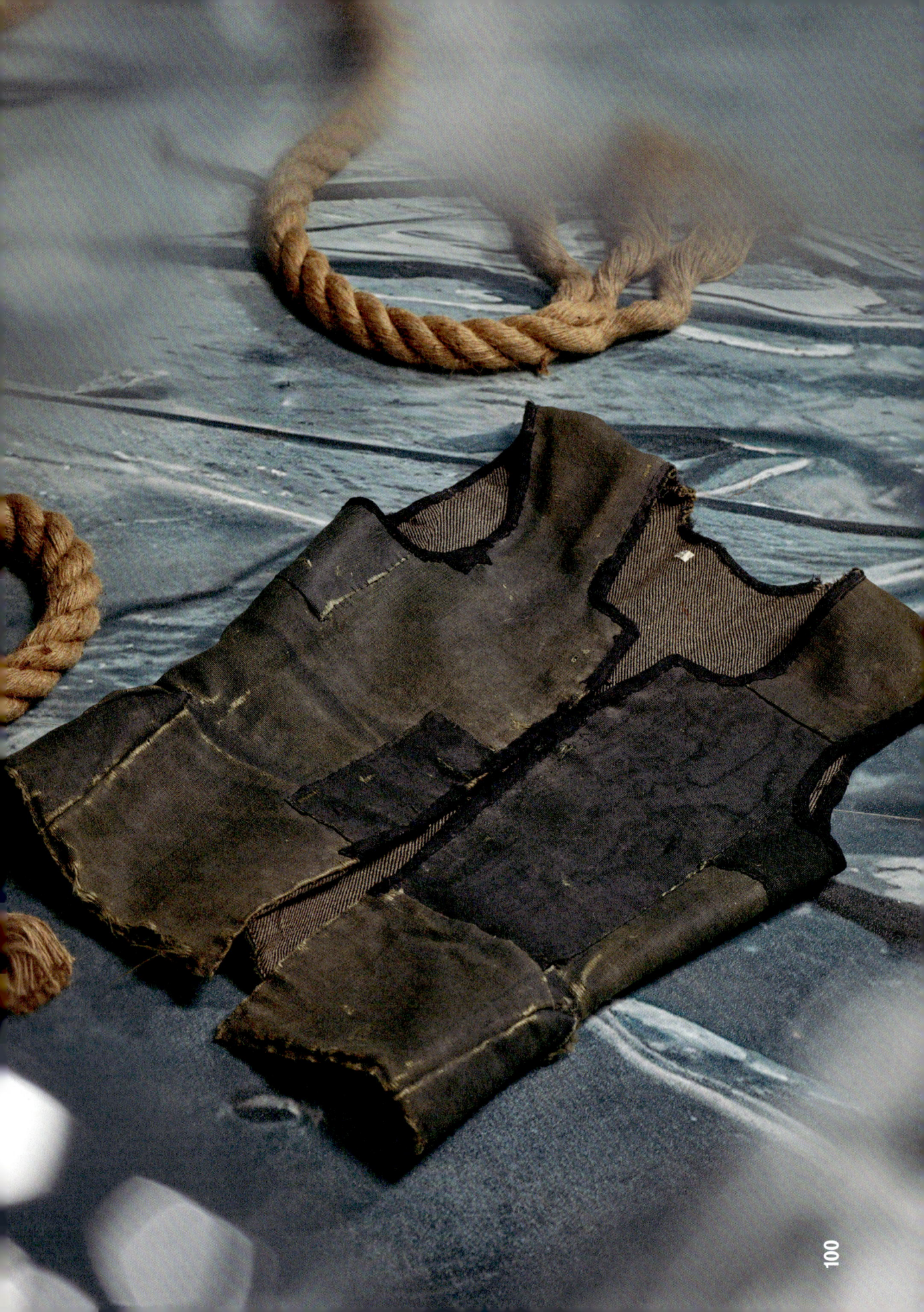

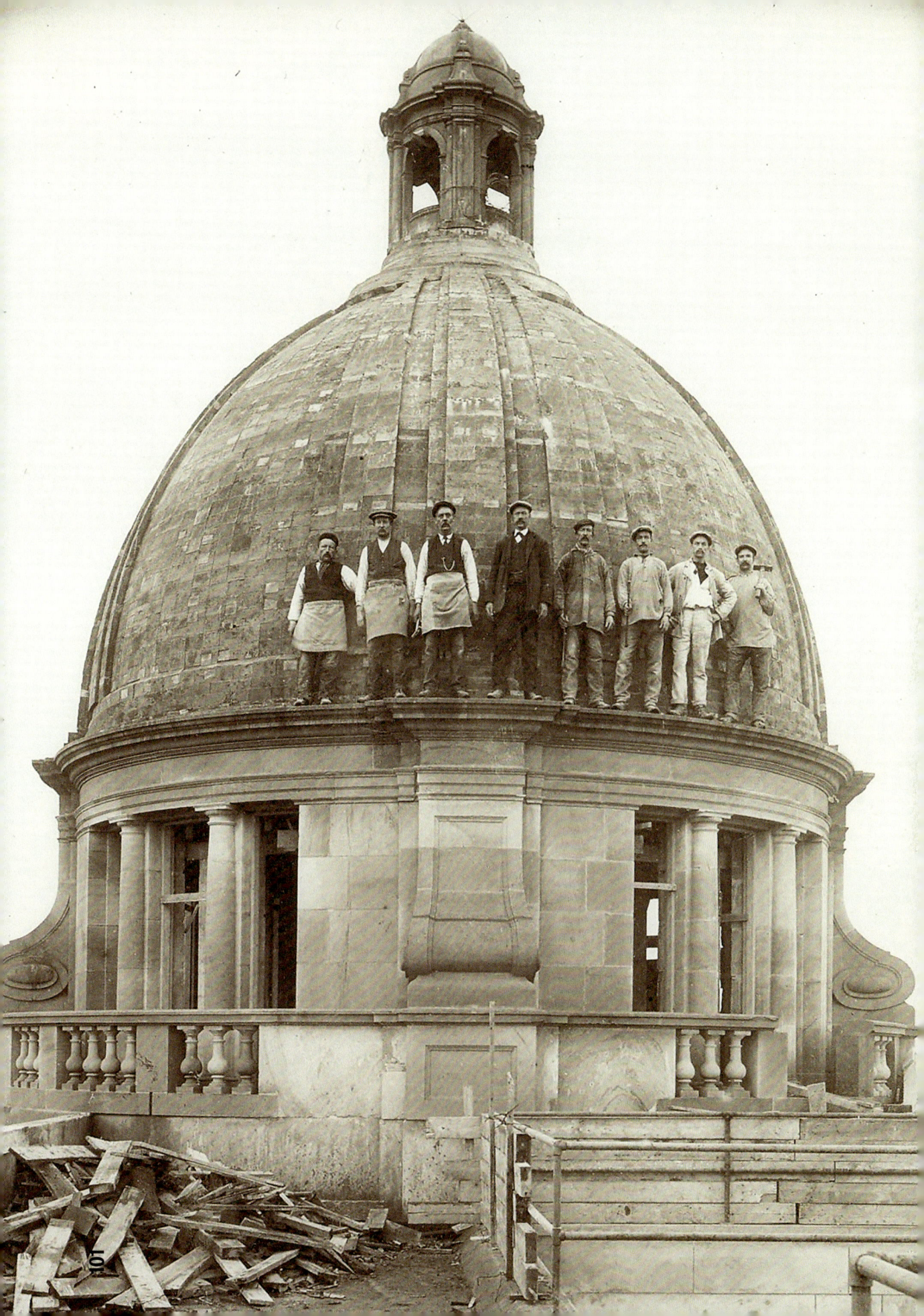

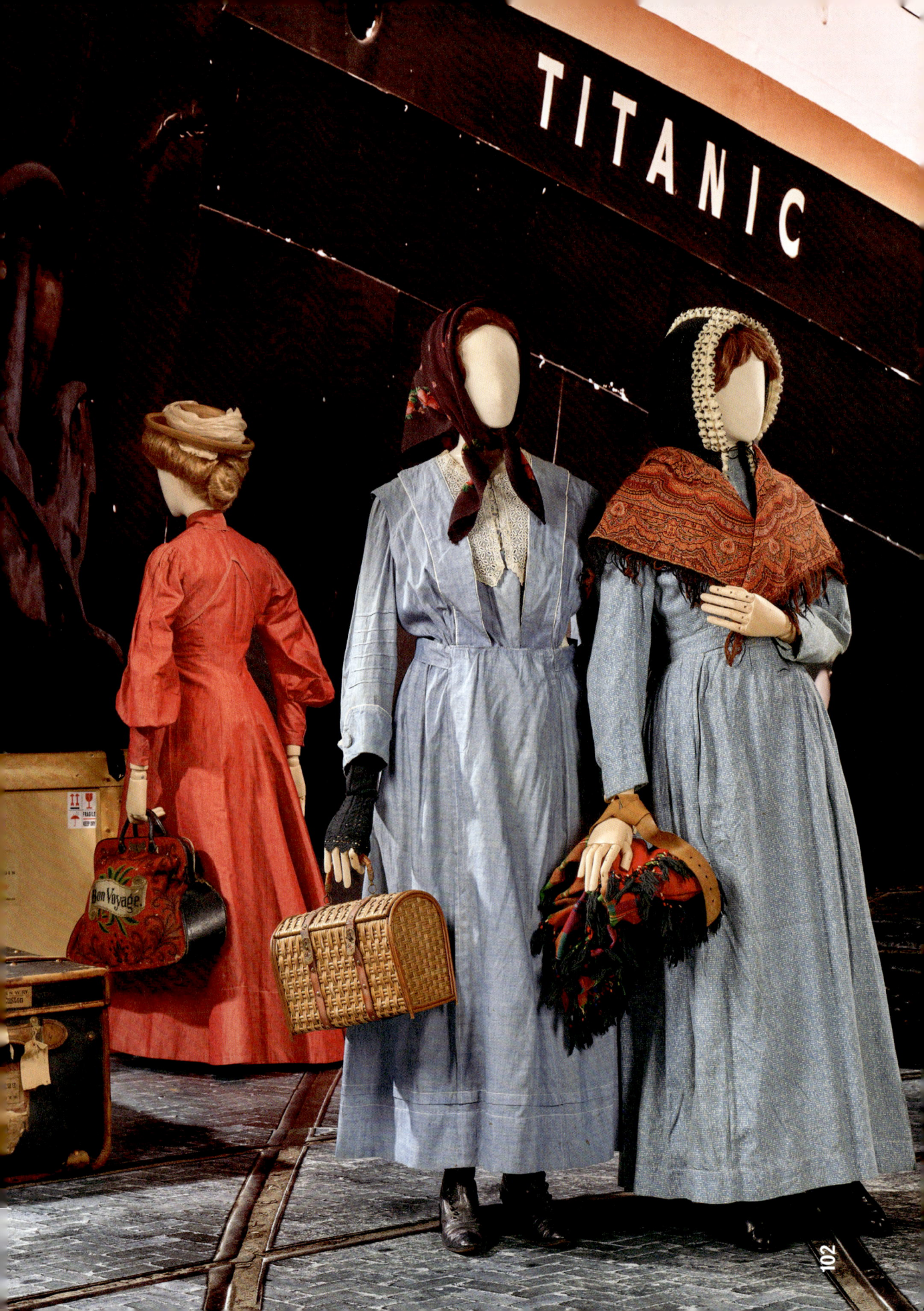

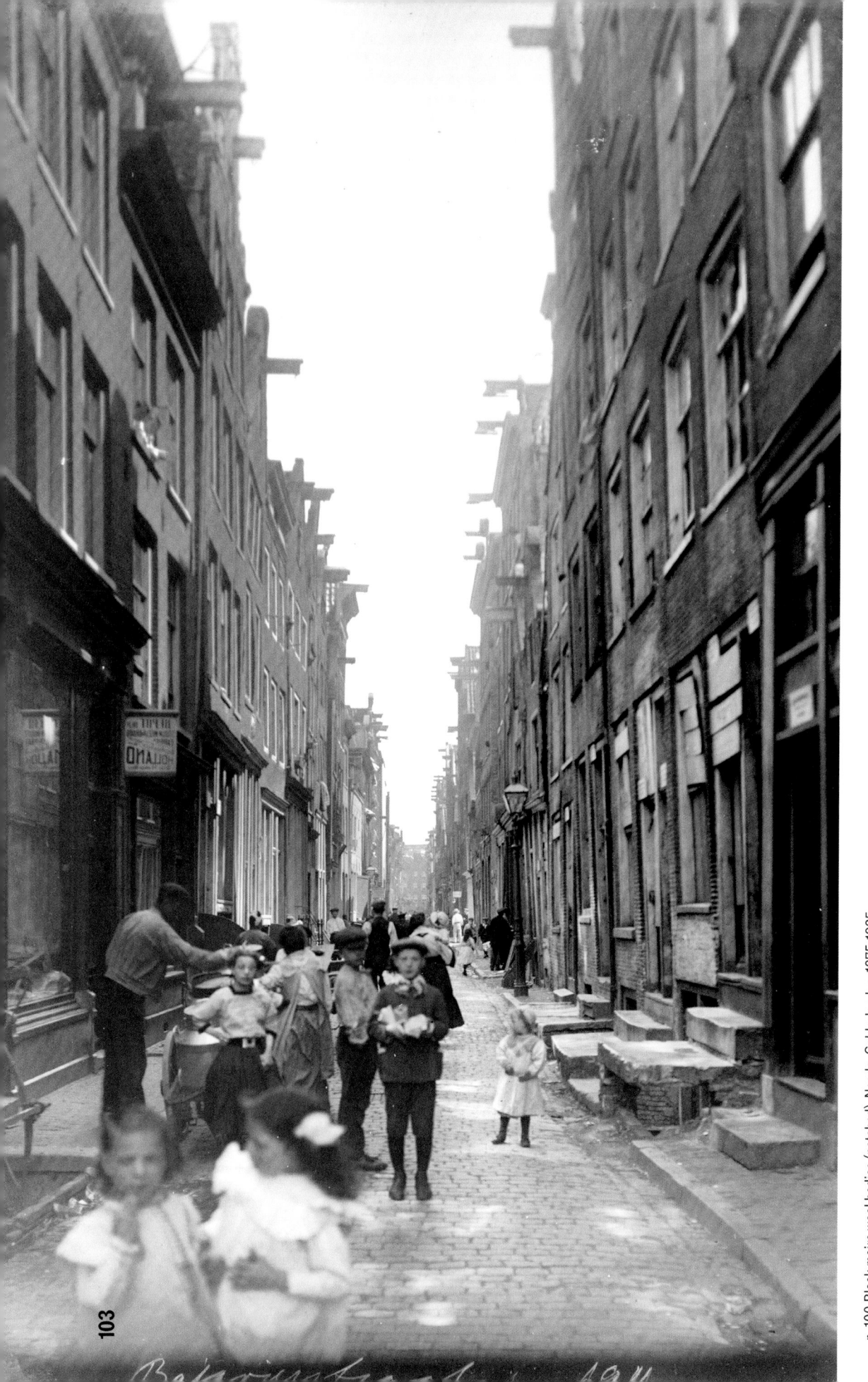

p. 100 Black moire wool bodice (patched), Neede, Gelderland, c. 1875-1925.

p. 101 Builders in work attire pose for a photographer during construction of the premises of Hirsch & Cie on Leidseplein, Amsterdam (opened in 1912).

p. 102 Reform dress (also used as maternity wear), red cotton denim, c. 1905; Dress in blue 'nurse's cotton' with white lace, c. 1910-1915; Maid's dress, white and blue printed cotton, c. 1880-1910.

p. 103 Locals in their everyday clothes on Batavierstraat, viewed towards Houtkopersburgwal in Amsterdam, photographed by the municipal public housing service, 1911.

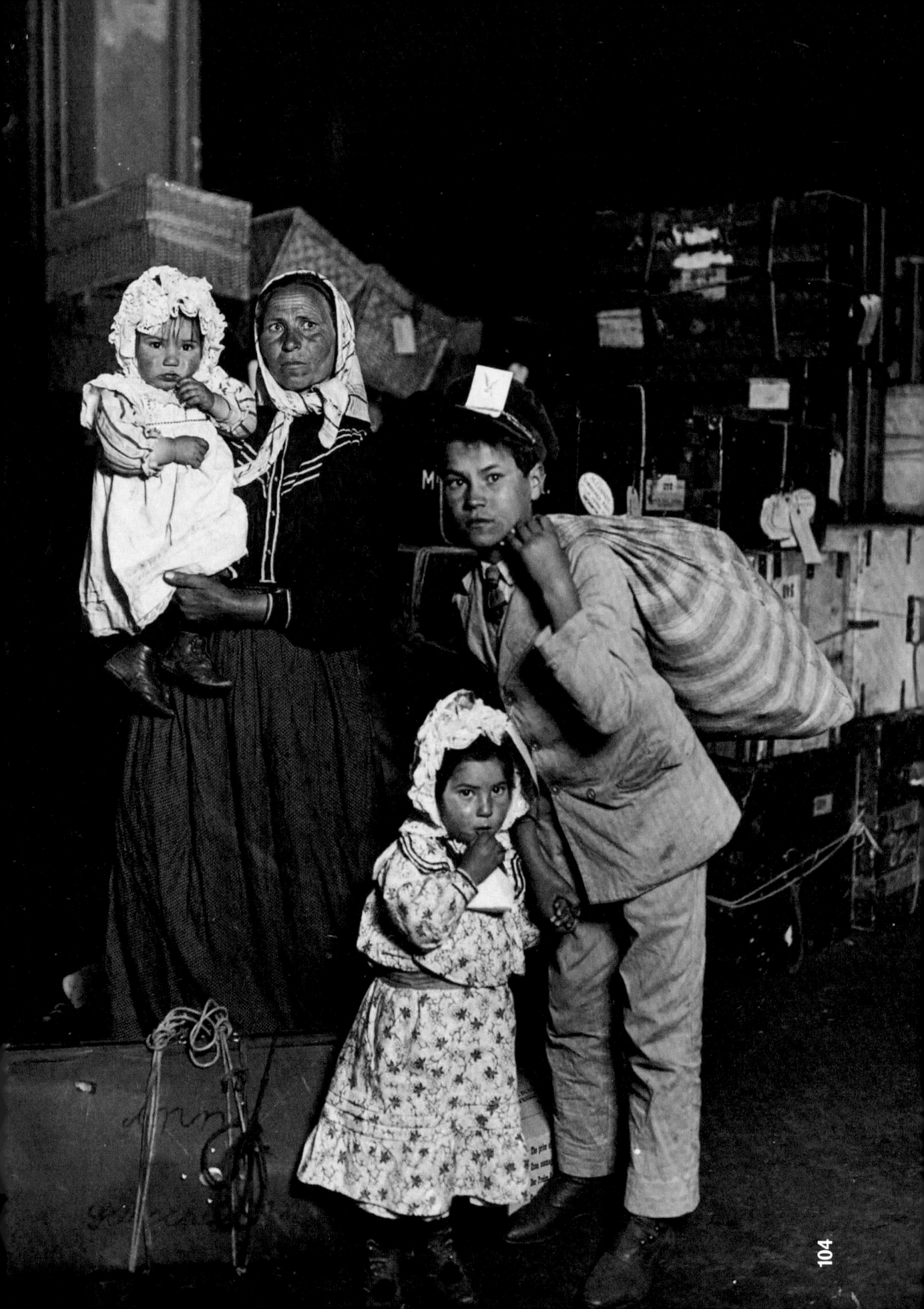

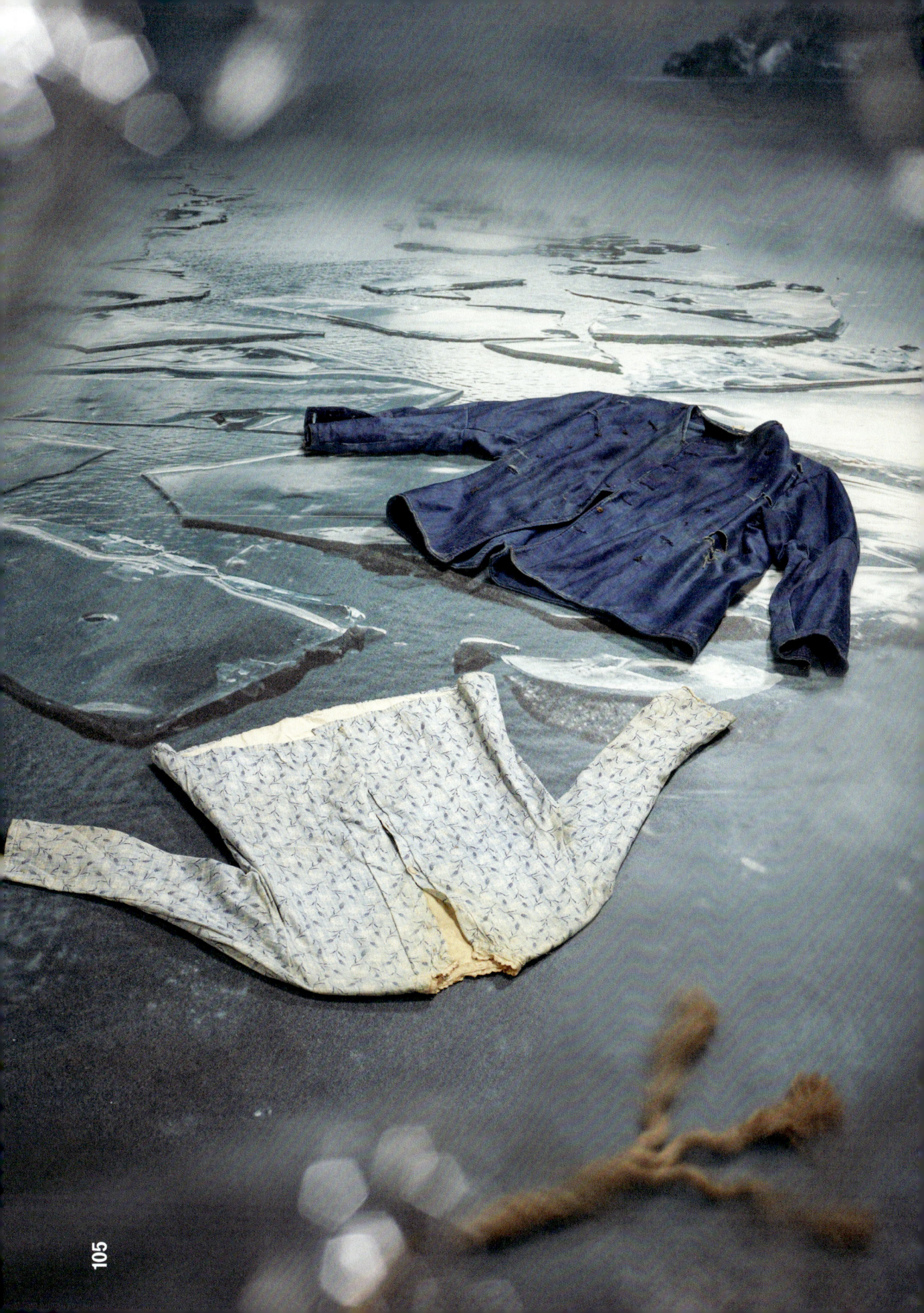

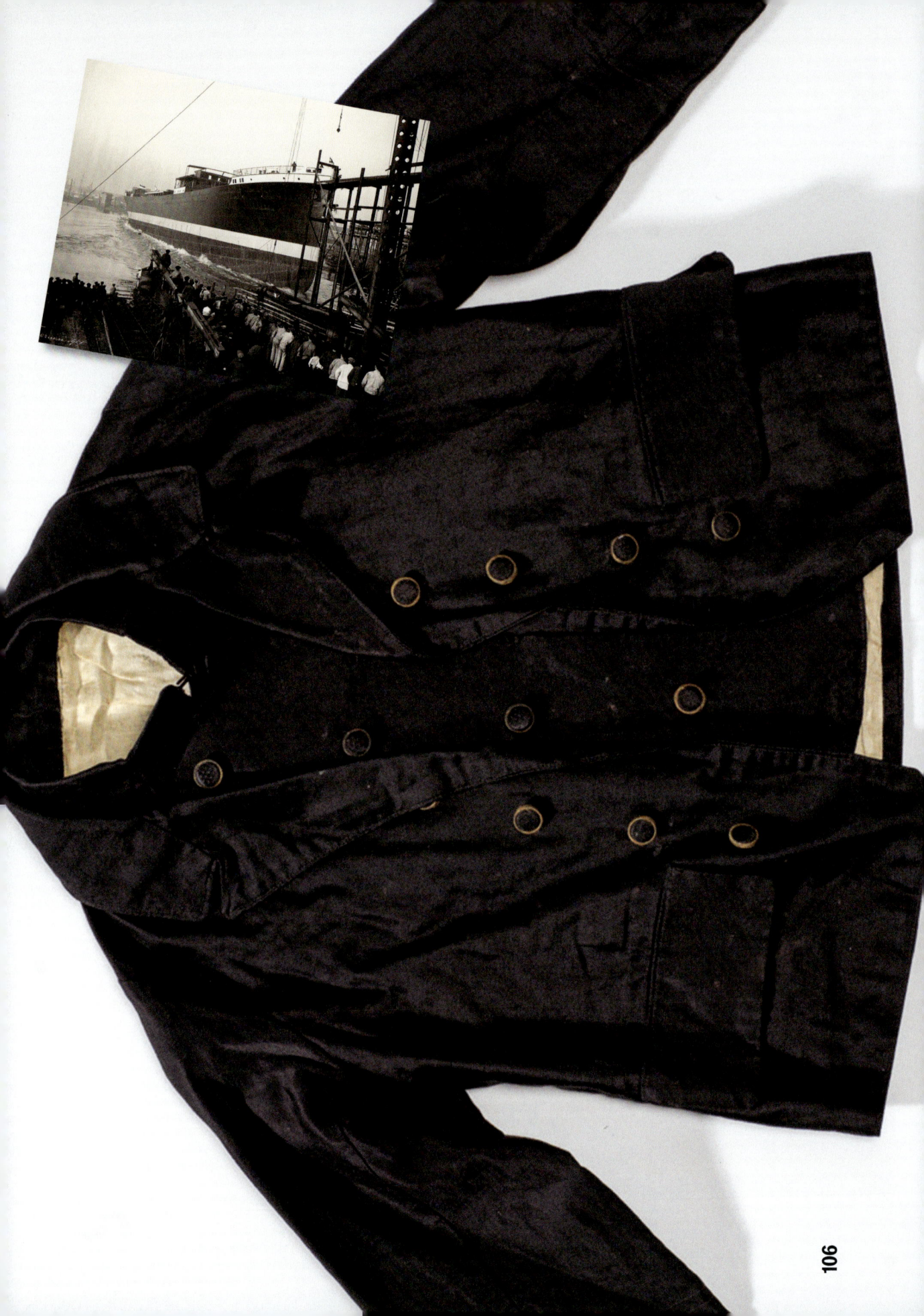

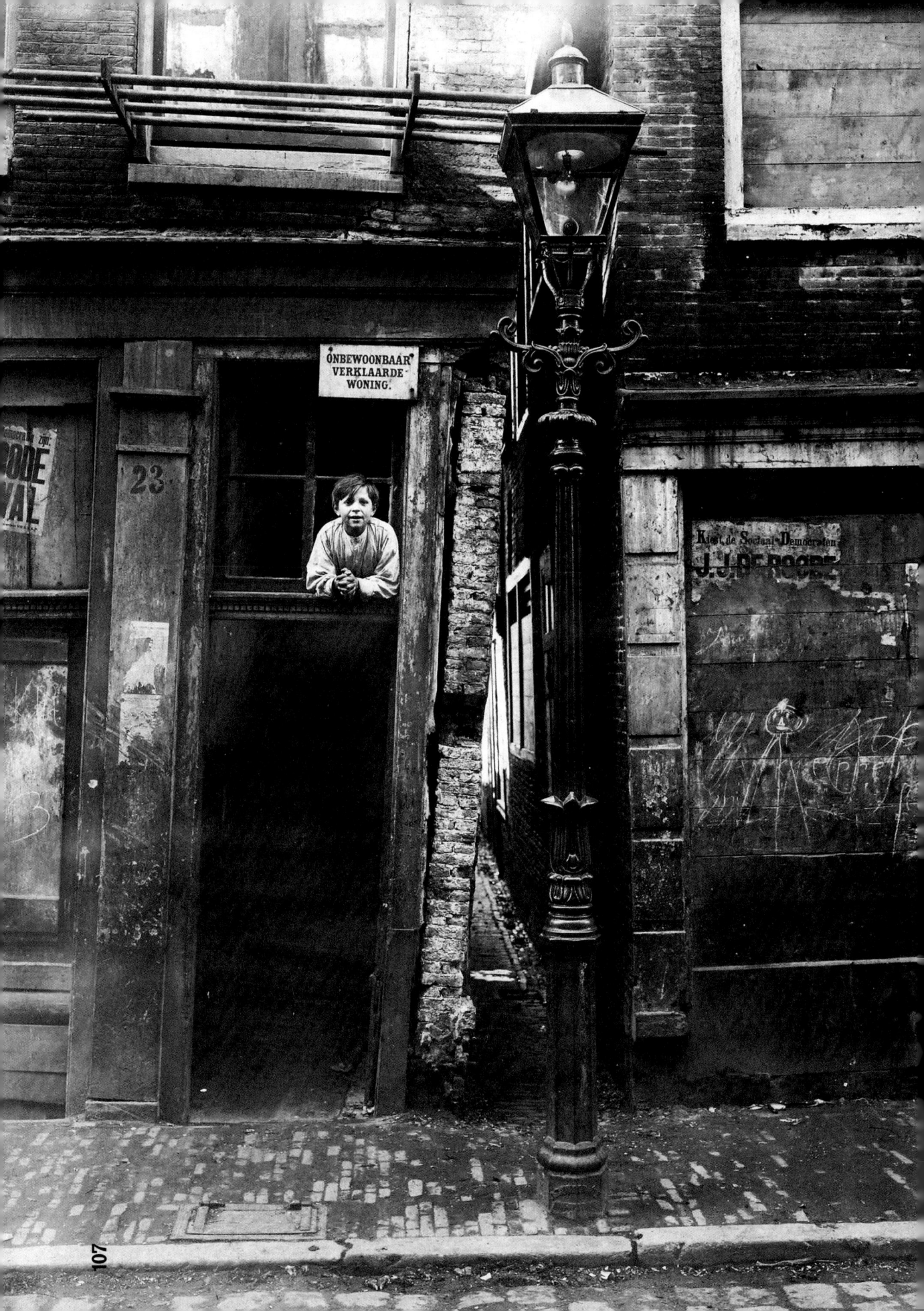

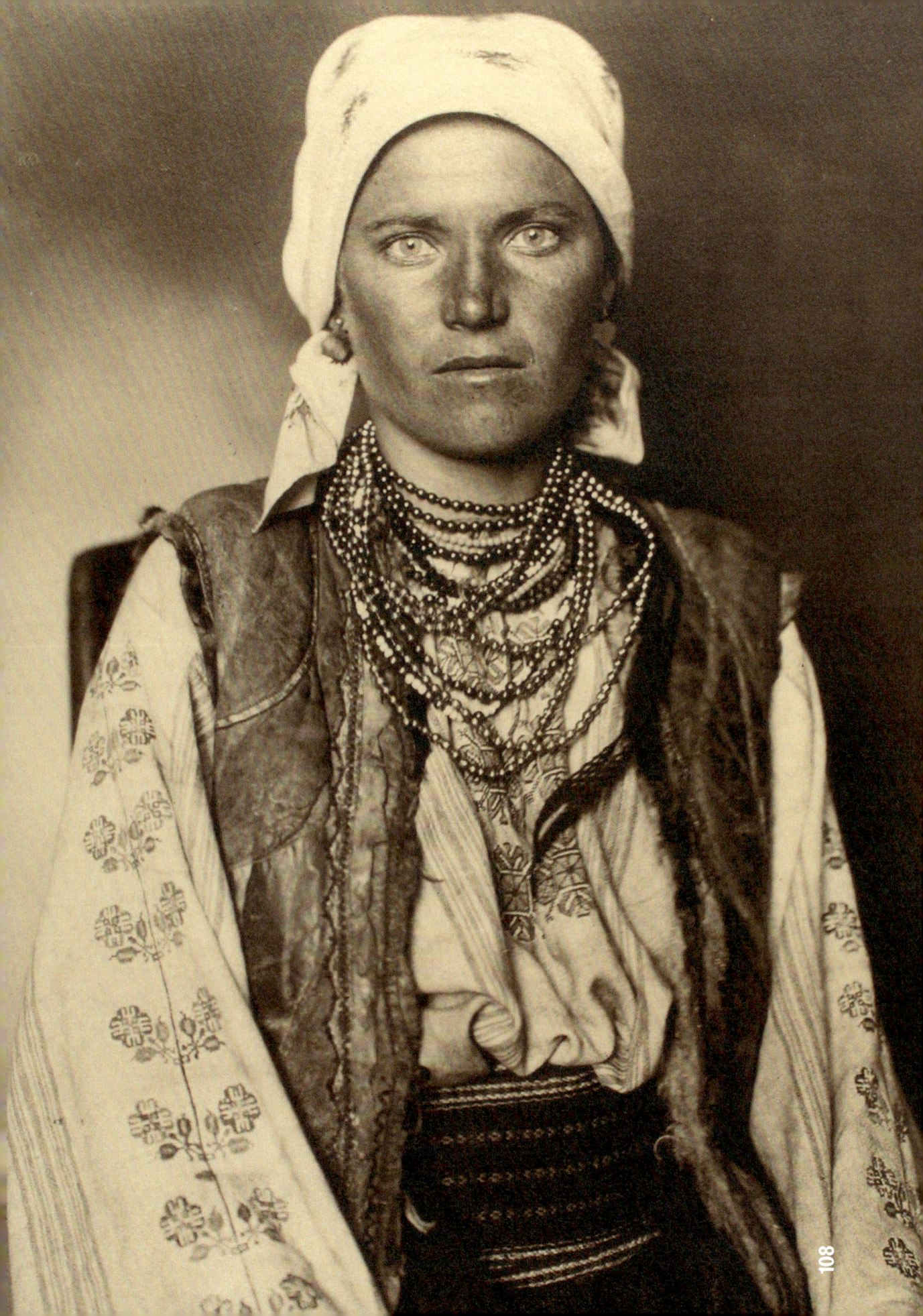

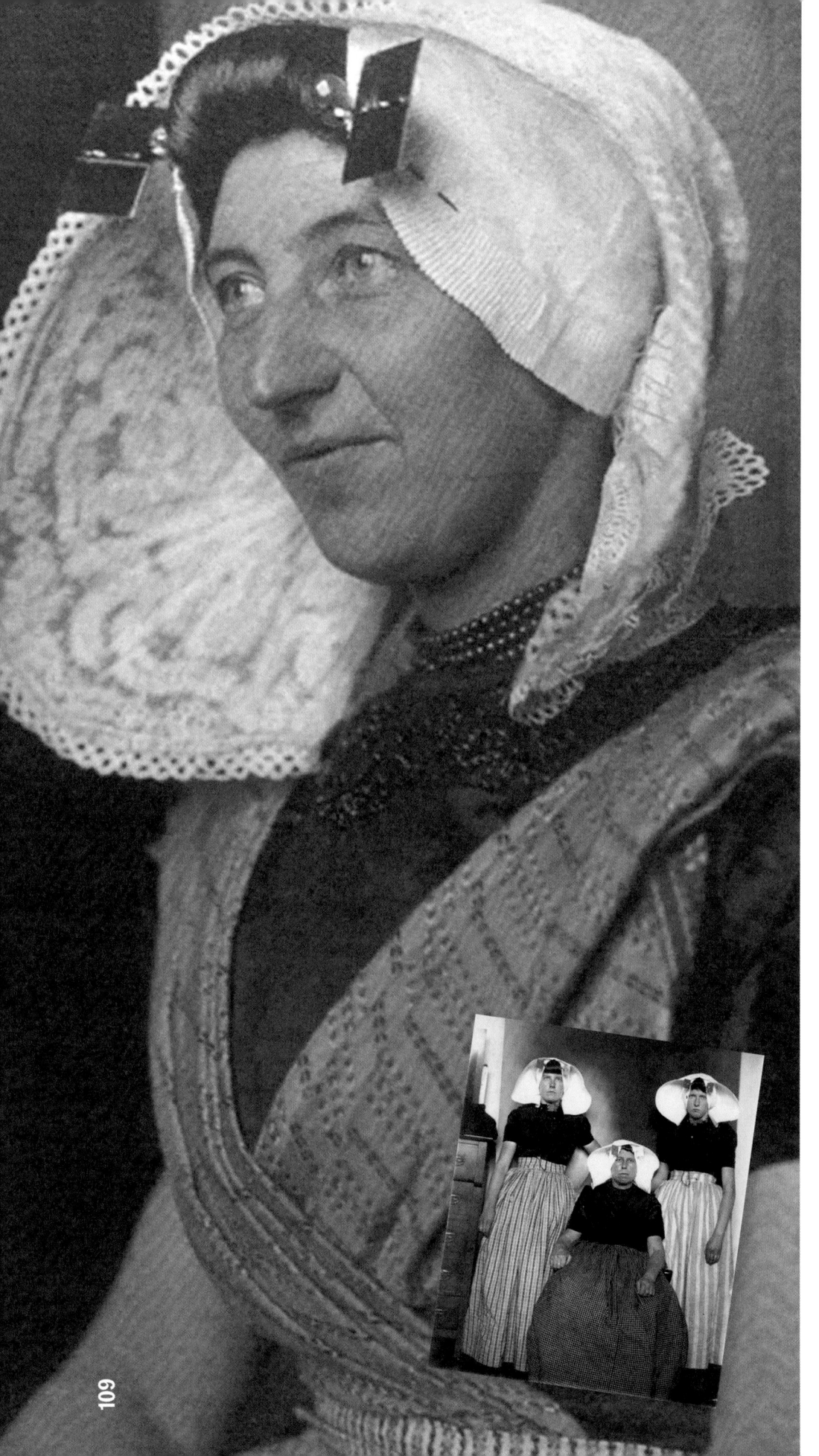

The photographs are fascinating: women in the Protestant traditional dress of Zuid-Beveland, Scottish boys in kilts and an Austrian in lederhosen. They have just arrived on Ellis Island, off wNew York City, where all migrants went to register. The new arrivals would be given a medical examination, and questionnaires would be completed, recording their personal details and information on their financial situation and their destination.

Astonishing numbers of migrants made the crossing in the age of the great ocean liners like the Titanic. Over twelve million migrants entered the country between 1892 and 1954. A small percentage of them came from the Netherlands. And a few of them were dressed in regional costume when they arrived. Why did they choose to enter their new country dressed this way? And why did others not do so? And how long did they continue to wear traditional dress?

There are few sources on the subject. The clothing worn by the newcomers is not recorded in the official register. It was individual photographers working on Ellis Island who picked out among the crowds the migrants who were wearing costumes typical of the region they hailed from. Later migrants from the Netherlands would sometimes be sent a shopping list, as well as travel tips. Around 1860, a Mr Snoeyenbosch wrote to a relative, requesting a large amount of linsey-woolsey fabric (a blend of linen and wool) for a woman's skirt, and a piece of fabric suitable for everyday trousers, as his relative saw fit.[1] How people would adapt their dress to their new situation was not, apparently, worth mentioning. Sometimes, however, one encounters snippets of information that are worth collecting. One Agnes Nestor from Michigan wrote, for example, in her 1880 memoirs about the newcomers who came to live in her town, describing how they could see the trains approaching and, if it was a train full of Dutch immigrants, they would rush to the station. She described newcomers arriving in national costume, wearing clogs.[2]

This must have been an impressive sight, but her impression is somewhat exaggerated. People left for the United States of America for all kinds of reasons, and decisions as to what to do with regional costumes were just as individual. Should on leave it behind in the Netherlands, exchange it as quickly as possible for civvies in America, or stop wearing it after a time? Most migrants exchanged their traditional dress for ordinary clothes before they left. A logical choice, as what would be the point of wearing clothing in America so closely associated with your hometown? Or of having a wardrobe that was so difficult to maintain in your new place of residence? It would not be possible to buy the things you needed for your costume there, and there was no one with the specialist knowledge required.

Several families from Zeeland were however forced to wear their regional costume in the initial period after their arrival in America, as they had spent all their savings on the voyage. There was simply no money left for a new wardrobe. Only after they had worked and saved for a time in their new home did they exchange their Zeeland traditional dress for ordinary clothes. The garments and jewellery were then probably cherished as heirlooms, as several American museum collections include items from Zeeland regional costumes from the late nineteenth century.

They were, however, the exception among Dutch wearers of traditional dress, as evidenced by the fact that, as far as is known, the Ellis Island collections only include photographs of people in the regional costume of Zeeland. No examples have been found from other regions. Correspondence with the home front reveals some urgent advice. Jacob Dunnink, for example, writing to his brother in Rouveen from America around 1855, warned that he should not bring many clothes, but as much underwear as possible. He presumably meant that this would be useful to have in America, but that his traditional Rouveen costume would not be much use. Migrants from the Veluwe region were also advised to swap their traditional dress for ordinary clothes before departure.

A woman who emigrated from Walcheren in Zeeland to Canada is known to have continued wearing her regional costume for almost twenty years, but she really was an exception.[3] For as Hendrik Barendregt wrote to his family in 1846, 'Everyone must envisage not being able to remain Dutch when they come to live in America; customs and manners must be followed.'[4]

Dutch regional costume in America

Jacco Hooikammer

[1] Herbert J. Brinks, *Schrijf spoedig terug: brieven van immigranten in Amerika, 1847-1920* [translated from English to Dutch, paraphrased here], The Hague 1978, p. 139.
[2] Idem, p. 48.
[3] Source: goldsmith Piet Minderhout of Westkapelle, who some years previously had spoken to a descendant of hers in his shop.
[4] W. Lagerwey (ed.), *Neen Nederland, 'k vergeet u niet: een beeld van het immigrantenleven in Amerika tussen 1846 en 1945 in verhalen, schetsen en gedichten*, Baarn 1982, p. 22.

The dress reform movement, supported by both women and men, gave rise to a new new style of dress in the early twentieth century. Anyone who was a radical cast off their corset and ('unhygienic') train. What exactly reformed clothing – an alternative to Paris fashions – should be like was the subject of debate. One solution was to look to classical antiquity, which resulted in gowns with lots of draping, often with a high waist resembling the empire style (which itself was based on classical antiquity). This was also a good design for gowns worn without a corset. Some drew inspiration from the Middle Ages, or the Art Nouveau style, producing gowns with elegant, sometimes asymmetrical, lines. There were also radical new gowns, very simple and straightforward. And in the 1910s, in particular, there were also modern artistic alternatives that mirrored developments in the decorative arts. Anyone who dressed alternatively often also preferred a modern interior and the artistic design aesthetic that went with it.[1] Such progressive tastes in fashion were often found among people of the social elite. Many reformed fashions – such as the elegant reform dresses that Madame De Vroye of Brussels sold in the Netherlands – and the avant-garde outfits from Liberty's sold at Metz & Co in the Netherlands were expensive.[2] A modern wardrobe of this kind was certainly not within everyone's means. (p.127)

A gown of brick-red cotton twill from c.1905 in the collection of Kunstmuseum Den Haag looks surprisingly modern. It was almost certainly worn as a reform dress, of the 'radical' kind, and was also convenient in light of the fact that the owner was pregnant with her daughter in 1905.[3] (p. 28) The design is very plain, worn with a small bolero. The loose fit not only made the dress suitable as maternity wear, it was also in line with the ideas of the dress reform movement, which promoted fashion without a corset. Other reform dresses in the museum's collection comes in a variety of tastes, colours and decorative elements. There are examples in softer pastel silks, but there are also vibrant purple dresses, the colour perhaps being associated with the purple, green and white favoured by the British suffragettes. But purple was also a fashionable colour at the time, so it may have been the result of a combination of factors.

All these alternative fashions were worn by women who, in different ways, were expressing their ideas about dress reform. The war and changes in society would accelerate these developments. Since the Netherlands remained neutral during the First World War, it was different for Dutch women than for women in France, Germany or Britain, who did 'men's work' out of necessity, often dressed in men's clothes. They adapted their wardrobe to their job, and so certain elements of men's fashions became a fixed part of women's fashion.[4] Women's suits, with jackets like those worn by men, became commonplace. But it would not be until the 1930s that trousers became at all acceptable for women, and then only when playing sports or on holiday. It was certainly not customary for lesbian or queer women to express their identity in the way they dressed. The few who did made a statement by, for example, having waistcoats made to go with their bespoke suits (as men did), like Countess Marie A.O.C. van Bylandt of The Hague. She was in a fortunate position, and opted to wear her hair as expected by her social circle, but to adapt her wardrobe to what she felt comfortable wearing.[5] (p. 128)

Feminists and other rebels

It is interesting to consider this, as it gives us a small glimpse of the liberties women were able to permit themselves at the time. Dressing alternatively by the standards of dress reform was one thing, but just how far could western women go in expressing their sexuality through their dress style? Fashion was above all modest, providing cover in all the right places, and focused on different times and occasions throughout the day. What was innovative in the 1910s was the more exciting underwear that was introduced into many women's wardrobe as a consequence of the new fashions. The fact that skirts became shorter, and that fewer high-necked gowns were worn, must also have felt like a liberation.

The modest attire of fashionable ladies contrasted sharply with the liberally dressed ladies on stage and in films. One popular way for women to express their sexuality, and to 'justify' it at the same time, was to dress in an 'oriental' style. This involved wearing a metal bra, headdress, some draped fabric, and very little else. One well-known example is the actress and dancer Mata Hari, the pseudonym adopted by Dutchwoman Margaretha Zelle, who also made this look famous around the world. (p.129) She was certainly not the only one who dressed in this way. Kunstmuseum Den Haag recently bought a costume that was worn on stage by German-Austrian actress Lili Marberg (1876-1962) when she played Salomé (1903-1908) in a production of Oscar Wilde's controversial play of the same name (written in 1891) at the Münchner Schauspielhaus in Munich. The fact that this was an 'oriental' story justified her skimpy costume, according to the ethics of the time. The same applied to Mata Hari. When she performed her so-called oriental dances (which she had in fact invented herself), dress scantily or even naked, at Musée Guimet in Paris, it was deemed to be art. But woe betide her if she had done so without the oriental link. She would probably have been arrested by the vice squad.

This fascination with the orient, partly fed by the all-too-obvious connection with female sexuality, was largely based on the famous stories in the *Thousand and One Nights*, a new French translation of which, including the original erotic passages, had been published in 1885-1888. The whole of Paris was captivated by this mysterious unknown world, which was also represented on stage. These fairytales were a huge source of inspiration for Paul Poiret, and in 1911 he gave his own thousand and one nights party in his garden, with the help of his artist friends. Guests were asked to come in 'oriental' costume, and anyone who did not received personal assistance from Poiret to change into appropriate attire. The fact that this 'oriental' alibi was needed to justify the sexuality of western women provides an interesting glimpse of the colonial world view that predominated at the time.

[1] We see this, for example, in the wardrobe of Miss Fokker at Kunstmuseum Den Haag. She wore modernist dresses, with matching modern hats from Metz & Co, combined with simple coats in kimono style. She will have cut an unusual figure at the time. See also Madelief Hohé, *Art Deco Paris*, exh.cat. (Gemeentemuseum Den Haag) Zwolle 2017, p. 27.

[2] Madelief Hohé, 'Esthetisch en Elegant. Art Nouveau en reformkleding in Nederland', in: Jan de Bruijn et al., *Art Nouveau in Nederland*, Zwolle 2018, pp. 144-163.

[3] The dress was almost certainly worn by Mrs C.A. Ruivekamp, the mother of the woman who donated it, who married Mr W.P. Laarman Jr. in 1904. The donor was born in 1905, which means that the gown was most probably worn during pregnancy. Research on the collection by Tirza Westland and Jacoba de Jonge in 2022. Inv.no. kos-1973-0070.

[4] Maude Bass-Krueger, Sophie Kurkdjian, *French Fashion, Women & The First World War*, New York 2020.

[5] Saskia Hoogervorst, *Tussen strik en das. Een visuele analyse naar de stijl van Nederlandse lesbische vrouwen in de jaren 1930*, (unpublished Master's dissertation, Faculty of Humanities, Curating Arts and Cultures MA), Vrije Universiteit Amsterdam 2022. Countess Marie van Bylandt's clothes are preserved in the collections of both Kunstmuseum Den Haag and Rijksmuseum Amsterdam. See also the forthcoming publication by Alies Pegtel, *'De vervlogen wereld van Marie, gravin van Bylandt'*, Zwolle 2025.

Madelief Hohé

What do Scarlett O'Hara (*Gone with the Wind*), Esther Smith (*Meet Me in St Louis*), Mary Crawley (*Downton Abbey*) and Prudence Featherington (Bridgerton) have in common?[1] They are all film and television characters who appear in a scene where they are being tightly laced into a corset. This seems to be a favourite among makers of costume dramas. Understandably so, as it provides an opportunity to show the characters in a more intimate setting. At the same time, it is also a way of signalling their social status, true 'fashion victims' of their time. Women who were literally limited in their freedom of movement. The film *Titanic* (1997) has a similar scene, albeit less excessive, where Rose complains as she is being laced into a corset by her mother. 'Of course it's unfair, we're women', her mother chides, as she pulls her daughter's corset tighter.[2] The act of lacing up emphasises her point.

These scenes play into the 'corset myth': the persistent notion that women were laced up so tightly that it was physically uncomfortable, and sometimes resulted in fainting fits.[3] Fortunately, the reality was somewhat less extreme. Despite what Hollywood would have us believe, corsets were not instruments of torture. For a long time, they were a part of a woman's foundation garments, along with a chemise and drawers (or 'combination') and, usually, several underskirts. Like a modern bra, a good corset provided support and could shape the body into a fashionable silhouette. Though tight-lacing, as often shown in films, did happen, it was more the exception than the rule. Most photographs from the time that show women with extremely small waists have therefore been retouched – the Photoshop of its day.[5]

But the corset was no panacea, and in the late nineteenth century it increasingly came in for criticism, including from the medical profession. The undertone was often sexist. It was, for example, said that corsets hampered women in their marital duties, and tight-lacing was used to argue that women had inferior characters, allowing fashion to take precedence over their own welfare.[6] It was such claims that gave the corset a negative image, which lives on today in the stereotypes we see in costume dramas. More considered criticism of the corset – and constricting clothing in general – came from the dress reform movements, like the Vereeniging voor Verbetering van Vrouwenkleeding (Association for the Improvement of Women's Clothing, V.v.V.v.V), established in the Netherlands in 1899. With prominent members who included doctor and activist Aletta Jacobs, this organisation considered what clothing would actually be appropriate for women's changing role in society.[7] More movement, more freedom was the goal. Many supporters of the dress reform movement exchanged the classic boned corset for foundation garments made of sturdy cotton, which supported the body without shaping or distorting it.[8]

Sans corset

Calls for the corset to be abandoned also came from the world of fashion itself. The preference for a more natural silhouette towards the end of the first decade of the twentieth century meant there was less need for corsets, particularly for women with a slender figure. Corsets were increasingly omitted so that gowns would better follow the shape of the body.[9] French designer Jeanne Margaine-Lacroix made figure-hugging gowns her trademark, though she was certainly not the only one to produce such designs. Photographs of her gowns in magazines were often accompanied by a caption pointing out 'se portant sans corset' (to be worn without a corset).[10] Rather than a gown being worn over a corset, the garment itself would include an in-built corset that shaped and supported the body, even more than the standard structured inner bodices.[11]

One example is an ice-blue evening gown by an unknown maker in the collection at Kunstmuseum Den Haag. (p. 87) The gown has a robust longline inner bodice, with an elastic band that would be passed between the legs, to ensure that the gown fitted closely to the body. At the same time, the band made it impossible to wear a classic underskirt, which suggests that the wearer wore little to nothing underneath the gown. The increasingly revealing evening wear fashionable at the time made it more and more difficult to wear traditional undergarments. The same wardrobe includes an evening gown by Gustav Beer from circa 1918, with a translucent bodice with strategically positioned embroidered flowers over a light-coloured lining. (p. 17) Little will have been worn under this gown.[12] All in all, these were bold choices, though also consistent with the fight for more freedom for women and their right to make their own choices.

[1] *Gone with the Wind* (1939), *Meet Me In St. Louis* (1944), *Downton Abbey* (2010-2015), *Bridgerton* (2020-).

[2] *Titanic* (1997).

[3] Valerie Steele, *The Corset. A Cultural History*, New Haven 2001, pp. 69-71.

[4] Steele 2001, pp.100-109.

[5] A faint grey patch can often be seen beside the waist in photographs – a sign that it has been retouched.

[6] Steele 2001, p. 83, p.111.

[7] Madelief Hohé et al., Mode <3 Kunst, exh.cat. (Gemeentemuseum Den Haag) Zwolle 2012, p. 70.

[8] There are several dress reform bodices in Kunstmuseum Den Haag's collection, incl. inv.nos. KA 78-1962 and KA 128-1955.

[9] Steele 2001, p. 141; *Les Modes: Revue mensuelle illustrée des arts décoratifs appliqués à la femme*, April 1907, p.25 and May 1907, p. 23. Accessed via gallica.bnf.fr in July 2025.

[10] In 1900, for instance, a newspaper referred to an empire-style gown under which no corset was needed: 'the entire internal waist section is supported with boning and lacing, so that the figure receives the required support'. *Rotterdamsch Nieuwsblad*, 17-04-1900. Accessed via delpher.nl in July 2025.

[11] There are two gowns from the fashion house of Jeanne Margaine-Lacroix in Kunstmuseum Den Haag's collection: K 132-1951 and K 125-300.

[12] See also: Tirza Westland, 'Uitdagend en uiterst modieus. Een studie naar twee 'gewaagde' japonnen in het Kunstmuseum Den Haag', in: *Kostuum*, Zwolle 2024, pp. 132-143.

Tirza Westland

Fashion full speed ahead

At the start of the twentieth century, fashion evolved faster than ever before. Paris was the epicentre of the fashion world, and each season the famous fashion houses attempted to introduce novelties and outdo the competition with the quality of their designs. This environment fostered some truly unique creations. The Kunstmuseum Den Haag collection, for example, includes an evening gown of exceptional quality, with a very distinct structure that set it apart from other gowns of the time.[1] It has an innovative short underskirt to which the front panel of the skirt, which extends into a pointed train, is attached. A strip of embroidered tulle falls over the top of the skirt, and is gathered in a puff above the train. On the waistband of the lining is the label of the Paris fashion house Jérôme, which had its premises at 104 Rue du Faubourg-Saint-Honoré, known for its luxury shopping. (p. 75)

Although the structure of the garment is unique in the collection at Kunstmuseum Den Haag, the gown itself is not entirely unique. Research has revealed that several versions exist. In 2015, for example, an almost identical gown by an unknown maker was auctioned at Augusta Auctions in the US. It is now in the collection of the Fountainhead Antique Auto Museum in Alaska.[2] The collection of the ASU FIDM Museum (FIDM) in Los Angeles also includes a version of the gown, made in vibrant chartreuse satin, from the fashion house of Gustav Beer.[3] The gowns are virtually identical, the only difference being the way the fabric is used on the bodice.[4] There is a fourth version of the gown at the Metropolitan Museum of Art in New York, although in this case the design has been interpreted a little more freely.[5] At the time of writing, a fifth version of the gown with a more traditional structure and a label from the fashion house Brooks in Philadelphia, is being offered for sale online.[6] Almost all the gowns are in the US, which suggests it was a popular design there.

The gown is not only well represented in terms of surviving examples, it also featured in a number of magazines from the time. It appeared in the 15 October 1912 edition of American *Vogue*, with an illustration and fairly detailed article, which reveals that the design was called *Déesse* (goddess), and originated at the fashion house of Gustav Beer.[7] Several days later, on 3 November 1912, the French magazine *La Mode Illustrée* carried a photograph of a model wearing the gown, confirmed that it was indeed a design by Beer, and informed its readers that the silk came from the British firm Liberty.[8] *Les Modes* of 1 February 1913 had a full-page photograph of a model in the Beer gown.[9] Although the model is seated, it is clearly the same design.

If we believe the magazines, the design originally came from Gustav Beer and not from Jérôme. The great similarities in terms of fabric, embroidery and, above all, structure between the Kunstmuseum's gown, the FIDM gown with the Beer label, and the Augusta Auctions gown by an unknown maker, suggests that the Kunstmuseum gown is a legal copy, for which fashion house Jérôme presumably purchased a licence from Beer (a big name at the time).

Fashion houses were very protective of their creations. At the start of the fashion season, every design would be registered, with a photograph, at the 'conseil de prud'hommes' (labour court).[10] Publishing designs in fashion magazines before they were launched was a criminal offence, as it allowed copies to be made. For this reason fashion house Paquin took two fashion magazines to court in 1909 after one of its staff had presumably leaked a number of designs. It was a controversial case, which led to the tightening up of regulations in the fashion world.[11] Only once the fashion houses had sold their creations to their clients would they be made public, after which photographs and prints could be published in the media. When clients appeared in public in their new purchases, they would immediately be captured in photographs and prints that were subsequently published in the press.[12] The fashion house would already have profited from its design, and any copies subsequently made would not harm them. The gown made by the fashion house in Philadelphia is probably an example of this. It follows the design of the gown on the outside, but the maker was apparently unaware of the original internal structure.

Once a photograph or print had been published, it would be endlessly copied in various magazines, both legally and illegally.[13] In June 1909, for example, the Dutch fashion magazine *De Gracieuse* used a costume that had been shot by famous photographer Reutlinger as inspiration for a fashion print. The same design, in an adapted version, was used by the magazine for a print on its title page in August 1909.[14] Reutlinger's name was mentioned, which suggests that these were legal copies. Interestingly, the photograph was also used as the basis for an undated advertising poster for the Italian department store Mele & Ci.[15] Never before had fashion spread so rapidly: fashion news really was moving full speed ahead.

1 Kunstmuseum Den Haag, inv.no. BSC-0330.

2 Augusta Auctions, auction in New York, 11 November 2015, lot 217. The gown was purchased by the Fountainhead Antique Auto Museum in Alaska, inv.no. 2025-001-029.

3 FIDM Los Angeles, inv.no. 2017.5.54.

4 Contact with curator Kevin Jones of FIDM revealed that the FIDM gown actually has the same unusual structure as the gown in Kunstmuseum Den Haag's collection.

5 A lace bodice has, for example been added, upon which only parts of the embroidered satin has been used. With a bluish-purple waistband and the addition of several pink beads, the gown is more colourful than the examples previously mentioned. Metropolitan Museum of Art New York, inv.no. C.I.X.56.2.3.

6 Offered for sale by Tovasvintage on online marketplace Etsy. July 2025.

7 *Vogue*, 15 October 1912, p. 23; thanks to Kevin Jones, FIDM.

8 *La Mode Illustrée*, 3 November 1912; thanks to Roberto Minozzo, Titanicprops.

9 *Les Modes*, 1 February 1913, p. 15; thanks to Kevin Jones, FIDM.

10 *Annales de la propriété industrielle, artistique et littéraire*, 1909, art 4809, p. 234-244. Via gallica.bnf.fr, accessed in July 2025.

11 Idem.

12 Kunstmuseum Den Haag's collection includes a fashion print from the magazine from 1909 (PRK-1978-0054) showing a costume in which Mata Hari was photographed at Longchamp in 1908.

13 Sophie Kurkdjian, "Copying is Stealing!": The Fashion Press and Counterfeiting', in: Maude Bass-Krueger & Sophie Kurkdjian (eds.), *French Fashion. Women & The First World War*, New York 2019, pp. 414-433.

14 *Gracieuse* juni 1909, p. 192 and August 1909, p. 224, Kunstmuseum Den Haag; Album Reutlinger de portraits divers, vol. 52, p. 16. Via gallica.bnf.fr, accessed in July 2025.

15 Dario Cimorelli (ed.) *Moda e pubblicità in Italia 1850-1950*, Milan 2022, p.147. See also the author's blog (in Dutch) on modemuze.nl: *Modefotografie & modeprenten in de vroeg 20e eeuw*.

Tirza Westland

Hats

In the early twentieth century, no outfit would be complete without a hat. One was simply not dressed for the outdoors without something covering one's head. This applied to men, women and children. But there was a big difference between the headgear worn by the fashionable wealthy, and what the poorer members of society wore. Those who followed fashion would wear a voguish hat, while the poor simply tied a shawl around their head. A gentleman of good standing would wear a fashionable bowler hat or top hat, the ordinary man in the street would wear a cap. The turn of the twentieth century was the heyday of women's hat fashion. France, particularly Paris, set the tone in fashion, including for hats. Women's hats were relatively small at first, with a flat brim, and were worn straight or tilted slightly forward. Gradually, hats grew larger, reaching their peak around 1910-1911. Besides large hats with large brims, tall hats (consisting mainly of a high crown with no brim) were also in fashion. These 'toques' appeared larger at the top than at the bottom. After 1912 hats became steadily smaller and more manageable. Hairstyles also became less voluminous, and hat fashions changed along with them.

Given the importance of hats in a person's wardrobe, the role of hatmaker, or milliner, had become gradually more prominent in the nineteenth century. They signed their hats in the manner of fashion designers, so the names of late-nineteenth-century milliners can be found in the crown or on the brim. Several fashion designers, including Gabrielle 'Coco' Chanel and Jeanne Lanvin, started out as milliners. There were many potential variations on the design and decoration, for relatively little investment. Clients loved hats in the latest style. The basic materials used to make hats were mainly felt (for winter) and straw (for summer). Hats were frequently imported without decoration, mainly from Paris, and could then be decorated locally according to the client's taste, using a whole range of decorations. There were hats that featured trimmings made of feathers, wings, bird bodies and sometimes entire birds. Paris had artisans who specialised in making silk flowers (*fleuristes*) and others who processed feathers (*plumiers*). Around 1900 there were 800 *plumassiers* (feather workshops) in Paris employing some 7000 people.[1] Exotic birds on hats became so fashionable that some species were threatened with extinction. In the Netherlands, this eventually led to the establishment of the society for the protection of birds in 1899.

The giant hats of the 1910s appeared even bigger as a result of the ostrich feathers – known as *willow plumes or pleureuses* – that hung over their brims. From 1915 onwards, hat designs transformed, moving towards a smaller brim and higher crown. Extra height was created by trimming the hat with *aigrettes* (heron feathers) and ostrich feathers positioned vertically. The large bow on the hat of Rose in the arrival scene of Titanic (1997) was no flight of fancy – it was the height of fashion in the 1910s. The fashion for extremely large hats may have been inspired by a hat designed by Lucile for actress Lily Elsie in *The Merry Widow* (1907). In the play, she wore an exceptionally large hat with ostrich feather, which went down in fashion history as the Merry Widow Hat.[2] Large hats required large hairstyles. Here, again, theatre actresses were the role model. Lillie Langtry (1853-1929) and other theatre stars were responsible for the popularity of large hairstyles.

The hairstyle would be fixed in place using tortoiseshell combs and hairpins, sometimes decorated with imitation diamonds. The hatpin was another vital accessory. The pins were dangerous; Germany introduced a law requiring a protective cap or guard on the tip for safety, a practice subsequently adopted by other countries. Women who did not comply risked a fine or imprisonment.[3] French designer Paul Poiret made the turban and bandeau (a wide headband) fashionable in the 1910s, as an alternative to the huge hats that had defined fashion up to that point.

[1] Susie Hopkins, *The Century of Hats: Headturning Style of the Twentieth Century*, London 1999, p. 12.
[2] Madeleine Ginsburg, *The Hat: Trends and Traditions*, London 1990, p. 103.
[3] Ginsburg 1990, p. 112.

In the opening scene of the film *Titanic* (1997) we see passengers from the different classes gathered on the quayside. Dressed in travel outfits, they stand among piles of trunks, crates and hatboxes. The clothes the passengers are wearing reveal their social class – as did all clothing at the time. Anyone who could afford it would wear special travel clothing. For the lower social classes, they probably simply travelled in the clothes they normally wore outdoors. Besides a coat and skirt, a woman would wear a woollen shawl tied round her head, a cap or a straw hat known as a boater, with a ribbon tied round it. Anyone who could not afford feathers or flowers to decorate their hat would use paper decorations.[1] A woollen cape or wrap would be worn around the shoulders, rather than an expensive tailored coat.

In the early twentieth century, a growing number of modern modes of transport became available for long journeys, including the steam train, steam ship and automobile, allowing people to travel greater distances. And though travel became more modern, faster and more comfortable, the reality was that a traveller's outfit would suffer greatly during a trip by train, boat or car. It would not only be exposed to the elements, but also to the dust and soot emitted by steam-powered trains and boats. The 'Ulster' was a practical travelling coat for men, a warm, waterproof woollen garment. It was not uncommon for those who could afford it to wear a special travel outfit on a trip or voyage. Passengers were advised to 'pack a handy bag or suitcase for the voyage, and leave the rest of one's clothing in trunks. On arrival at one's destination, travel clothing could be handed over to the travel company for safekeeping until the return voyage.'[2]

What did the fashionable wealthy travellers wear? A modern woman would wear a 'tailor-made' suit, like the one worn by Rose in the film, when the Titanic sets sail. A tailored suit was also worn for more sporting occasions. Initially, little distinction was drawn between clothes for travel and for sport. The concept of sport was broader in those days, akin to what we would call leisure nowadays – things like travel, walking, hunting, cycling, driving, strolling by the sea, sailing. The hemlines of women's sports clothes were shorter than those of fashionable suits, to afford more freedom of movement. Car driving was also regarded as a sport. A 'duster' (so called because it protected the wearer from the dust in the air), or *manteaux automobiles*, was useful. It would be worn over other clothes.[3] Goggles protected the eyes from the dust and the bright sun. Hats would be tied to the head with a shawl or veil, and large hat covers made of fabric were also developed, with a hole for goggles, which made women look like beekeepers. Sport clothing like tweed suits, hunting outfits and driving outfits were made by tailors, whose clientèle were mainly men. From 1900 female clients increasingly turned to tailors to have riding habits and suits made.[4]

The growth in the popularity and seriousness of sport as a leisure activity over the course of the twentieth century is evidenced by the fact that there were even sporting facilities on board the hypermodern Titanic in 1912. First-class passengers had access to a gym that had training bikes, a mechanical horse (to practise riding), a squash court and a saltwater indoor pool.[5] It is said that John Jacob Astor IV (JJ Astor) spent his final hours on board the Titanic distracting himself on the mechanical horse, knowing that the ship was about to sink.[6]

[1] Susie Hopkins, *The Century of Hats: Headturning Style of the Twentieth Century*, London 1999, p. 94.
[2] Janneke Budding, *Mijnheer de Baron is op reis. Buitenlandse reizen van de adel, 1814-1914*, Zutphen 2021, p. 55.
[3] *Mode Sports Paris*, exh.cat. (Palais Galliera Musée de la Mode de la Ville de Paris) Paris 2024. 'Au Louvre' coat, Palais Galliera, p. 80.
[4] Cassie Davies-Strodder et al., *London Society Fashion 1905-1925: The Wardrobe of Heather Firbank*, London 2015, p. 64.
[5] Cathalijne Boland, *Reuchlins reis*, Amsterdam 2023, p. 283.
[6] *Encyclopedia Titanica* online Victim John Jacob Astor IV (JJ Astor) First Class Passenger.

Travel clothing

Kathleen Mahieu

Perishable Clothing

The new century brought significant changes in fashion and also in the discovery of new materials. The female wardrobe evolved from separate bodices and skirts to one-piece dresses, with the invention of 'tea gowns', afternoon dresses, day dresses and evening gowns.[1] Made with expensive materials, many of these dresses were embellished with colourful fabrics trimmed with lace motifs, embroidered designs, fur, or even faux flowers.[2] However, most of the materials used were as fragile and ephemeral as in past fashions.

Silk (*soie grége*, *chappe*, *tussah* or *bourette*) was for instance widely used in the form of chiffon, taffeta, satin or even velvet, dyed bright colours. It dominated Paris fashion from 1910 onwards.[3] Dark blues and black became very prevalent during 1909 and into early 1910, switching to lighter hues in 1913 to 1914.[4] Of all of these fabrics, chiffon was without doubt the most useful material for fashion designers at the beginning of the century. Nowadays, it is the source of structural problems due its poor condition, having lost its original strength and disintegrating when handled.

Paul Poiret and Lucile were very inspired by these materials and the opportunities the new dye industry offered them, specially the colour combinations that now ruled the fashion scene, in the designs of Leon Bakst for the Ballet Russes.[5] This achievement was only possible thanks to the diversity of new synthetic dyes available at that moment. Despite the pioneering role played by Britain and France, with the discovery of *Mauvine* and *Fuchsine* before 1860, Switzerland and Germany became the new leading producers of synthetic dyes after 1880.[6] The new century brought an enormous diversity of new colorants (*basic dyes*, *acid dyes*, *mordant dyes*, *sulphur dyes*, *azoic dyes*) which did not always bring good results as regards long-term stability. Many of those fabrics are currently in a very fragile condition, so that the dresses cannot even be displayed on a mannequin.[7] (p. 134)

Following on from the experience gained with the first synthetic dyes, new processes were introduced after 1900, leaving behind the weighted silk processes that caused so may problems due to the use of heavy metals in the form of tin chloride, lead acetate and aluminum nitrate.[8][9] The new processes were now focused on new metal components such as sodium phosphate, chrome or zinc chloride in combination with natural tannins (such as sumac or logwood) to achieve better results.[10]

These dyes were also used to imitate luxury materials such as fur on evening dresses, hats or coats, which became very fashionable at the beginning of the century.[11][12] Rabbit fur, for instance, was widely used at this time to imitate expensive materials such as seal or otter. It was coloured with black dyes (such as diamines) and exposed to different oxidation processes with hydrogen peroxide or sodium dichromate.[13] Sometimes, the fur was submitted to further processes by the addition of metallic components (*iron copper*, *iron sulfates*, *potassium*, *chromates*), along with vegetal tannins (*logwood*), with the aim of obtaining darker hues. In the press, designers such as Lucile promoted the use of synthetic dyes for colouring furs to make them more fashionable '*...we are dyeing and painting fox, why instead of dyeing fox brown, should we not dye or paint it purple, green or blue?...*' or '*...I have seen a delightful pink chiffon evening gown trimmed with bands of pink ermine...*'[15]. However, as seen with silks, the submission of the material to these harsh alkaline conditions affected the long-term condition of the fur. It weakened the attachment of the hairs to the skin and caused strong delamination of the support.[16][17]

The use of these dyes was also extended into the field of fashion in the form of decorative elements. This was the case, for instance, with green acid dyes (such as *Green-Blue S*, *Green-Neptune S* or *Green-Neptune SB*), which were very expensive to produce compared to other dyes like blue alkalis (e.g. *Blue 6B*) or palatine blacks (e.g. *Black-Palatine 4B*). Due to their lower cost, the latter dyes were typically used to colour buttons, feathers, or even embroidery materials.[18] Sequins made of gelatin (collagen), for instance, which were widely used until the 1920s, were subjected during manufacturing to harsh acetic acids and alkaline environments. This exposure affected their longevity, particularly because of their low glass transition point.[19] This effect was documented in the Gustave Beer dress, where the embroidered sequins had deformed from their original cup shapes into flattened forms. (p. 17) As with fabrics and furs, sequins were also an experimental field for the new dye technology. However, as has been seen, their adoption later caused problems for textile conservators.

1 Jenny Lister, London Society Fashion 1905-1925: The Wardrobe of Heather Firbank, Victoria & Albert Museum, London 2015, pp.7, 27.
2 Lister 2015, p. 50.
3 Clare Rose, 'Rough wolves in the sheepcote: the meanings of fashionable color, 1900-1914', in: Colours in Fashion, London 2017, p. 162.
4 Anne Katherine Reilly, 'Conservation of a Lucile LTD. Evening dress, circa 1910-1914', unpublished MA diss., Fashion Institute of Technology, New York 2010, p. 15.
5 Rose 2017, p. 158, 159.
6 Matthew Winterbottom 'The Triumph of Colour': the Synthetic Colour Revolution in: Colour Revolution, Victorian Art, Fashion & Design, Melton 2023, p. 93.
7 Analysis carried out in 2023 by Alina Krotova and Chiara Vettorazzo from the University of Antwerp as part of the 'safe silk' research project.
8 Ralph Leoce, 'A study in textile degradation: the conservation of an 1899 Jeanne Paquin gown', unpublished MA diss., Fashion Institute of Technology, New York 1994, p. 37.
9 Silvia Montero Redondo, 'La "seda cargada" en la indumentaria entre 1880 y 1930. Metodología de estudio y propuesta de conservación-restauración', in: GE-Conservación, N2, 2011: p. 81-98 / Marei Hacke, '"Weighted silk: history, analysis and conservation', in: Reviews in Conservation, N9, 2008, pp. 1-15.
10 These combinations were registered in dye manuals from the time such as 'Colores de Anilina, Badische Anilin & Soda Fabrik, 1902' or Cassella & Co., Frankfurt, A.M¹., Die Diaminfarbe" (1895/96)¹.
11 Kunstmuseum Den Haag has several objects with fur as decoration, such as the evening coat (inv.no. K74-1987) worn by Virginia Pearce Delgado and accessories such as the hat BSA 444 (circa 1908), among others.
12 Lisa Charlotte Lardeau, De fibres et de poils', Etude et conservation-restauration de la robe "Tolédo" de Paul Poiret MA diss., Institut du patrimoine, Paris 2020, p. 94.
13 Lardeau 2020, p. 99.
14 Lardeau 2020, p. 100.
15 Lady Duff-Gordon 'Rainbow faces and painted furs!' in: The Times Dispatch, Richmond September 21, 1913.
16 Dignar Carole, Gaelen Gordon, 'Metal Ion Catalyzed Oxidation and collar on a velvet cape', in: Journal of the Canadian Association for Conservation, vol. 24, (1999), pp. 11-22.
17 'La Perse' by Paul Poiret in collaboration with Raoul Dufy (1911) from MET Costume collection (2005.199 a) was one of the cases of damaged fur, where the hairs came away from the skin support. Information gathered by conservator Glenn Petersen during the installation at Kunstmuseum Den Haag in September 2017 of the exhibition Art Deco Paris, (14.10.2017-04.03.2018).
18 Badische Anilin & Soda Fabrik, 1902, pp. 26–40.
19 Chris Paulocik, R. Scott Williams, "The Chemical Composition and Conservation of Late 19th and Early 20th Century Sequins." Journal of the Canadian Association for Conservation, 2010, Volume 35, pp. 46–61.

César Rodríguez Salinas

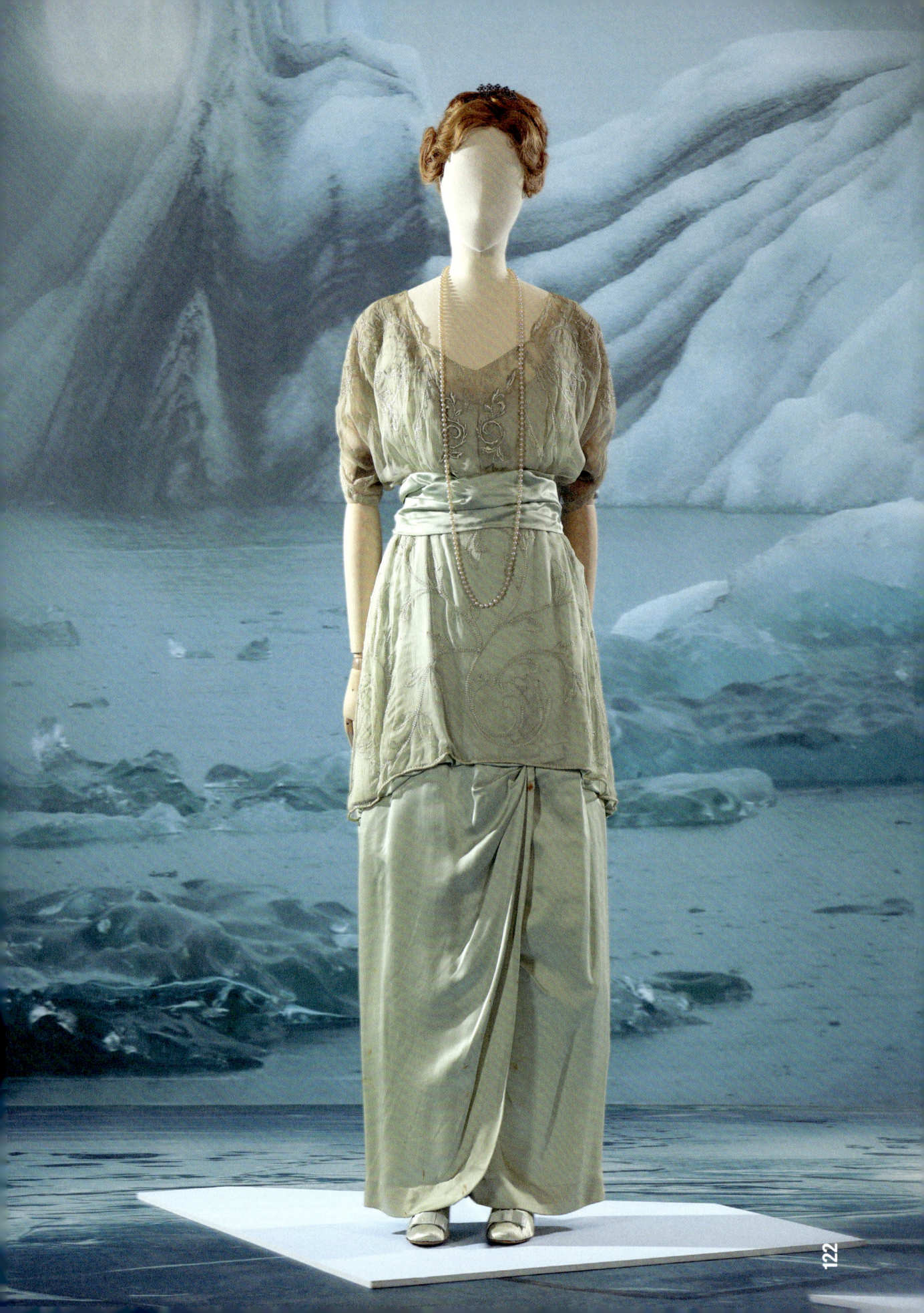

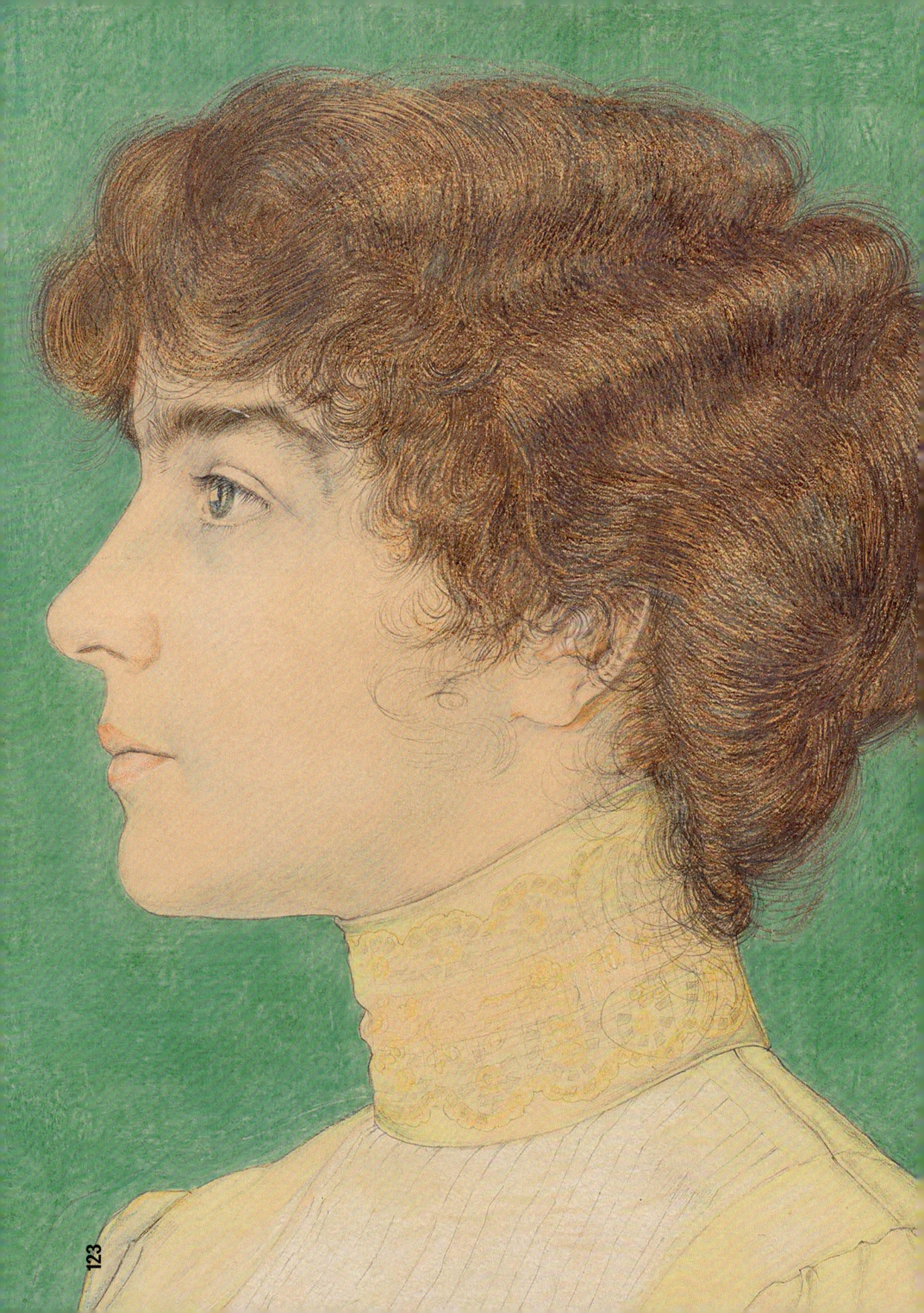

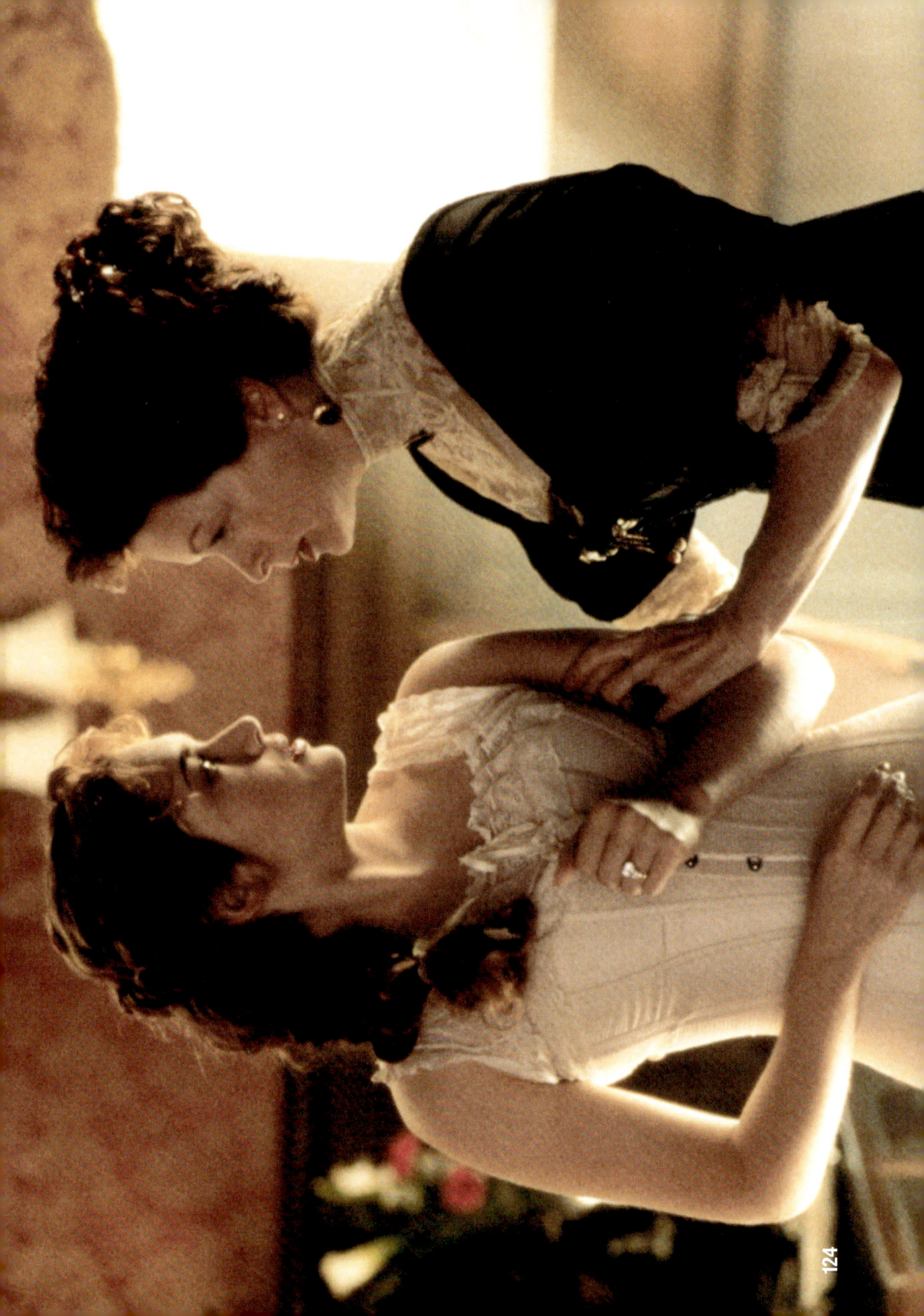

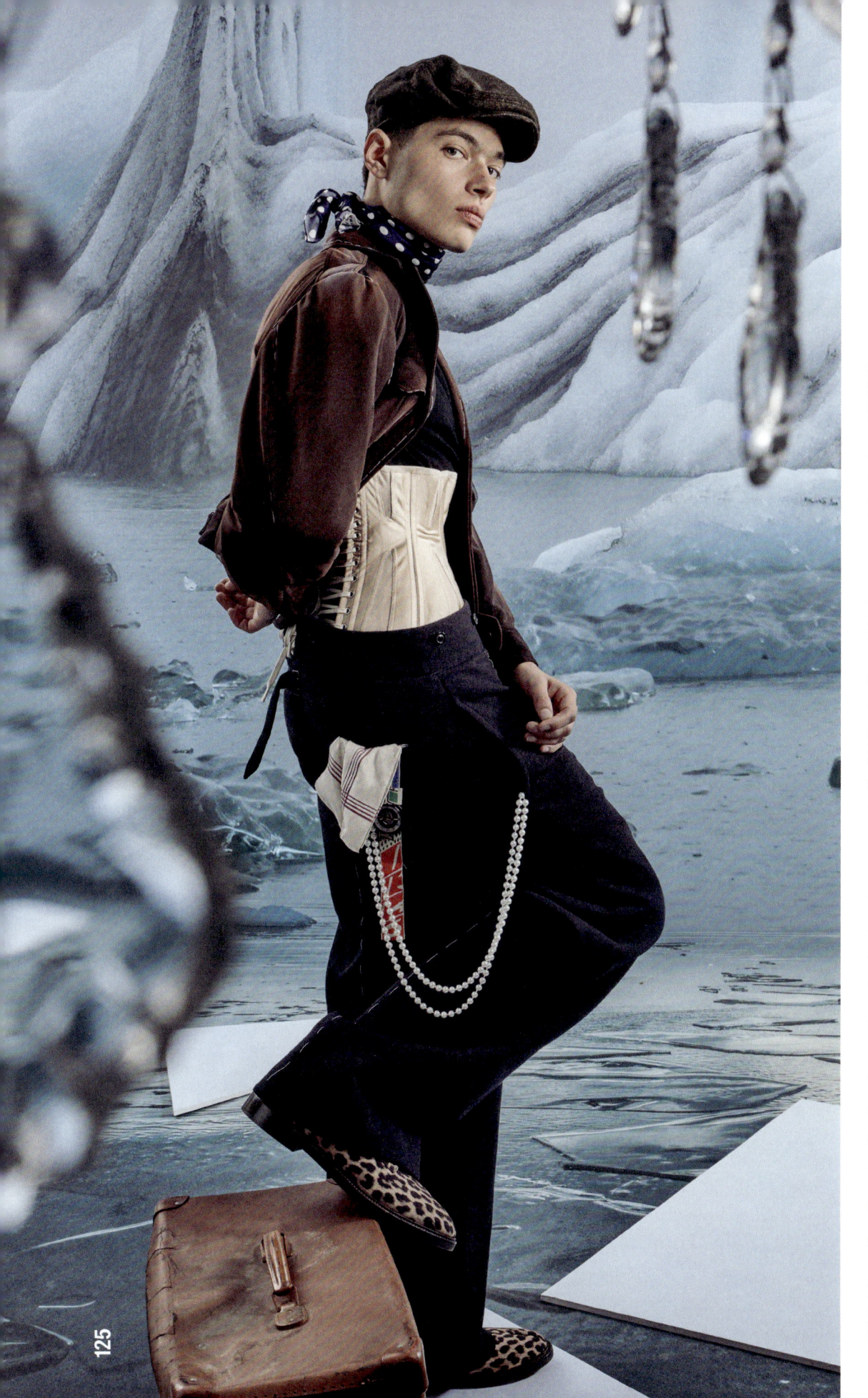

125

p. 122 Mejuffrouw Haag, Turquoise silk satin and mousseline embroidered evening gown, worn by Mrs A.H. Hondius-Crone during her engagement, Amsterdam, c. 1913-1914.
p. 123 Jan Toorop, Portrait of Lily Clifford (1884 –1960), wearing a high-necked day dress; she travelled a lot and taught modern languages, 1902.
p. 124 Rose (Kate Winslet) wearing a corset, with her mother Ruth Dewitt Bukater (Frances Fisher) in *Titanic* (1997).
p. 125 John Galliano for Maison Margiela, Ensemble with corset, Artisanal Co-Ed 2024, courtesy of Maison Margiela, Paris.

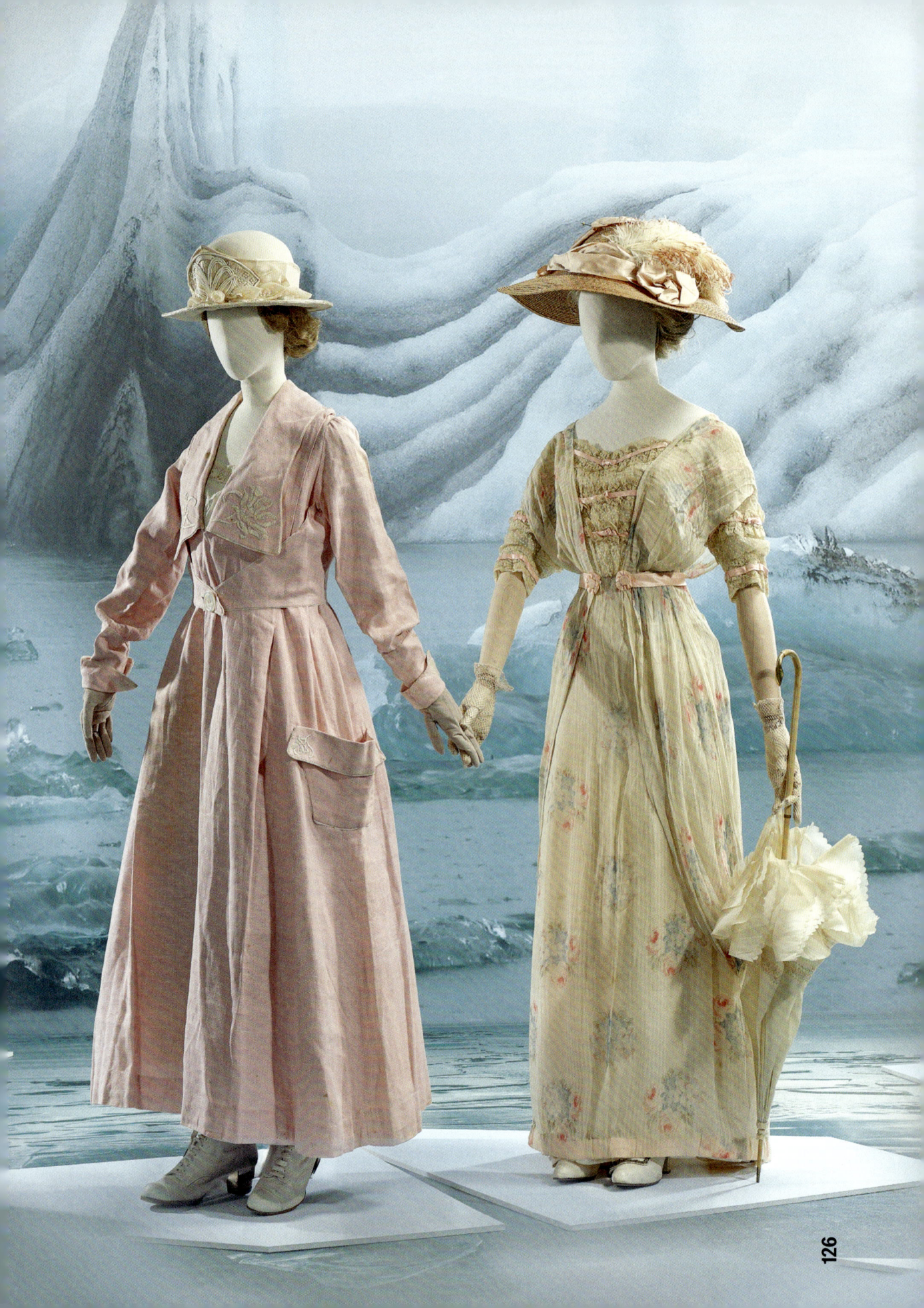

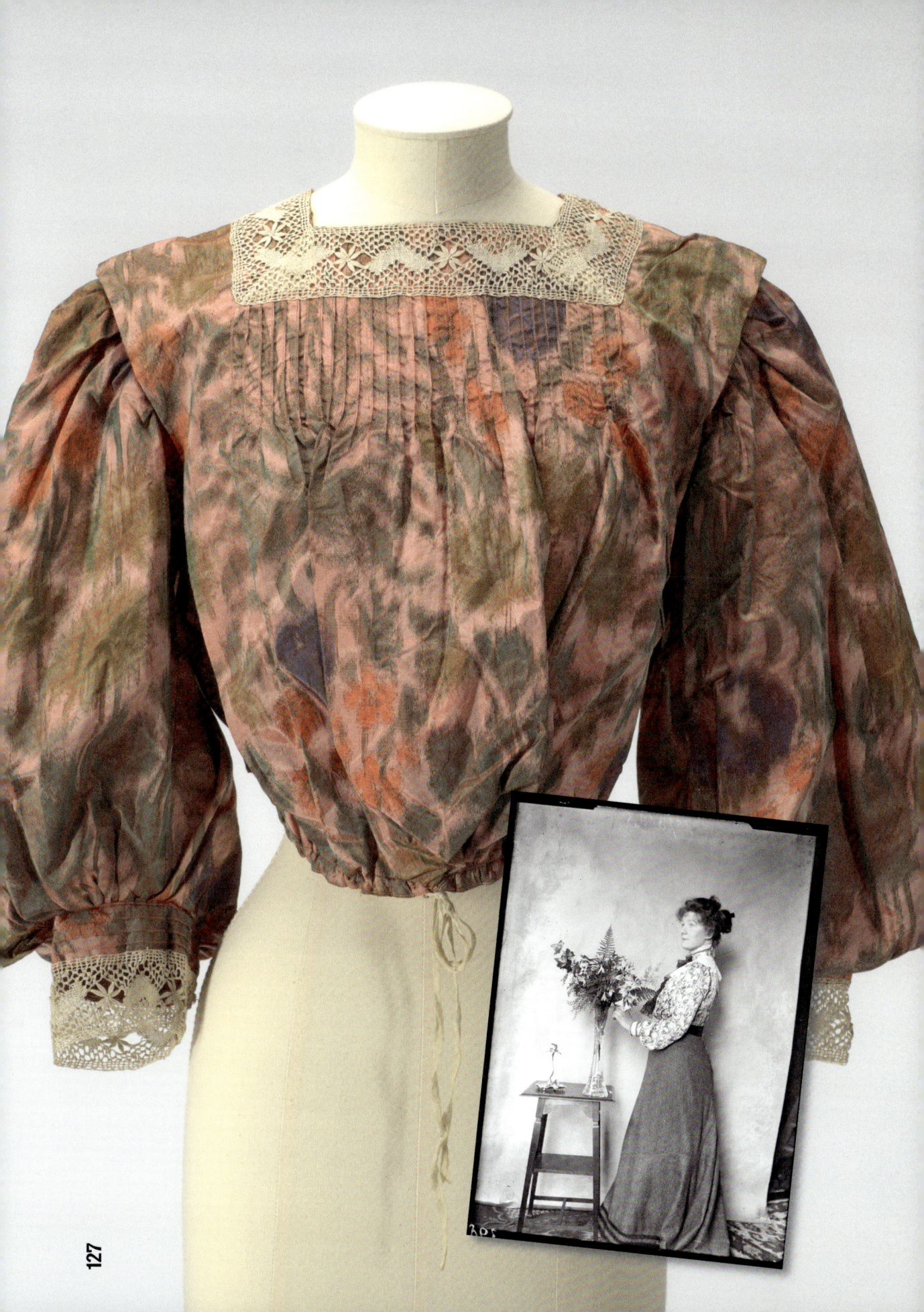

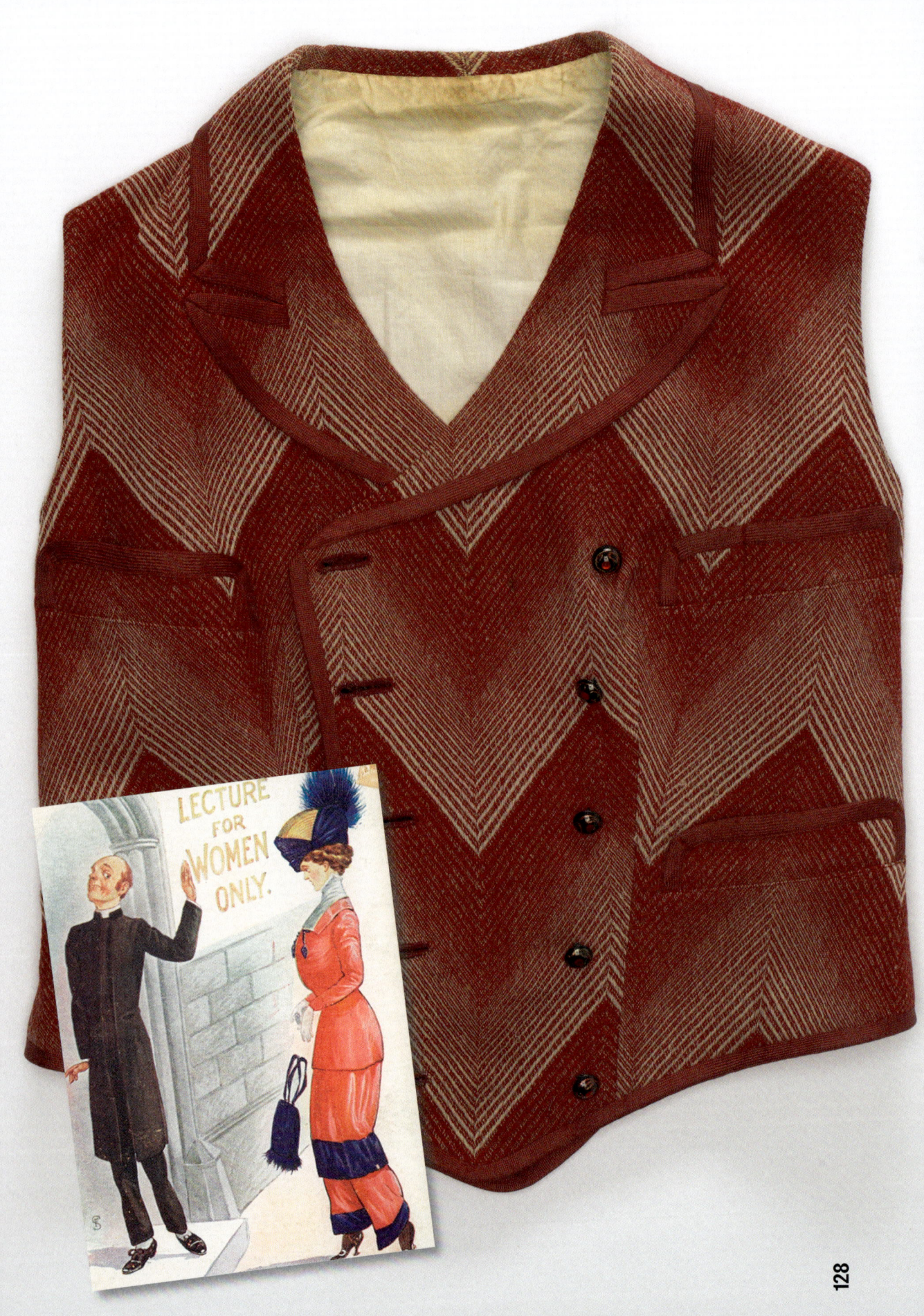

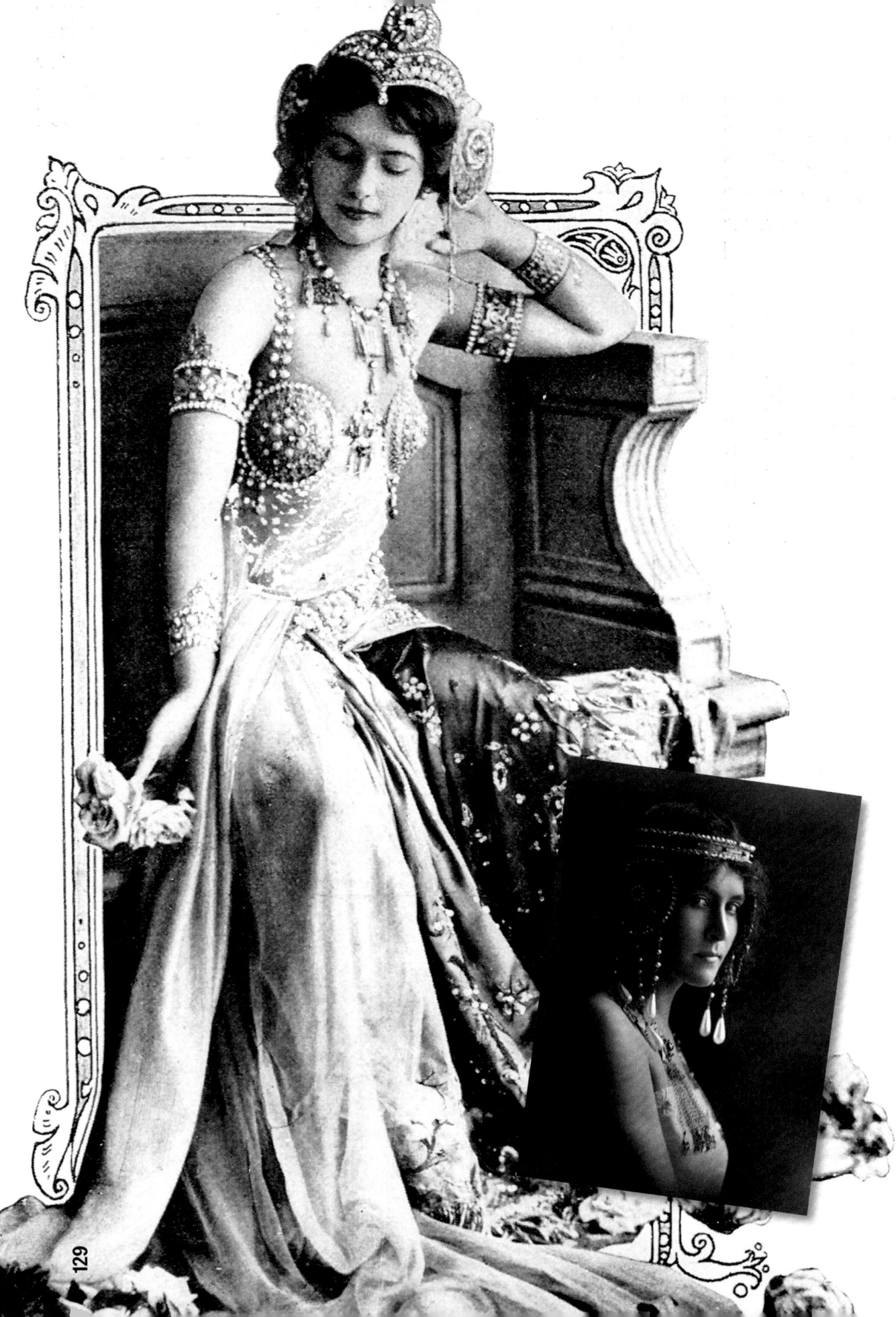

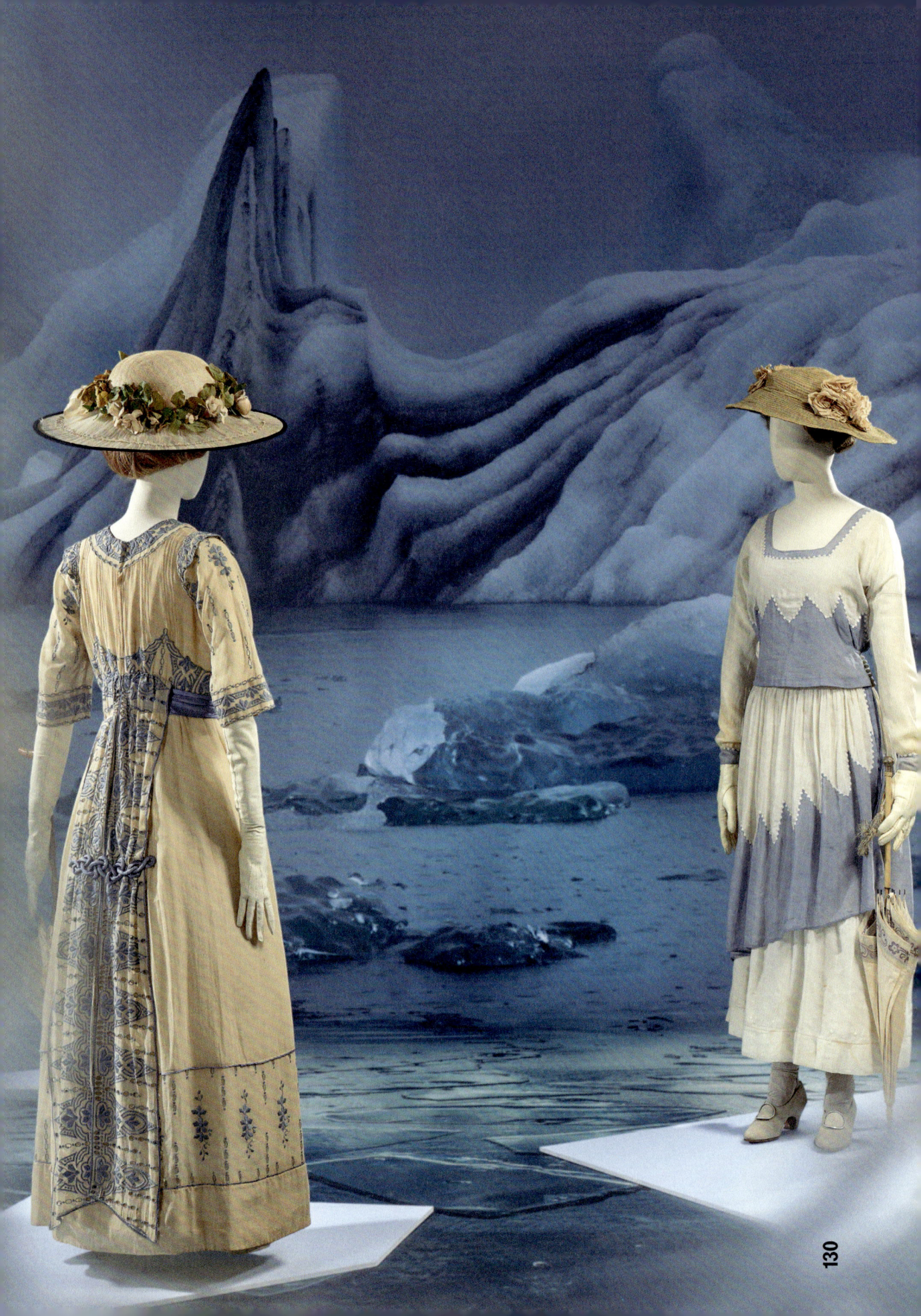

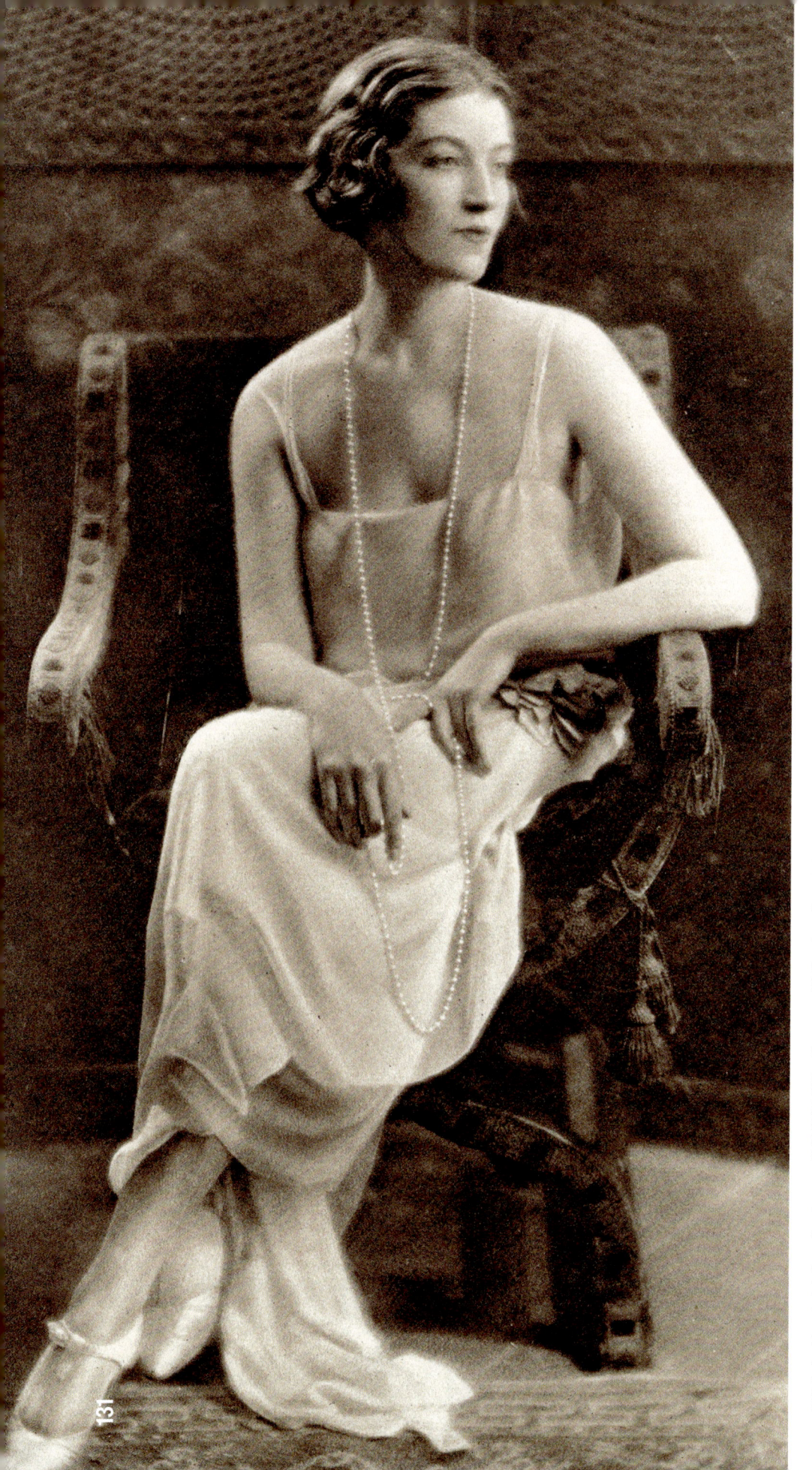

p. 126 Embroidered pink linen day dress, c. 1915-1917; Silk voile gown with floral motifs and pink trim, c. 1913, both worn by Virginia Pearce Delgado-Orth (1891-1985) in New York.

p. 127 Marie Drukker, Reform blouse made of Liberty crepe de chine, purchased at Metz & Co, Hilversum / Amsterdam, c. 1907-1908, worn by Mrs H.W. Zeverijn-Wichers (1869-1912).

p. 127 Ms Coelen wearing a blouse and skirt, c. 1908-1910.

p. 128 Red wool and satinet waistcoat (woman's), The Hague, c. 1912-1918, worn by Countess Marie Alexandrine Otheline Caroline van Bylandt (1874- 1968).

p. 128 Cartoon showing a woman being refused entry to a lecture 'For Women Only' because she is wearing jupe-culottes, 1911.

p. 129 Mata Hari (Margaretha Zelle) (1876-1917) wearing her oriental dance costume, 1906.

p. 129 Actress Lili Marberg as Salomé (in the play of the same name by Oscar Wilde), production in Germany, 1903-1907.

p. 130 Day dress, white cotton with blue silk embroidery, Indonesia, c. 1910-1913; Day dress in white and blue cotton, Indonesia, c. 1916-1918.

p. 131 Daisy Fellowes (Marguerite Séverine Philippine Decazes de Glücksberg) (1890-1962); society figure and editor-in-chief of *Harper's Bazaar* (French edition), 1922.

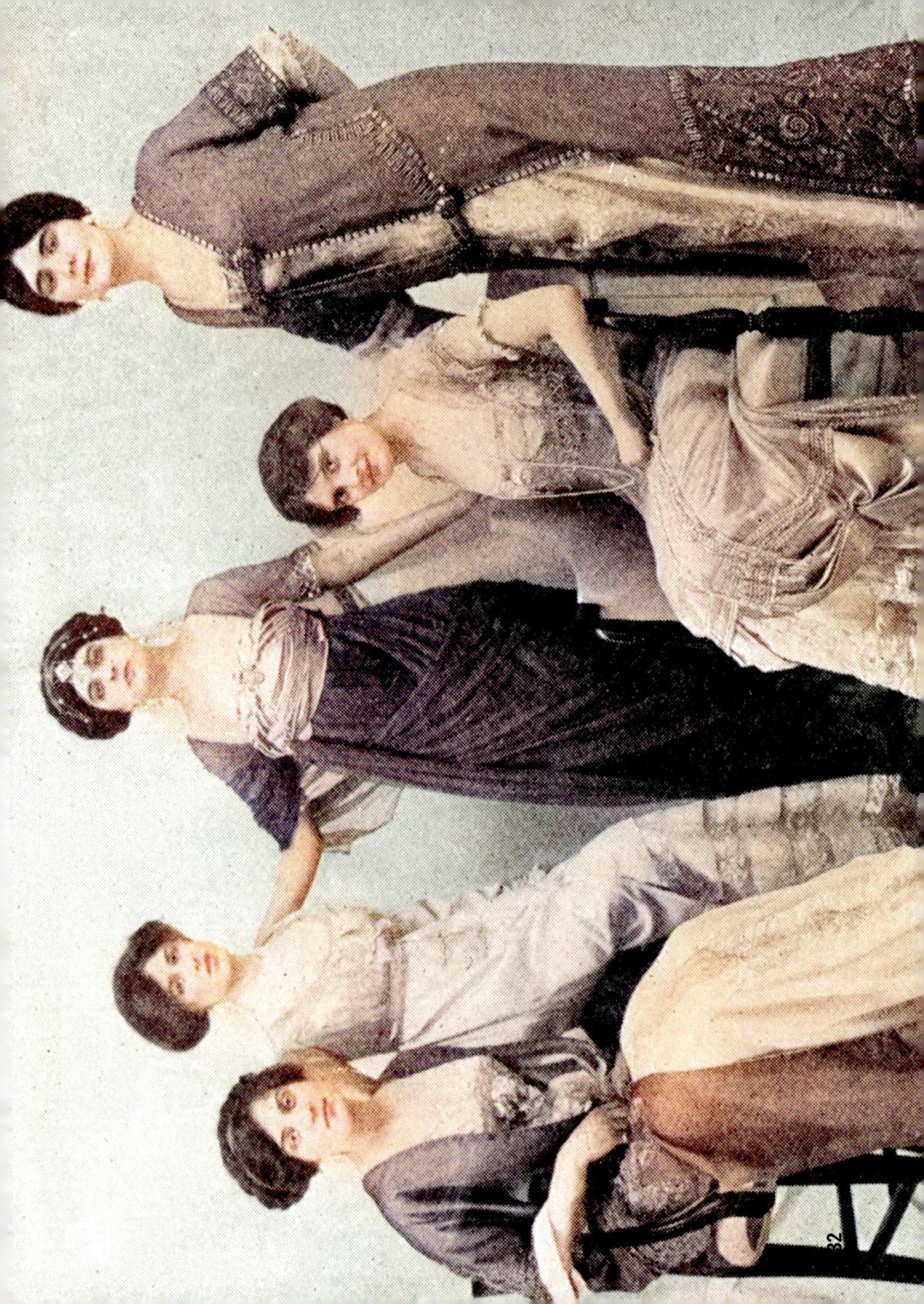

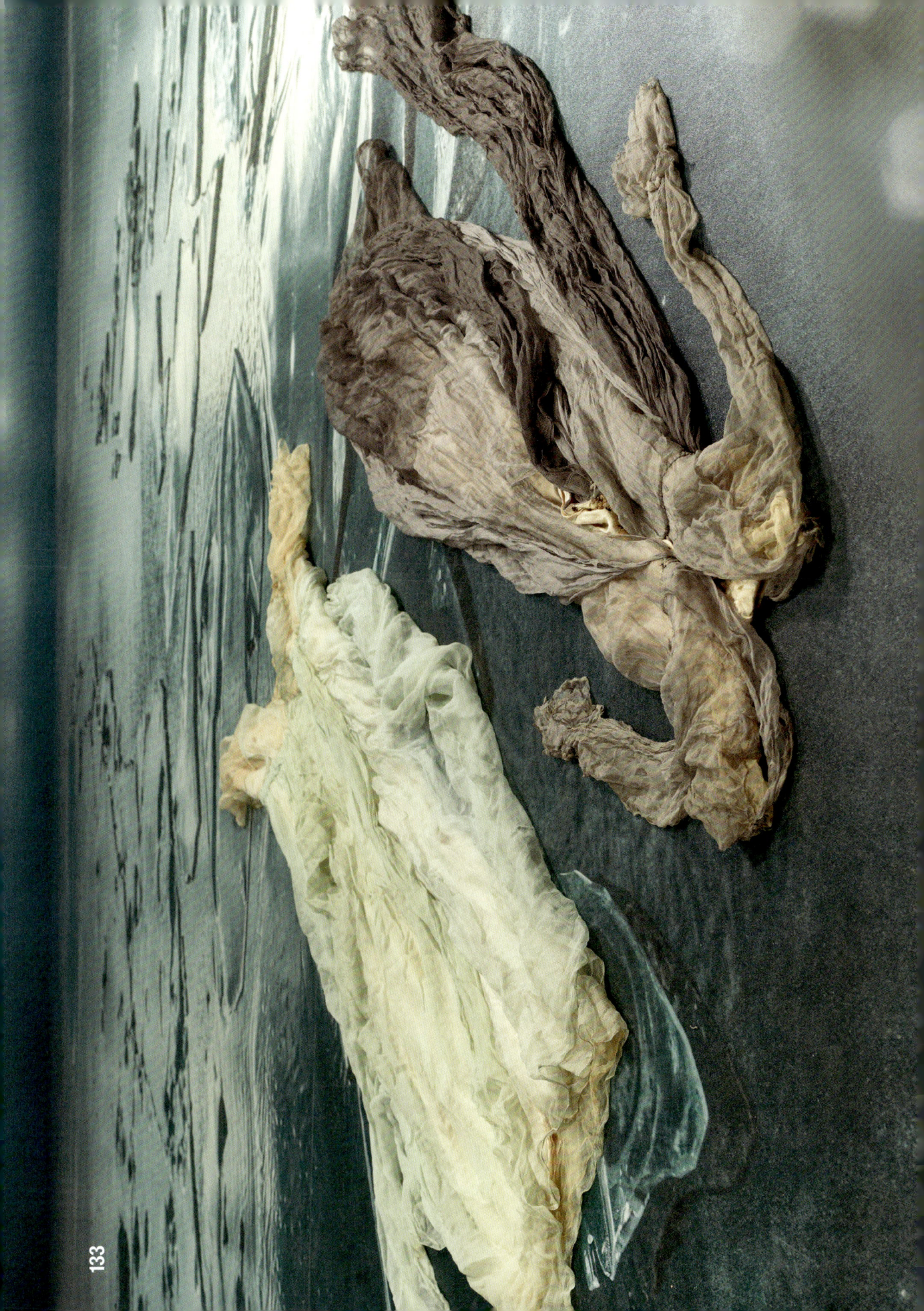

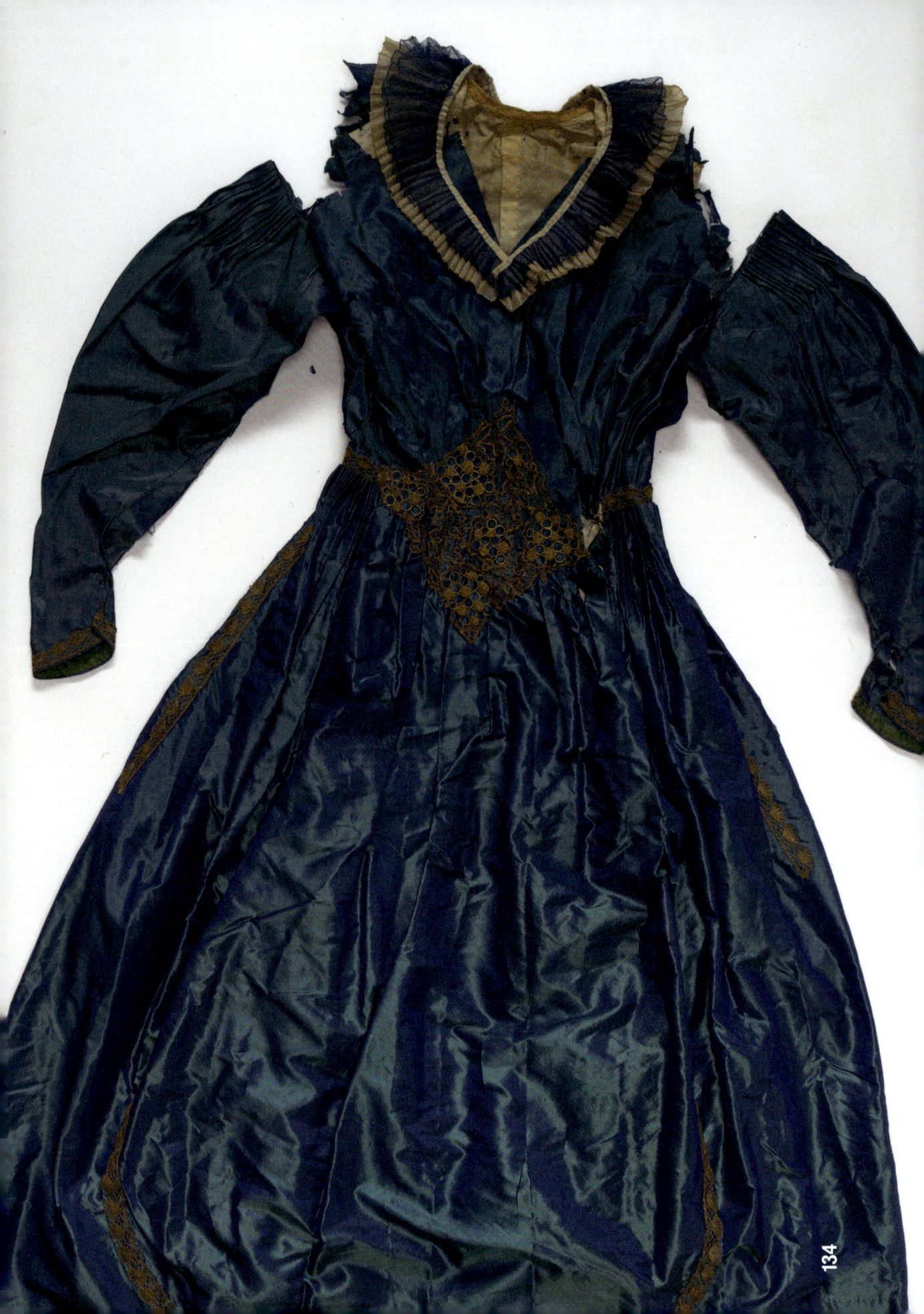

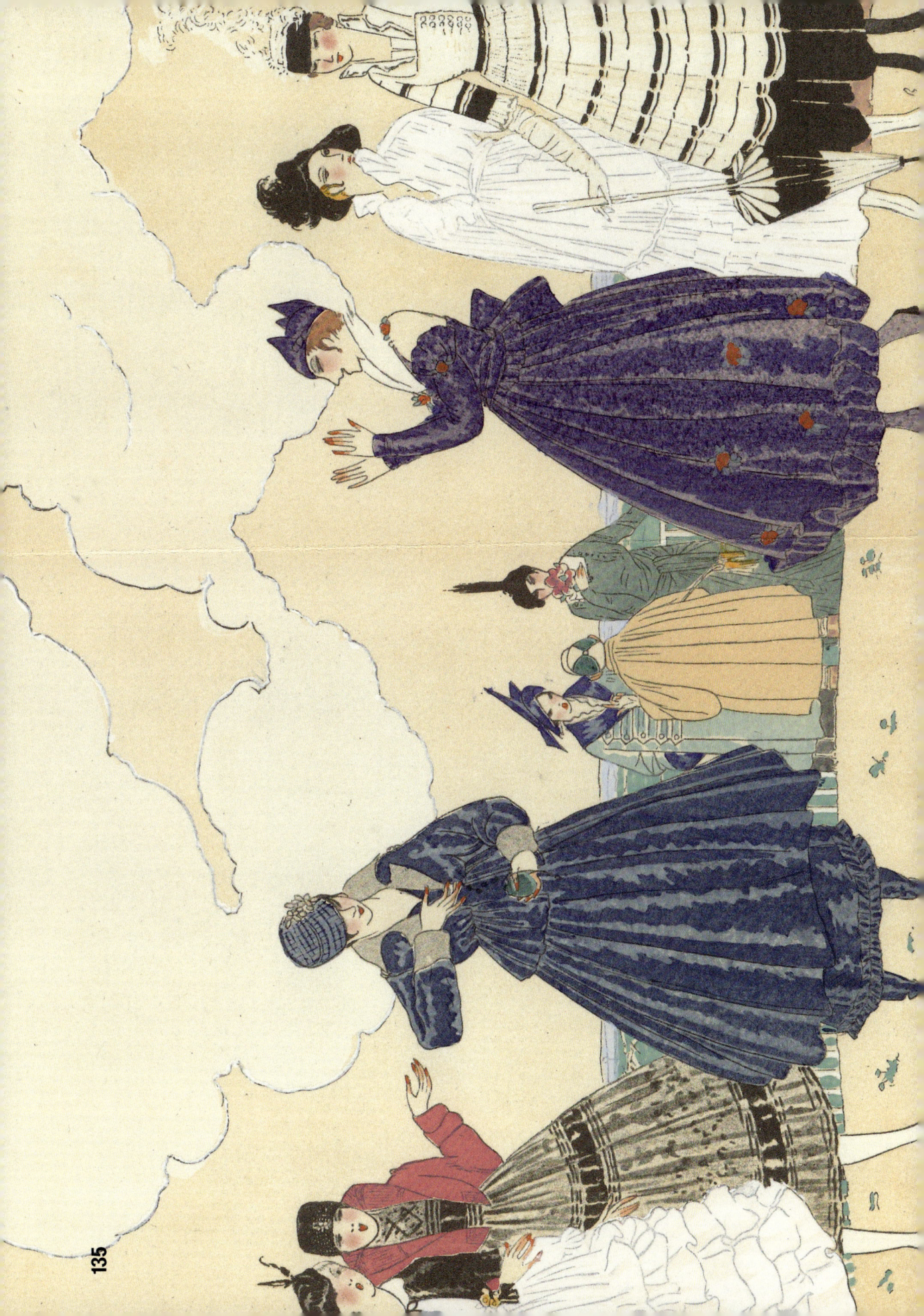

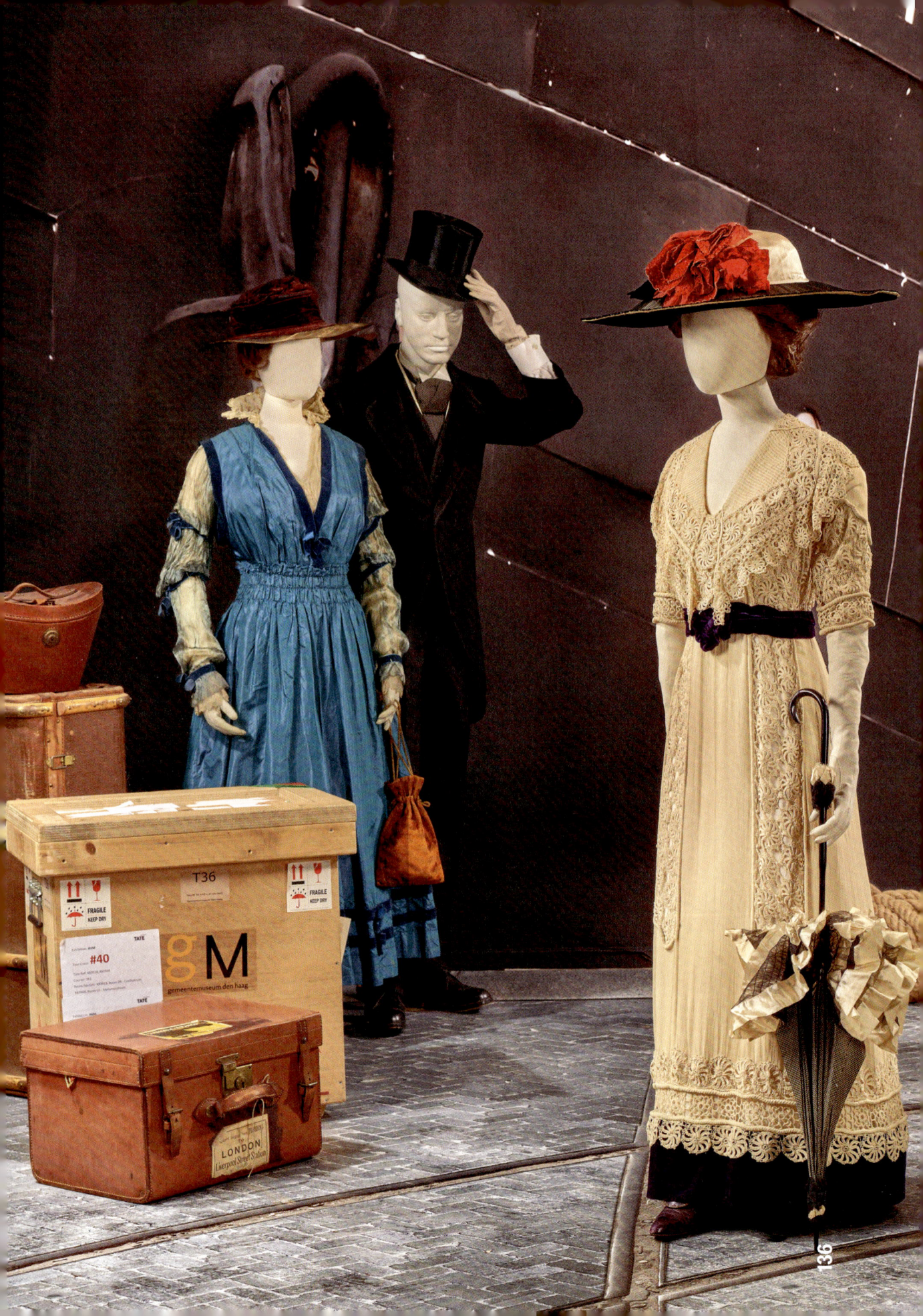

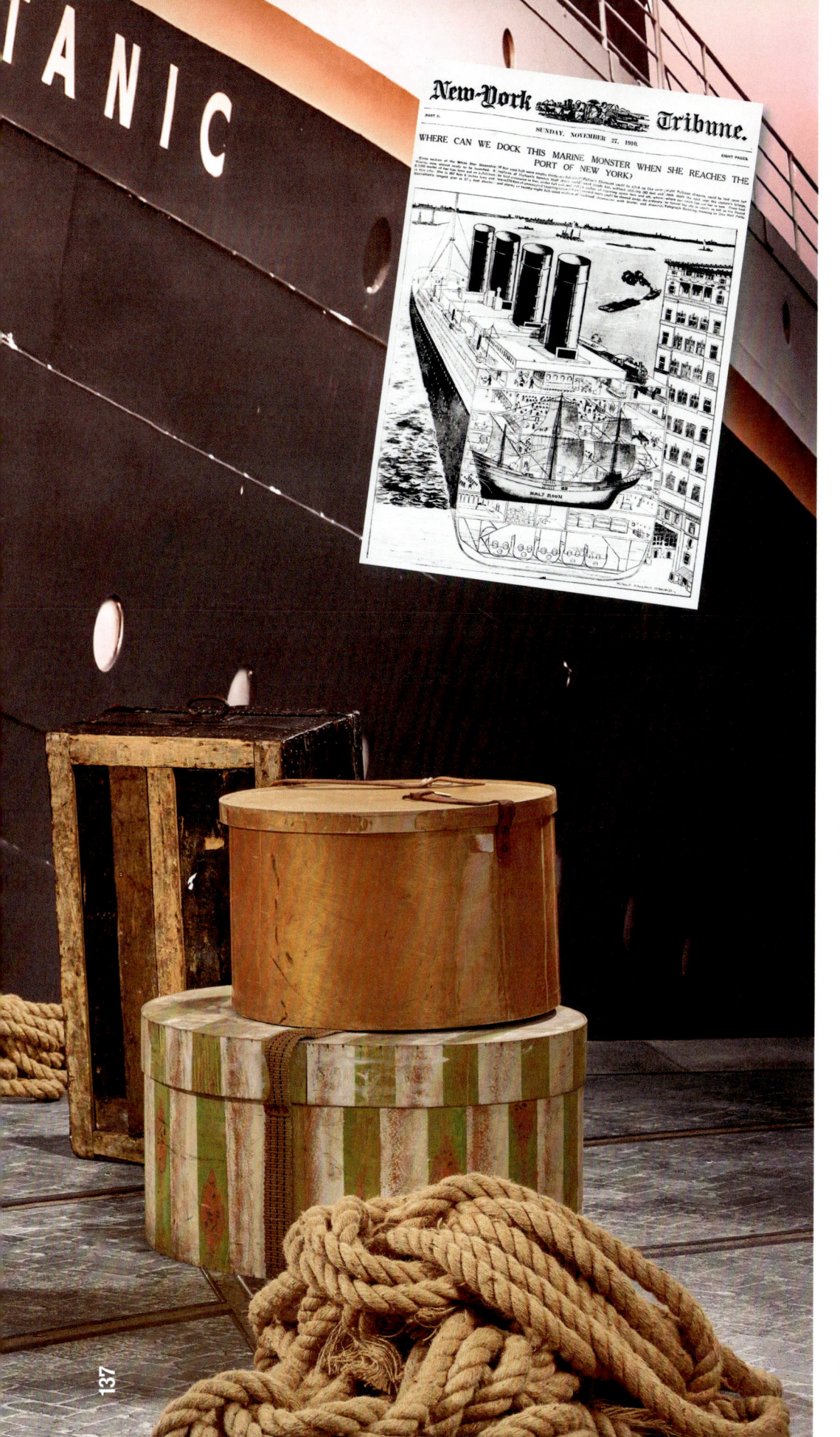

p. 132 Models from fashion house Lucile, run by Lady Duff-Gordon, on their way to New York in 1910. They are all wearing one of Lucile's 'emotional gowns', based on their own personality.

p. 133 Lucile, Two silk gowns from the wardrobe of 'it girl' Daisy Fellowes, c. 1911; they were discovered in a trunk, courtesy of Lewis Orchard.

p. 134 Maison Stuttman, Blue silk tafetta dress with conservation problems, Amsterdam, c. 1916.

p. 135 Fashion plate featuring designs by Paris couturiers; the blue dress by Lanvin resembles the Stuttmann dress, in: *La Gazette du Bon Ton*, summer 1915, collection Rijksmuseum Amsterdam.

p. 136 Petrol blue silk faille gown with gauze sleeves, c. 1915-1917; Morning suit with top hat, wool, silk, 1904, worn by L. den Beer-Poortugael Esq.; Afternoon dress, white cotton and purple silk velvet, c. 1912-1914.

p. 137 The Titanic (built 1909-1911) on the front page of the *New York Tribune*, 27 November 1910: 'Where Can We Dock This Marine Monster When She Reaches The Port of New York?'

Titanic: The Last Dance?

Just as the loss of the Titanic and the First World War prompted changes in the 1910s, the world has changed since the COVID-19 pandemic. During the pandemic, fashion was full of bright, optimistic colours – to keep our spirits up, perhaps? Since then, things have become soft, comforting, romantic, in a style redolent with emotion and soft embraces. The shops are full of lace dresses that could easily be from the 1910s. Simone Rocha, Dries van Noten and Comme des Garçons are just a few of the designers producing soft shapes and colours, many with historical references. Tess van Zalinge often combines them with corset structures that signal empowerment. So why is it that fashions are so soft and romantic, while the world grows harder, and conflict spreads? While people are at odds more than ever before. How come the shape and feel of the fashions of the 1910s has such resonance in our day and age? Is it a form of escapism? And did the hard world of that time need the same romantic fashions we seem to need now?

John Galliano's 'artisanal' collection for Margiela in spring 2024 was a real moment in fashion of the kind that occurs only a few times in a decade. A collection that attracted universal attention, and which will go down in fashion history as a turning point, because it explored a new aesthetic – one that was also surprisingly historical. The setting was a Parisian basement café by the Seine full of colourful characters. The models entered the mist-shrouded set among the customers, men and women dressed in fashions inspired by the 1910s and 1920s. Wasp waists, but now not just for the women – also for the men. A man's suit that would not have looked out of place on Jack in the film *Titanic* was now worn with a corset, a string of pearls as a watch chain, and leopard print shoes. (p. 125) Dresses in the war crinoline silhouette of the 1910s, long lace gowns through which 'merkins' (pubic wigs) were visible. A quintessentially romantic style, but one that played with historical male-female roles, combined with drama and nostalgia to produce a new, desirable aesthetic. Galliano – who fell into disgrace some time ago after making controversial statements – had also referenced the 1910s in previous collections. A striking gown from the 'artisanal' summer 2020 collection combines a trench coat – worn in the trenches of the 'Great War' – and a black lace evening gown with jet beads. The perfect blend of male and female, a duality that also made it perfectly fluid.

Alongside this mellow, luxurious aesthetic, work clothing is currently another source of inspiration. In the Netherlands we see this in the designs of Bonne Suits and Jacques Hullekes: gender-neutral suits inspired by boiler suits and altered garments. British designer Craig Green has been fascinated by work clothing for years, and produces highly innovative and original menswear collections. In his summer 2019 collection, Green created an 'aura' for some pieces, following the line of the figure, in collaboration with David Curtis-Ring. This was inspired by a photograph of a woman that Green had seen, in which the shadow of the person beside her gave the woman an aura, which also resembles a body outline at a crime scene. The collection was also based on the clothes worn by anonymous care and rescue workers. Cleaners, surgeons, police officers: the collection is full of references to their work outfits. 'They're the modern-day saviours or angels,' Craig Green explained.[1] In light of the COVID-19 pandemic that began shortly afterwards, this is certainly an interesting thought. The pandemic prompted a renewed appreciation of nurses, doctors and others in jobs where they devote themselves to the well-being of others.[2] It is also interesting to consider this notion in relation to the stokers and other workers on board the Titanic who, as recent research has established, continued to work in the bowels of the ship to keep the lights on even as the ship was foundering, for the safety of others.[3]

The resilience and strength of women was the theme of the *Carte Blanche* collection that Iris van Herpen presented online during Paris haute-couture week 2024. She worked with French filmmaker Julie Gautier, using the female body as 'a tool to claim freedom as well as a weapon to oppress and control. It is an ode to the ongoing resilience and strength of women

Soft powers in a hard world

Madelief Hohé

worldwide [...].'[4] This is a story of taking control and finding freedom. Van Herpen's optimistic view of the world and her desire to innovate and connect also come together in the *Sympoiesis* collection which she presented in Paris in June 2025. One of the designs was made in collaboration with bio-designer Chris Bellamy, who packed 125 million algae in gel which – under the right temperature and light conditions – will live on in the dress.[5] A way of drawing attention to the need for humans to reconnect with nature, in this case the ocean, 'the largest and most important ecosystem on our planet that generates more than half of the oxygen we breathe,' as Van Herpen explained. 'This collection is a collaboration with nature itself. In this time of ecological emergency and biodiversity loss, biodesign invites us to rethink the way we 'use' materials, to visualise a future where all human design is not just inspired by nature, but integrated with it. It highlights the interdependence between humans and nature, viewing the body not as isolated, but as an ecosystem – where fashion becomes alive, responsive, and deeply connected with the natural world.'[6] Could this be more poetic, or more appropriate to a story about the Titanic & Fashion, the last dance?

Amidst all the tumult in the world, creative, original designers look to the future with positivity, and bring poetry to fashion. 'The soft powers will surely win in the end', poet Henriëtte Roland Holst wrote hopefully in 1918, the year the First World War came to an end. I choose to believe in her optimism, and that of the designers discussed above: fashion always points to the future.

1 https://hero-magazine.com/shows/craig-green-ss19; Katya Foreman, 'Craig Green Men's Spring 2019', *Women's Wear Daily*, 14 June 2018, accessed in July 2025.

2 The pandemic evoked associations with the Spanish flu pandemic (1918-1920) which broke out just as the First World War came to an end, costing millions of lives, more even than the war itself. In 2020 there was a frightening familiarity in the photographs of the time showing people wearing face masks. History was suddenly repeating itself, with the arrival of a global pandemic.

3 Rebecca Morelle, Alison Francis, 'Titanic scan reveals ground-breaking details of ship's final hours', *BBC online*, 8 April 2025, accessed in July 2025.

4 Information from Iris van Herpen, *Carte Blanche* film, Paris Haute Couture week, 23 January 2023.

5 Information from Iris van Herpen, show on 7 July 2025 in Paris, and collection viewed at Atelier Néerlandais, 9 July 2025. Thanks to Iris van Herpen and her team.

6 Information from Iris van Herpen, July 2025.

We all experience the moment, the decision of what to wear today. How do we feel, or how do we want to feel? And above all, what impression do we want to make? What we wear is not a decision to be taken lightly. It says who we are, where we come from and where we want to go. In a world where visibility is still unequally shared, clothes are a way of showing yourself and claiming space. The body not only wears fabrics, it also articulates history, vision, identity, resolve and pride. It sends a powerful message. Just a single garment can be used as a tool to lay claim to space, question boundaries and show that who you are does not fit within a single outline, style or norm. Each item tells its own unique story. *Titanic & Fashion* is about the different passengers who travelled on the iconic Titanic in April 1912, and collided with an iceberg.

The ship was a loaded setting. A floating microcosm. An opulent, multilayered bubble, in which clothes precisely reflected who you were and where you 'came from'. Onboard the ship, identity was not only the name in and nationality of your passport but, above all, what you wore. For the elite, the ship symbolised grandeur, privilege and spectacle. For others, it held the prospect of a new life, an escape or the hope of something better. And it was precisely at this point of friction that sparked something. Then, as now, clothes determined who was seen and who was not. Who was given space and who had to fight for it. The Titanic may have sunk, but its impact remains afloat. It still echoes today, like a timeless mirror that confronts us with ourselves.

Today, we are not on a ship, but in a society or culture with systems that divide us, where people have to fight for visibility and it is not always safe to express oneself. Clothes can provide protection, but they can also present a risk. They can declare, 'Here I am, and this is my story'. In an ideal world, this message should be visible, open to discussion and understandable. This exhibition is more than an ode to fashion. It is a plea for the right to be visible, for people to be able to show themselves in whatever form they choose. A plea for the expression of identity, even if it is at odds with the norm. The body as the medium and clothes as a language in a free, safe culture without discrimination.

Those who wear the clothes are not only style icons or public figures. They are bringers of stories. What they display is not outfits, but layers of time. Their choices tell us about origins, about the future, about how they want to be in the world, and what they want to do with it. As long as we continue to create space for diversity of appearance, we also create space for diversity of ideas, feelings and being. Clothes are not a side-issue in this, they are a powerful form of expression. Evidence of existence, of autonomy and of empowerment. For if we forget the power of simply being there, as we want to be, we will lose the essence of what it is to be human.

Clothes as the visualisation of a powerful message
Cathelijne Blok

Titanic, Remixed

Traveling the deep sea, deep space of *Drexciya's Wavejumper*, I contemplate the watery depths, the world of whale calls like the undulating elocution of Saturn's rings. Our bodies are made of stars, light particles zooming trillions of miles to Earth, mini universes exploded into orchestrated synchronicities reformed, moved by fluctuations of planetary pulls in orbit.

The moon waves and sun rays reflect our primeval nature, cooled in moonlight, warmed in sunlight. The Black Arts Movement poets of the 60s and 70s enacted a necessary symbolic reversal, reminding us of the African origins of humanity from whom all others are variations. They wrote of Blackness as all the colors of the sun's illumination, as projectors of light embodied Yoruba orisas like Osun, golden goddess of beauty and sweet waters whose symbols include a shimmering mirror, the fan, sunflowers, a gourd of honey, and in some cases, a bow and arrow.

The Sun and Moon Camo Coats represent a dynamic and cyclical duality. The foundations of Yoruba cosmology ascribe primacy to eijwapo, the concept of twoness seen in the two halves of the sacred calabash. The pantheon of orisas is shaped by Yemaya, blue- and white-adorned goddess of the oceans, mother and creator of humanity, and protective warrior whose machete is decorated with cowries of abundance. Through her balance of nurturing and protective qualities, the ocean's power becomes a divine tool arising from purple-blue depths like the liberatory mythology of *Drexciya*. In this narrative, a reclamation is enacted upon the history of centuries-long holocaust by European kidnappers of African peoples transported in horrific conditions across continental waters toward the waiting nightmare of chattel slavery. Pregnant African women thrown overboard into Atlantic waters en route to this fraught future enacted the ultimate liberation. Whether they were thrown or whether they jumped to freedom – the latter as I prefer to imagine it – the story goes that they survived in the watery depths, giving birth to Afronaut aquatic beings known as Drexciyans, generations of whom are thriving in the ocean's world, biding their time, poised to return 'to deliver Whitey a beatdown'. In Afrofuturism-inspired exhibitions over the last couple decades, contemporary artists have engaged with this mythology as a historical reparation, a futurist world-building reflecting an Africanist shapeshifting legacy rooted in diverse traditions, and a resistance and 'thrival' technology.

Iconic musician/composer Sun Ra and the Solar Arkestra recorded the classic *We Travel the Spaceways*, opening portals to interplanetary journeys through the language of music. In 1980s Detroit, Michigan, new methods and materials were being employed to shape a new music, techno, utilizing emerging technology and expanded forms of instrumentation to travel sonic pathways, inhabiting and sculpting the code, the dots and the dashes, as sublime dislocation away from the weight of the body into a realm of digital synesthesia, post-corporeal abstracted expressionism of Blackness like playwright Ed Bullins' critical play *The Theme is Blackness*, pushing outside of objectified frames of identity into fresh methods of creation and the experience of sound.

Kunstmuseum Den Haag tries to explore subjects from multiple perspectives. We therefore invited D. Denenge Duyst-Akpem, artist, historian, cross-disciplinary designer, and founder of the *Camo Coat Collection* to reflect in essay and exhibition forms on the mythological and historical connections to themes of water and the vessel throughout Black, Indigenous, Diasporic traditions. With her monograph *AFRIFUTURI 02022020*, a commemorative project and community/education portal, she coined the syncretic term 'Afrofuturity' to reflect an Africa-centered global aesthetic and methodology rooted in reclamation and reparation of the past, honoring of the trailblazers, and engaging empowered future visioning.

She is core faculty in the Low-Residency MFA Program at SAIC where she has offered courses centering Afrofuturism, postcolonial studies, and graduate studio practice in addition to presenting lectures worldwide including Victoria & Albert Museum London for the critically acclaimed *Africa Fashion*, Smithsonian Institution, Goethe Institute, Zurich University of the Arts, ARTEXTE Montréal, and many more. Denenge describes her work thus: 'As a scholar and practitioner, I utilize the teaching of Afrofuturity as a methodology of (Black) liberation, the foundation of which is the exercising of visionary and imagination muscles in sculpting new futures that affirm the present and are rooted in the past.' In this article, she writes about her *Sun and Moon* designs in connection with the Titanic themes.

The group *Drexciya* adopted this moniker in honor of the mythology, harnessing the power of this historic reclamation through the oratory power of the name, activated upon its every repetition. Appearing publicly only rarely and masked when so, *Drexciya's* members preferred to foreground the mystery of their music. Compositions wove sonic synapses and cross-temporal tapestries of watery codes like the quilts that communicated messages from covert abolitionists to those labelled fugitive, always making a way out of no way, embracing alternative frequencies, new forms from the old, reworked and re-presented, reclaimed and remixed. The two, four, eight, sixteen squared to 256 possible divinatory readings in Ifa tradition whose gateways are opened by the lobes of the sacred caffeinated kola nut as a ritual portal to Ancestral information in transcendental balance and aesthetics of the cool. The Dogon people of Mali call their amphibious celestial ancestors 'Nommo', communicating through cosmic waves. Amongst the Dagara of Burkina Faso, the elemental wheel's water people are the communicators, those who bring balance and say what must be said. In the dance of duality, heating and cooling, the entities of Sun and Moon come into conversation with the essential element of water.

Aquatic lore and maritime mythologies connect cultural threads to global traditions. We hear tales of sirens and mermaids, but how many know Mami Wata, the name for a group of African and Caribbean water spirits who embody dualities of both abundance and misfortune? Mami Wata represents beauty and the divine feminine principal. Yet, note the uproar and backlash in recent years when the beloved Disney character of The Little Mermaid was depicted by a young Black actress. How dare we place Blackness or Black femininity as a representation of beauty? Like the purple-blue-black of Mother Octopus known as the guardian of the depths, Pulitzer-prize winning poet Gwendolyn Brooks was praised in poetic oriki by Black Arts Movement great Haki Madhubuti as 'black doubleblack purpleblack blueblack beenblack.' Moving in the depths, sought-after, desired, often misunderstood, the eight-tentacled mystical ocho shapeshifts infinity, reducing her body to fit through spaces where her beak can shimmy to freedom, taking ever more fascinating forms, even changing the colors of her body in response to dreams as she slumbers, floating at rest in beauty sleep even though, at an instant, the protective mother may awake to enact rightful vengeance. The Black Feminine is constantly demonized and yet we are the blueprint, the origin from whom all others descend, containing infinite variations in our DNA. Medusa's beauty and trauma were reduced to fear, her locs re-constructed as snakes, her face frozen into a permanent expression of rage, reduced from producer of life to harbinger of stone-cold extinction, purveyors of death rather than life, story erased by her perpetrators. And Lilith who refused to submit to Adam's patriarchy and so was relegated to darkness and supplanted by Eve onto whom all of Humanity's sins were heaped.

The Divine Feminine is no one's bitch. The sea is not to be trifled with. She will call all that is hers back just as we see the mighty orca whales rising up against nefarious and destructive entities in the waters in present day. #TeamOrca! The ocean does not suffer fools. Humanity continues its so-called forward progress. Futurisimo. Bigger, faster, stronger. Ships as moving monuments, magnificent declarations. Man stations himself upon that prow, surveying what will be 'discovered', the ship itself an ecosystem floating precariously as testament to tenacity. Titanic Captain Smith ignored the warnings about the dangerous icebergs that ended up causing his ship's demise. Many stories were lost that day, many lives who haunt the depths for whom we hope for peace and oneness with the elements.

Mohau Modisakeng's three-channel video work *Passage*, whose name refers to life as voyage, 'an important concept in the Setswana language, where the experience of life is referred to as a 'passage' and human beings as voyagers, was exhibited at the 2017 Venice Biennale for the Pavilion of South Africa,

D. Denenge Duyst-Akpem

among other esteemed venues worldwide. The commission centers 'slavery's dismemberment of African identity and its enduring erasure of personal histories.' This work is described as a meditation 'on trans-oceanic slavery, a bustling trade that brought forced labourers from the Dutch East India Company's colonies in South and East Asia to work on plantations in the Cape Colony. Through that historical connection, he comments on current displacements of people created by political and economic upheaval.' I experienced this exquisite work as part of the exhibition I*n Their Own Form: Contemporary Photography and Afrofuturism* at the Museum of Contemporary Photography, Chicago, during the same summer that a ship capsized carrying hundreds of African asylum seekers and more light was being shed by media on the ever-growing conflict and contradictions around immigration in the Mediterranean.

The experience of the work was enhanced by its installation as three monumental projections positioned facing solid wood benches in darkened space, immersing viewers in dark blue-grey tones of the water that provoked a sensation of descent with the figures as the film progressed. We view at first from above: glistening water and figures in black and white ensembles, including a Trilby hat and a Basotho blanket, floating framed within rowboats, each carrying one possession. The boats filled slowly with water until we were visually submerged with the figures, navigating bubbles and the swirling of fabric undulating underwater, perceiving traces of memories, of collective fear and longing, threads of stories, glimpsed and lost, as we descended untethered into undefined space. Freeform textile folds enveloped their forms reshaped by the water, just as memory acts upon histories erased and forgotten, appearing as distant echoes or whispers recalled. The sea is a portal, a site of memory, lieux de mémoire.

Titanic's story is one that has captured the imagination of generations, most especially through the star-studded film told through the lens of doomed lovers, young love cut short, forever locked into fantasy by Celine Dion's vocal prowess pulling at the heartstrings. It has also come to symbolize a certain excess gone astray, that wealth cannot save you, and all the ways that warnings are ignored especially when nature is involved. Our present ecological crisis is case in point, with scientists who sound the alarm silenced. All in the name of the machine's forward progress that requires fresh resources to fuel its seemingly inevitable advance.

This is also a tale of design extravagance and innovation, of the ways that we have manifested into existence new forms of living, traveling, being. The finest of everything, a hotel on water, high society in garments spun from the most exquisite fabrics, a most glorious and elegant display. Layers of luxury, especially for the upper echelons of society in first and second class. The latest in marine engineering, heralding the new age in mechanics, of possibility formed of metal, wheels, cogs, fire, smoke, steam, and all the people required to serve its function. There are stories hidden, yet to be revealed. When people of the Global Majority think of ships, it is often through the lens of slavery. Of course, there were sailors from Africa and other continents who predated any European contact—in fact, even 'Europe' as a concept—with many of these histories deliberately erased to construct the myth of white supremacy and manifest destiny. In 'The Moan' from *On My Journey Now: Looking at African-American History Through the Spirituals*, celebrated poet Nikki Giovanni traces the most elemental sound of grief and despair echoing through the belly of those ships. She writes about how even the sharks began to alter their paths, drawn by the bodies of dying Africans. Consider these moans in relationship to the cries of those sucked down into the icy waters of the Titanic's sinking. This is why mythologies of reclamation like Drexciya are so important to healing collective consciousness. As sci-fi writer Octavia Butler instructed, we write ourselves into existence, telling our stories and taking back the construction of narrative.

We reclaim our histories of water in all its forms including the accounts and identities of those who pioneered and invented. The Titanic was one of a new group of White Star Line ships. Seven years later in 1919, father of Pan-Africanism Marcus Garvey would launch the Black Star Line—referenced in the hip-hop album by Talib Kweli and Yasiin Bey formerly known as Mos Def—as a move by the wealthy shipping magnate to repatriate Black Americans back to Africa, Liberia to be specific. Multi-hyphenate Paul Miller aka DJ Spooky That Subliminal Kid wrote in *The Book of Ice* about Matthew Henson, who in 1909, three years prior to the Titanic voyage, was the first African-American to reach the North Pole as part of group of explorers led by Inuit guides. Miller details how ice has become a symbolic terminology within Black culture, notably within the music and monikers of hip-hop that arose as precursor to the digital travel of techno. From Ice Cube to Ice T to admiring exclamations of 'maaaan, that's cold!' to the anti-art rabble-rousing trickster magic of David Hammons with his famous *Bliz-aard Ball Sale* on the streets of New York and *Cold Shoulder*, an installation of fur coats draped over large blocks of ice. Ice, as in: not to be trifled with. Ice, as in: a warning, a statement of strength, the hardest, the best, the pinnacle of cool.

Was Titanic's demise a result of a combination of human error and arrogance, mechanical breakdown, perhaps spirits of the sea enacting a gesture of refusal against the gilded ship of excess created by industrial revolution, wrought from cheap labor and children's nimble fingers constructing intricate layers of a glorious monstrosity just as Congo's hungry children are conscripted today to procure the minerals to feed the world's bottomless hunger for 'progress' in the global goal of futurity? In the decades leading up to the Titanic disaster, Belgian colonialism enacted by King Leopold's henchmen would sever the hands and arms of children whose parents failed to meet quotas, then photograph them together. Museums in present-day are still adorned with decorative hands in a sadistic nod to this indescribably brutal past. Nigerian artist Otobong Nkanga's monumental exhibition *To Dig a Hole That Collapses Again* confronts colonial histories in part through a study of Namibia, centering the dust and detritus that remains after the imperial project, like the Titanic's sunken remains that provide clues to bygone times.

I like to think that the sea, the ice, and the storm do not necessarily act with malice or with the intentionally violent urges that so plague certain demographics of humanity. I like to believe that Nature simply functions as she does. Ice will ice, storms will storm, water will flow and overflow, expand and contract, shift its form time and again. We experience the more negative effects of this nature, of which we are part, when we neglect to respect its power. Simply put, we reap what we sow. There are many caught innocently in the crossfire of those decisions, of actions made generations and centuries prior to their birth or today. Cause and effect. As Otobong's title put it so poetically, to dig a hole that collapses again. The law of gravity, action producing reaction, if only by the shifting of volume from one location to another, the working of one entity upon another. In the end, we must question where lies our responsibility not only to ourselves and to our own communities, but to the larger global community and to the legacy of the future. How do we use these histories to learn and grow, to create an equitable and holistic life for all in harmony with nature?

The original Camo Coat Collection centers these questions through consideration of Yoruba orisa Osanyin, god of leaves and forest wisdom, the healer who studies and applies the knowledge of the natural world as protection and healing. Camo Coats grew from the Osanyin Commemorative Portrait Series which depicted 35+ Fellows of the National Endowment for the Humanities Institute on Black Aesthetics and Sacred Systems. I photographed each member at a tree or natural location of their choice on the Emory University campus in Atlanta, Georgia, USA, in the style of Osanyin who is often depicted as half human, half tree. The series referenced the autobiographical accounts of shaman Elder Malidoma Somé in *Of Water and the Spirit of* moments 'In the Arms of the Green Lady' during an initiatory tree-gazing exercise.

The textiles of this collection and its companion series, CCv2: The Garden Collection inspired by photography in gardens on four continents, are rooted in the concept of camouflage and pattern protection, connected to West African ankara and commemorative designs that highlight and preserve histories in the cloth. The Sun and Moon cloaks are layered in meaning and form a diptych in honor of these polarities with kaleidoscopic patterns arranged to align points of activation like the pyramids of Teotihuacan. The images and motifs are recognizable in part or in full to those who are familiar with the locations depicted or for whom the symbols have meaning. Together, as with King Agyeman Prempeh I's adinkra cloth from 1888, the combination tells a story, as historical document, garment, archive, and activation by the wearer. The coats allow for shapeshifting similar to both the biomimicry employed as evasion and hyper-visibility of color and pattern in the animal world. The designs serve as a new type of camouflage informed by the personal and the collective. This collection honors our bodies as sites, as physical and spiritual architectures that can be mobilized to manifest protection and empowered mobility, especially within contested or dangerous spaces where we see camouflage utilized as part of protest in service of the people instead of as a military indicator.

The Sun Goddess cloak employs dazzling color the way that the sun blinds at the height of the day with a swirling combination of symbolic motifs including a remixed collage of El Anatsui's gold coin pillars and jewel-studded cocoons punctuated by green diamonds alluding to ikarem, the snake friend and protector of Tiv people. In contrast, the Moon Goddess gown is a light cotton affair printed with mirroring images of the Chicago skyline at sunset, with blue sky and lake viewed from the waterfront in Bronzeville, Chicago's historic Black arts neighborhood and high-femme puff sleeves depicting flowering bushes and bees from the Lurie Garden in Millennium Park, capturing the floaty effervescent essence of nymphs called by the gardens to twirl under the emerging moon. Time stands still, and yet with the ever-evolving city landscape, this view will never be the same again. Commemorative textiles allow entry to a moment, a breath, a memory, reactivated through movement, motion, dance.

My work engages trace and memory in materials of the past and expressions of future vision. Textile encodes meaning, embedding clues to consciousness. Its form and presentation are a portal, an evocation of liberatory possibility, real or imagined. Through its shaping and wearing, we activate these connections like a spider's webbed strands tenderly pulled, synapses reaching gingerly across time and space, to envelop in sticky embrace.

One of the most high-profile passengers on the RMS Titanic was the American billionaire John Jacob Astor IV. Worth 2.8 billion dollars, he was the richest man on board. Astor, who came from a wealthy property dynasty, was not only famous for his flamboyant building projects in Manhattan, but also as an inventor and science fiction author. In 1894 he published *A Journey in Other Worlds*, a vision of life in the year 2000. This essay shows that much about the age when the Titanic was built, and set out on its first and only voyage, can be explained on the basis of Astor's book.

Astor's short book is a futuristic novel, a highly popular genre at the time, which offers a fictional glimpse of life in the year 2000. In the 106 years following the publication of the book, humanity has taken full control of life on Earth (and elsewhere). Like every futuristic novel, Astor's book is a hail of buckshot. Some of his predictions – including the advent of a global telephone network, planes, solar energy and space travel – are highly accurate. But others are very wide of the mark. In Astor's book, humans have colonised the planets Jupiter and Saturn, have straightened the planet's tilted axis and dammed up the Arctic Ocean. Humanity has the Earth firmly in its grip and is busy making its mark on the rest of the universe.

The first thing that strikes us about Astor's book is its almost adorable optimism, and its belief that human progress is a given. One of the key attractions of the Titanic, it is said, is that it embodies the optimism with which people in the west looked to the future in the late nineteenth century.

In the late nineteenth century, people believed they could shape the future. There would be no limit to the control humans would exert over the world. Mobility and travel were an important aspect of this, as the literature of the time reflects. In Jules Verne's novels, people travel under the sea, under the ground and through space. In those of H.G. Wells they even travel through time. In our current world, where we seem to have lost this unshakable confidence, this is a particularly attractive notion.

Humanity never sits still – we just do not seem to have it in us. We still make amazing discoveries that radically change our lives. But our enthusiasm for innovation is no longer as straightforward as it was in Astor's day. The planet and its resources have turned out to be finite, and trees cannot grow to the heavens. So we have become more aware of the downside of technological progress. Innovation comes at a price.

Major recent developments, such as the launch of the first consumer AI ChatGPT in 2022, are approached with more caution, more regard for their implications. AI promises hitherto unknown possibilities, but as with the internet and social media, we must also ask how it will influence our thinking, our creativity, and what it is to be human. The idea that innovations often come with a societal hangover is more obvious to us than it was to Astor, for whom the year 2000 was an absolute paradise.

If we ignore the fine detail, we can see something of the spirit of that age in Elon Musk's technological optimism, but that is also precisely where the pessimism lies. Musk wants to go to Mars because he expects the Earth will soon succumb to our collective consumption and human ambition. To him, Mars will be a refuge for a small number of fortunates, rather than a hopeful start to humanity's great galactic adventure.

Seen in this light, Astor's hopeful optimism is a more attractive fantasy.

It was this optimistic belief in neverending technological progress that inspired the building of the RMS Titanic and her sister ships, the Olympic and the Britannic. The ships would signify a new milestone in shipbuilding. They would be bigger, faster and more luxurious than anything that went before, but the designers also never doubted for a moment that their achievement would soon be surpassed by something even better.

If we overlook all the technological muscle flexing in Astor's book, we also see that it is full of his insights concerning global politics. The United States has come to dominate the world. The countries of Europe, including the

Jeroen Post

British Empire, have succumbed to socialist revolution and have ceded all their colonies to the Americans. Although the British Empire was still going strong in 1894, by around 1912 it was already clear that Britain's global dominance was starting to wane, and that the empire had passed its peak. The Titanic was built in the transitional period between the British and the American century, and Astor was right in his prediction that America would soon take over from the British.

This was also clear on board the Titanic. The ship was thoroughly British, designed in Liverpool and built in Belfast. She was the epitome of British maritime tradition. But she also resulted from the fact that the British could feel the Americans breathing down their neck when it came to the question of who would rule the waves in the future.

America was also becoming a financial superpower. The fact that American billionaire Astor dined on board with members of the British aristocracy shows that the United Kingdom would experience more competition in the future. The disdain with which the 'vulgar' nouveau riche were regarded could not hide the fact that the British upper classes were aware that America's new upper classes were beginning to outdo them. Wealthy American passengers like Molly Brown, Isidor Straus, Archibald Gracie and Astor himself were testimony to the fact that the global economy's centre of gravity was gradually shifting to America. Morganatic marriages with American industrialists were a way for the impoverished British upper classes to safeguard their own wealth for the future.[1]

Finally, Astor's book is written from the classic perspective of the well-read, white Anglo-Saxon bourgeois man. It is a perspective that still sets the tone in many stories about the Titanic, despite the huge diversity of nationalities on board. The world of 1912 was exceedingly colonial, and so were Astor's predictions for the future. Around the turn of the twentieth century, America was behaving increasingly like an imperial power, with wars of conquest against Spain (1898) and colonies in the Philippines. Regions rich in resources were being annexed and pillaged to fuel western industrial societies. In Astor's book, the United States not only takes over European colonies, it also continues its own colonial exploits in the jungles of… the planet Jupiter.

Yes, indeed, your eyes do not deceive you. In Astor's future, colonialism persists, and the frontier has shifted to the far corners of the galaxy. In his imagination, American colonisers fight flesh-eating plants, giant snakes and prehistoric elephants in the jungles of Jupiter. But it is well worth the fight, as the planet has huge reserves of iron ore, silver, lead, gold, coal and oil. Finally, the book is also a masculine fantasy. It has female characters, but the miracles of the future are mainly the work of men, as Astor sees it. Though he does say that in the future both men and women enjoy equal educational opportunities. Even someone like Astor could not deny the fact that, in the west, the women's movement was beginning to gain momentum. In the first-class section of the Titanic, he cannot have failed to notice Molly Brown, who a few years later would become the first woman to stand for election to the US Senate, and who worked for the Red Cross, serving US troops at the front. The struggle for women's suffrage turned out to be just as unsinkable as Molly Brown herself.

John Jacob Astor went down with the Titanic in 1912, and his irrepressible optimism about the future was also lost when the First World War broke out in the summer of 1914. The industrial meat grinder of the trenches brought the optimism of 'la belle époque' to an abrupt end. Many of Astor's predictions came true, but the optimism and bravura with which they were accompanied in *A Journey in Other Worlds* were often missing. In this brief exegesis of his book, we see that it was written during a transitional period in the western world. The old and the new are sometimes hard to reconcile – just as they were on the Titanic.

Perhaps that is the real attraction of the Titanic, a reminder of a world that believed anything was possible, before history proved otherwise.

[1] A morganatic marriage was when someone of noble or royal birth married someone of a lower rank. This was often frowned upon, but at the time of the Titanic it was a way of forming an alliance between a good name and the financial resources of the new upper classes.

John Jacob Astor and the future that never was

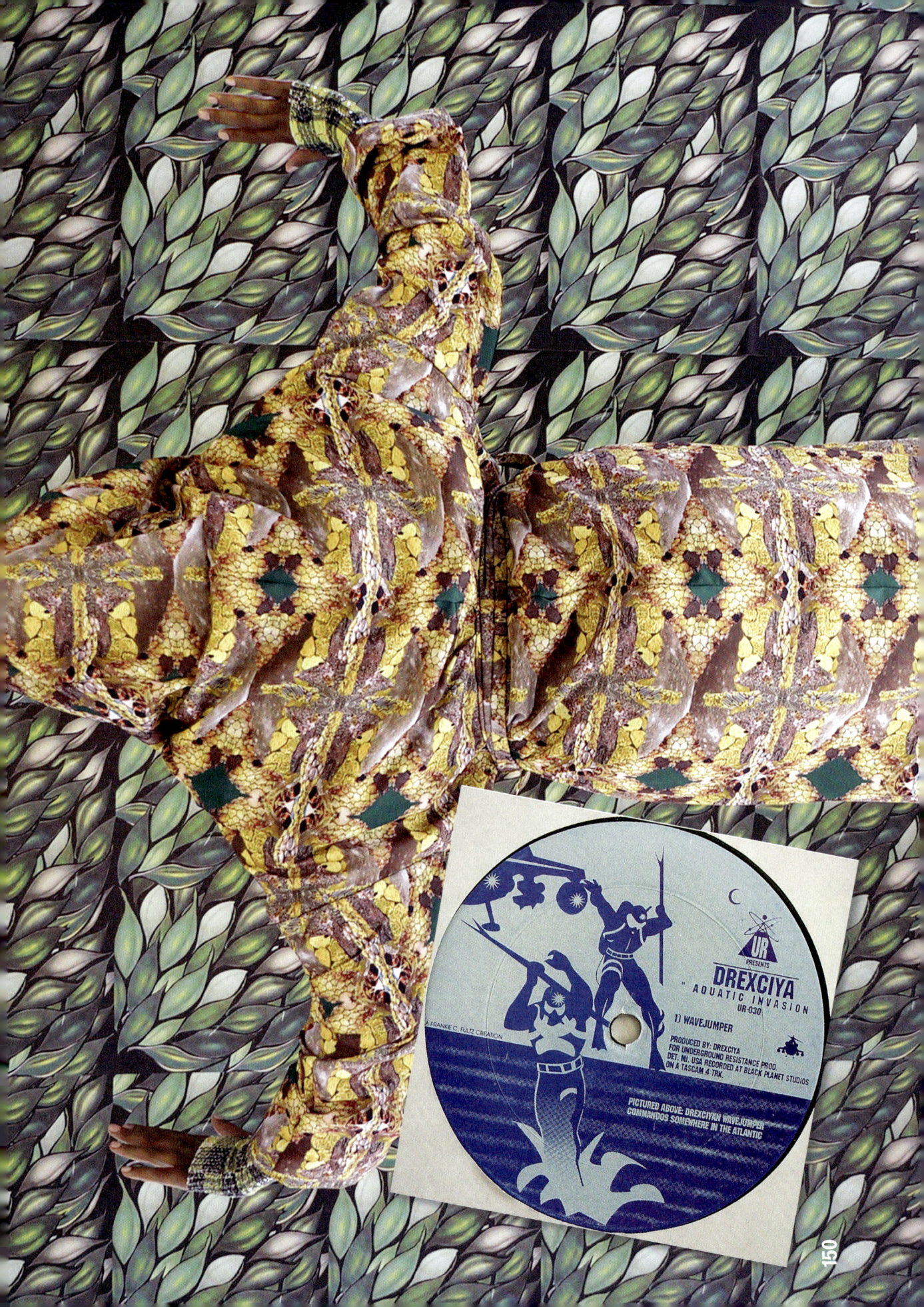

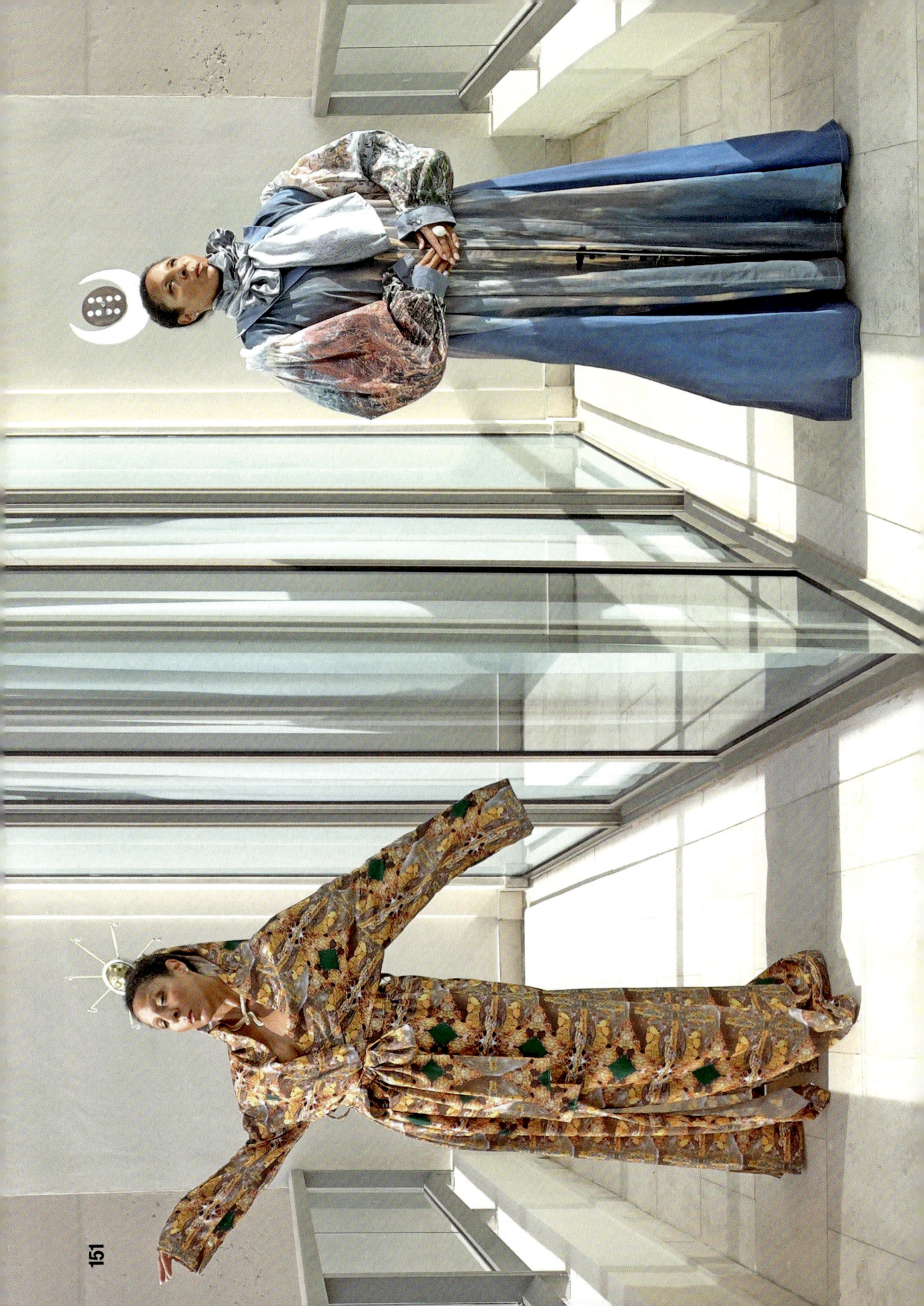

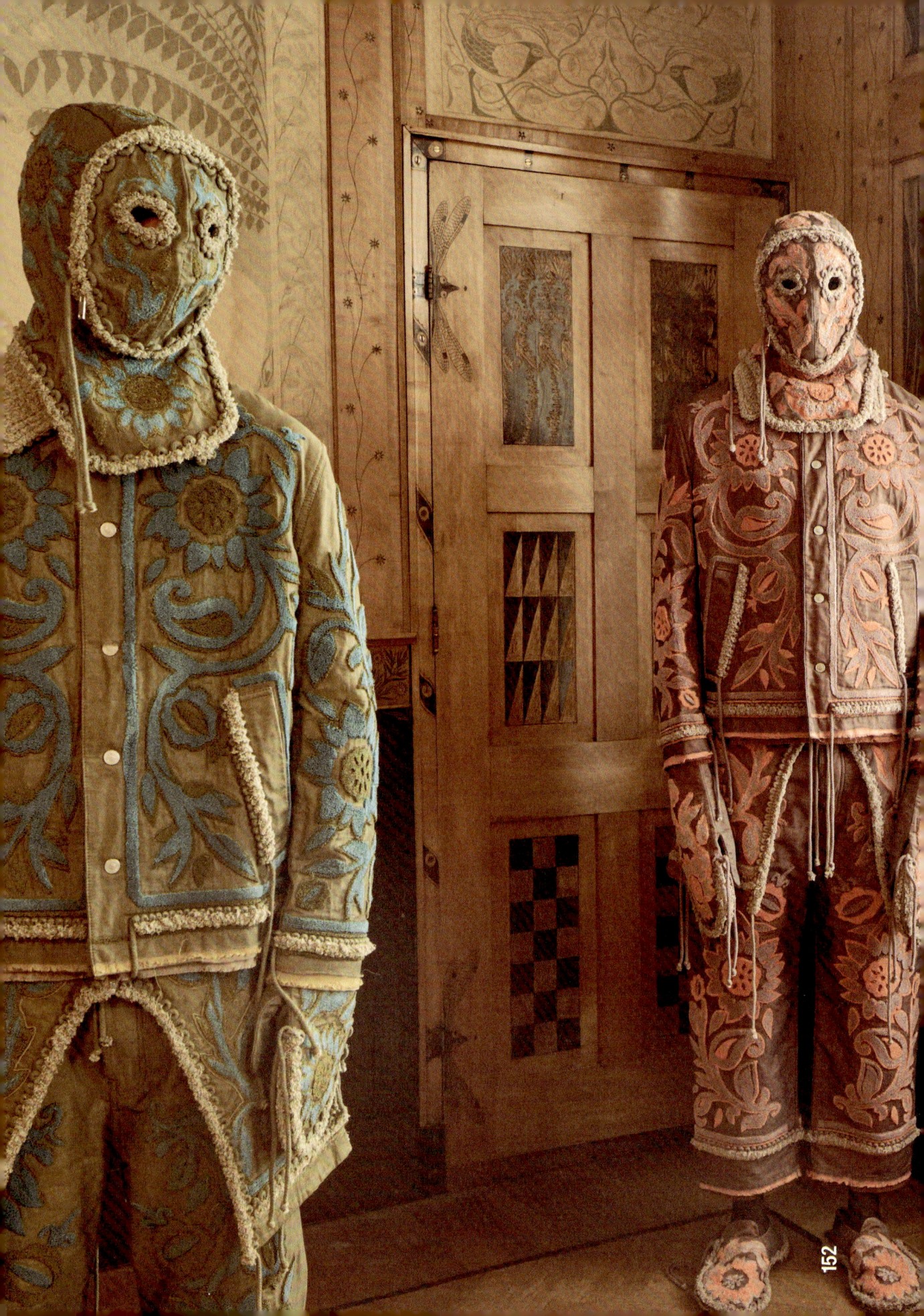

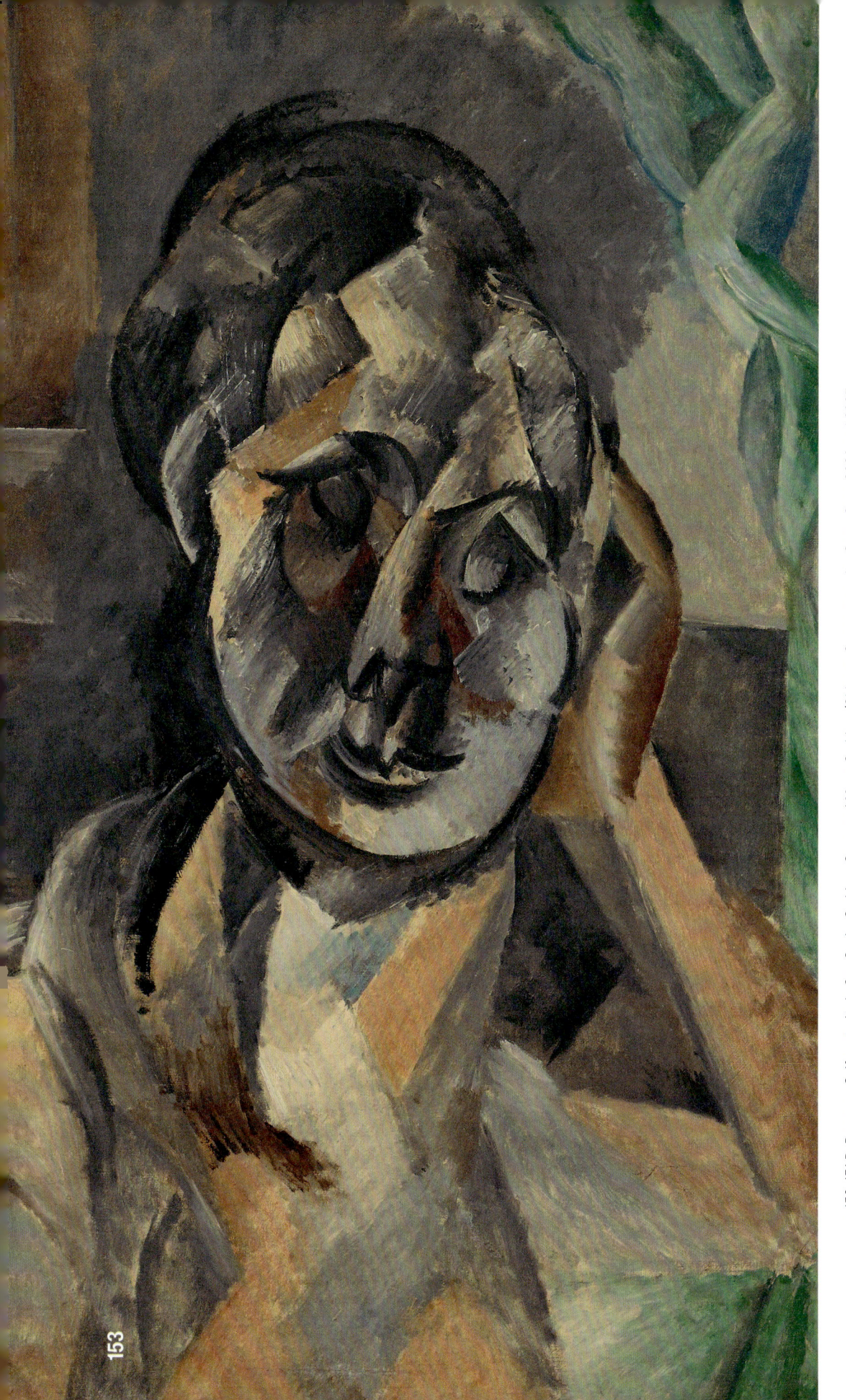

p. 150, 151 D. Denenge, Self-portraits in Sun Snake Goddess Gown and Moon Goddess/Chicago Commemorative Camo Coat, 2020 and 2025.

p. 150 Drexciya, LP of "Wavejumper", 1995.

p. 152 Craig Green, Two outfits with woven floral motifs, spring/summer 2024, courtesy of Craig Green, London.

p. 153 Pablo Picasso, *La femme au pot de moutarde* (Woman with Mustard Pot), Paris 1910. The woman depicted was Picasso's first great love, Fernande Olivier (1881-1961). She also appears once or twice among the five women in his famous *Les Demoiselles d'Avignon* (1907), which Rose takes with her on the voyage in the film *Titanic* (the painting was not in reality onboard). *La femme au pot de moutarde* did however travel from Paris to New York in 1913 for the legendary *Armory Show*, which introduced America to cubism.

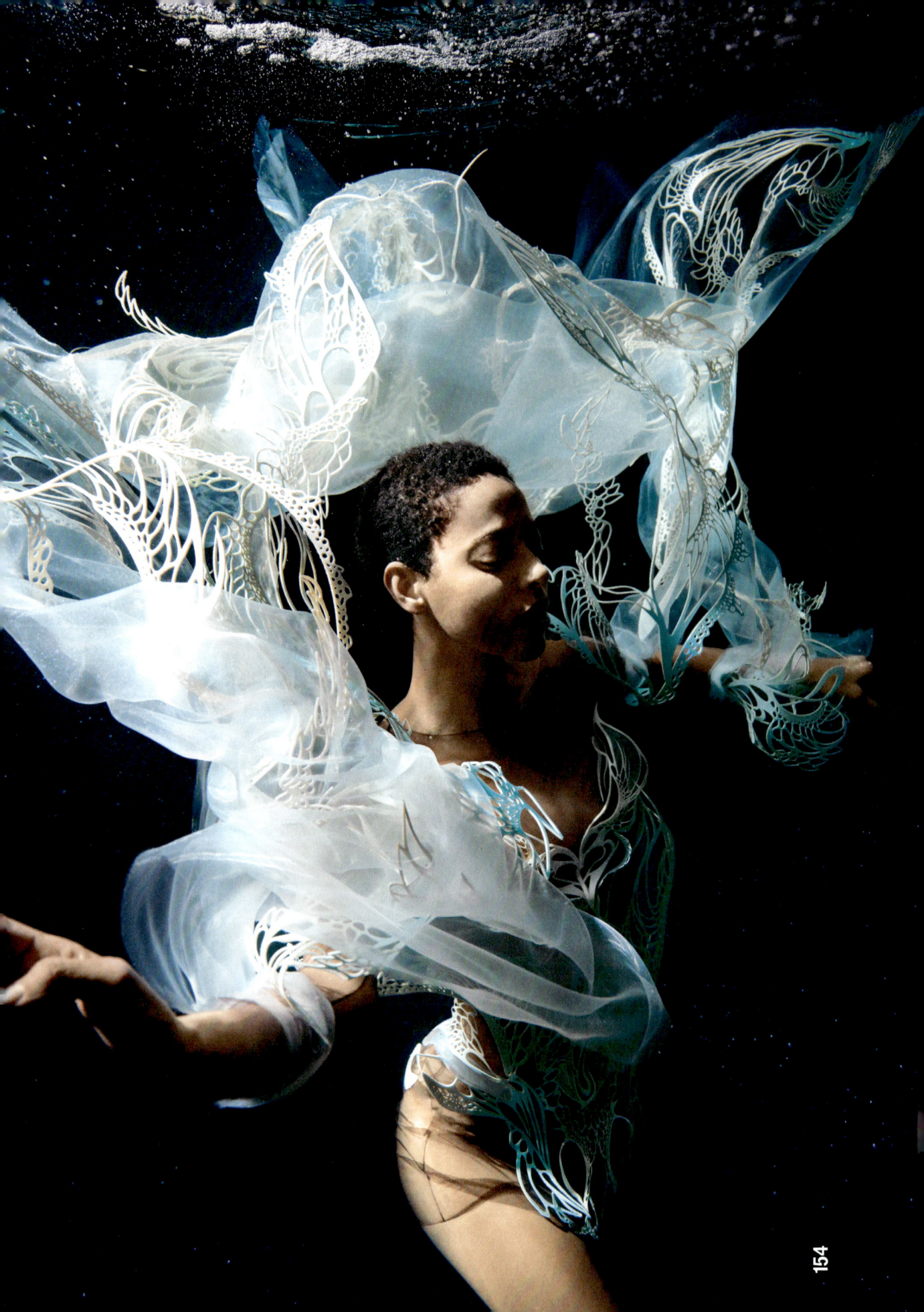

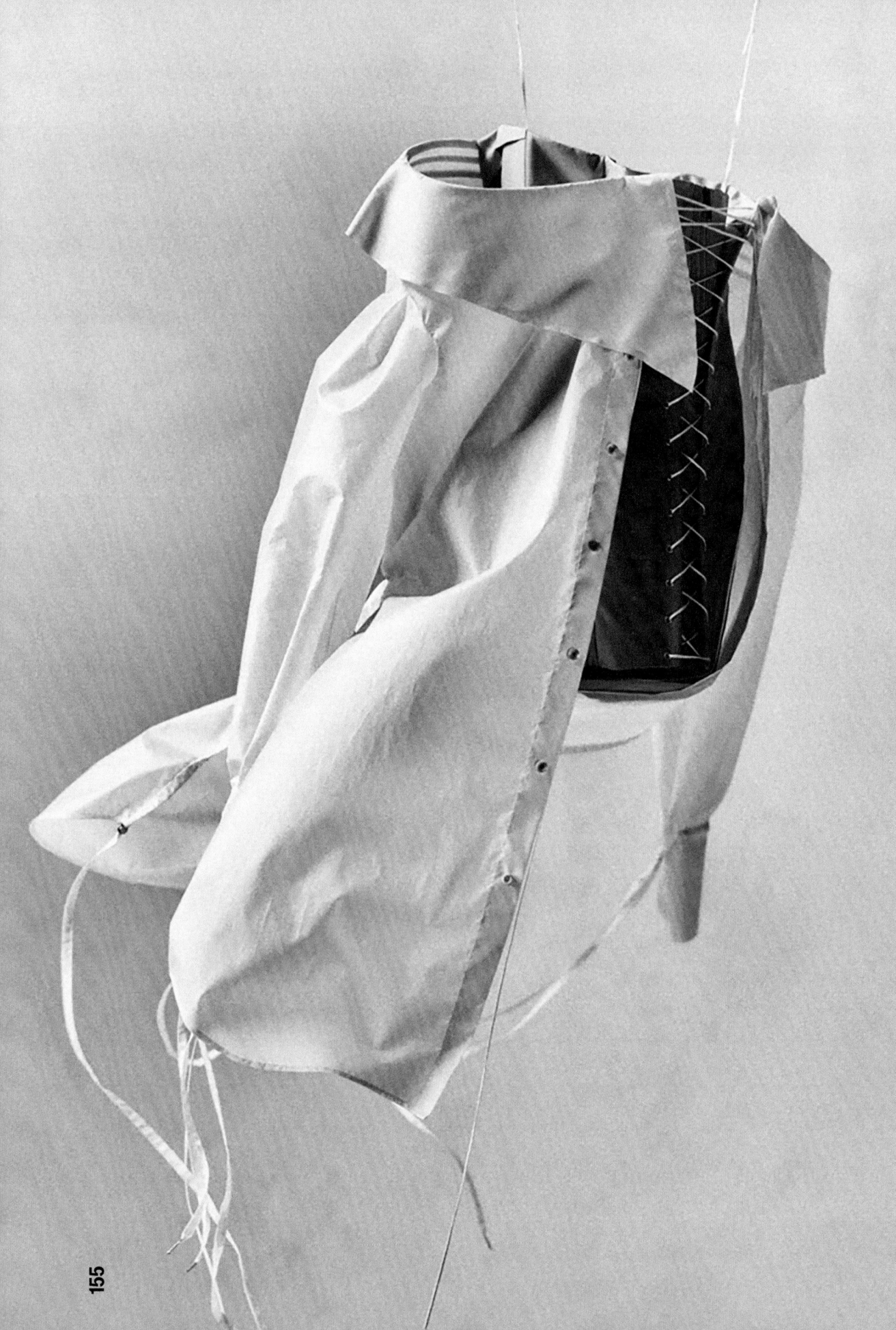

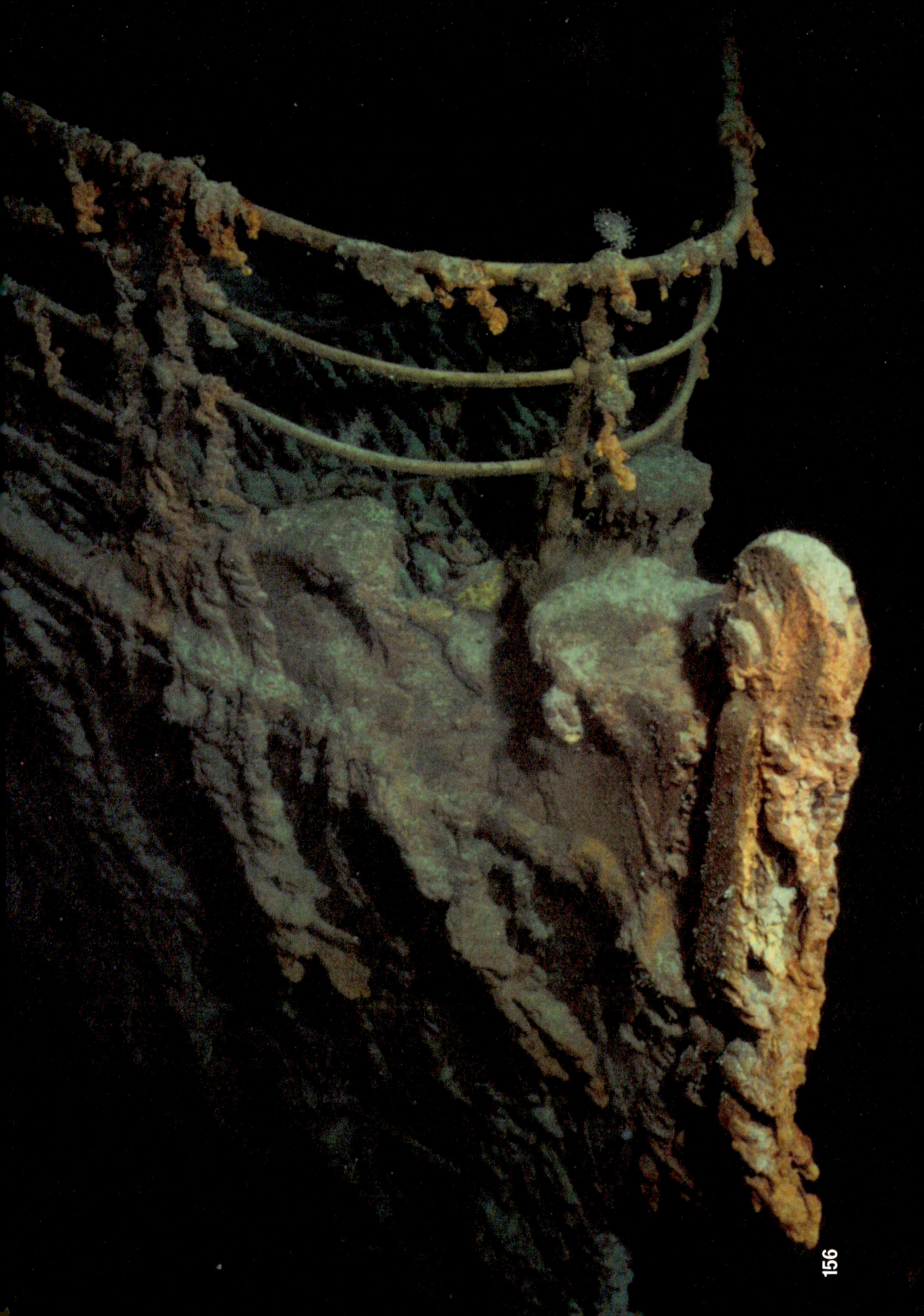

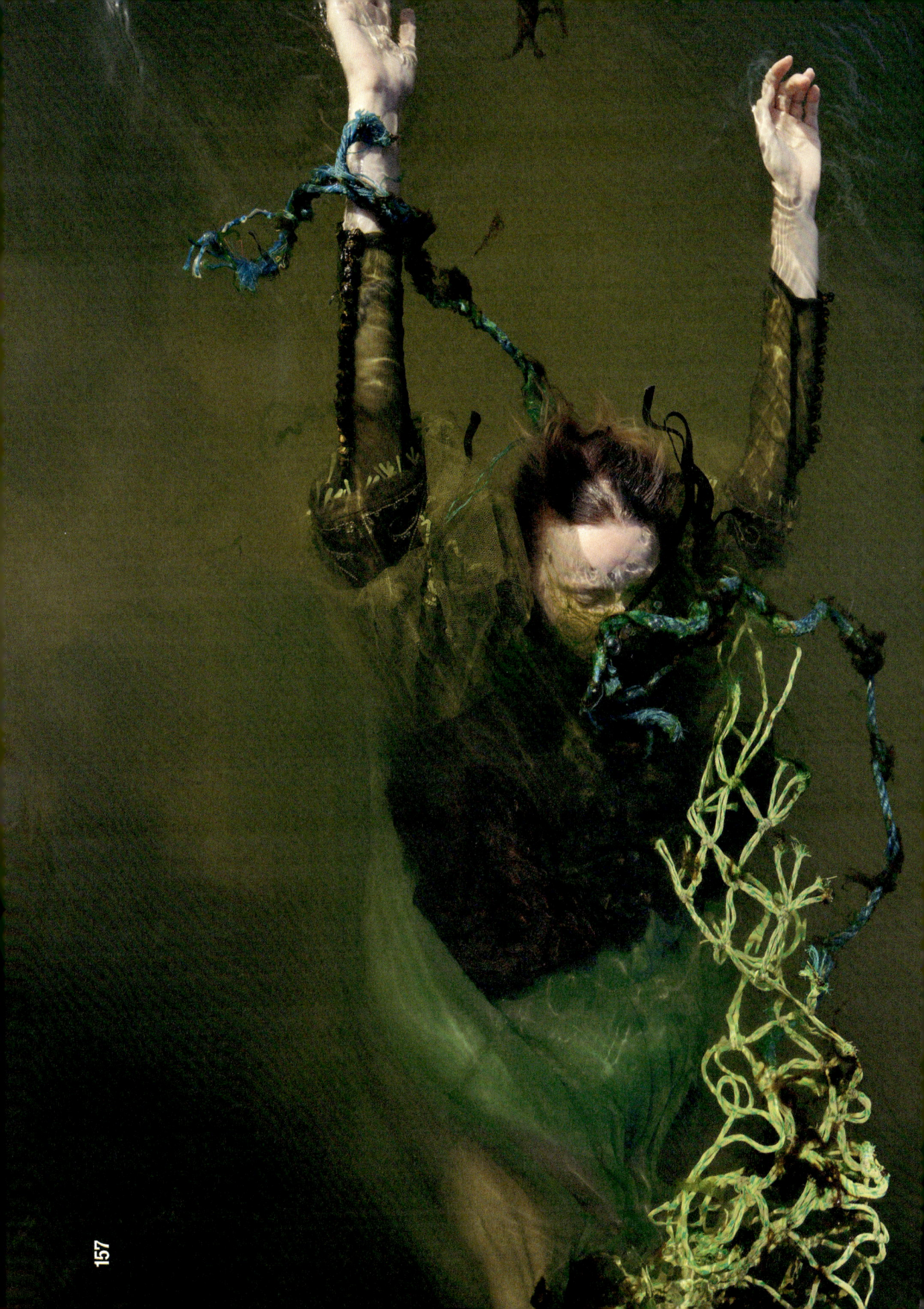

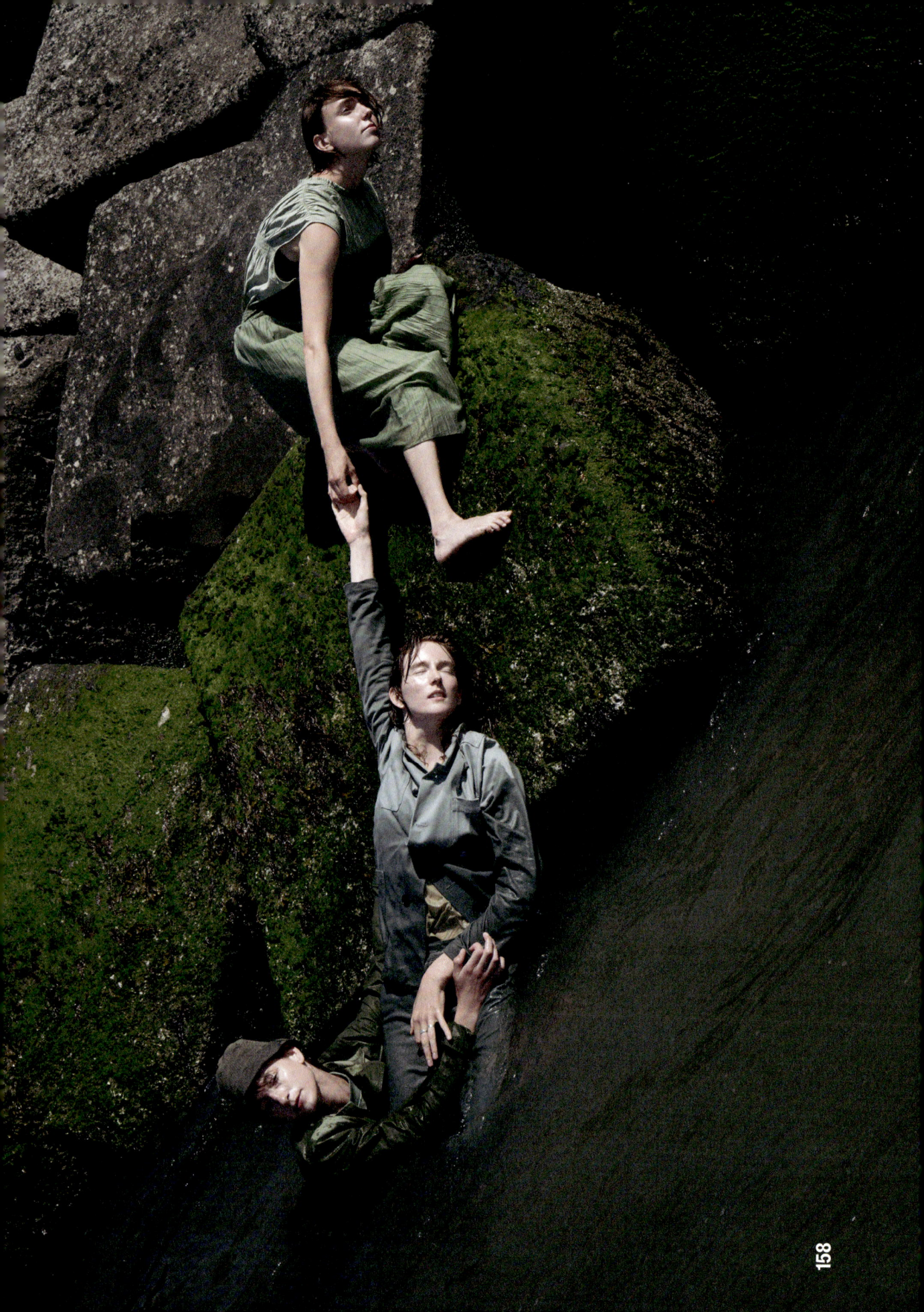

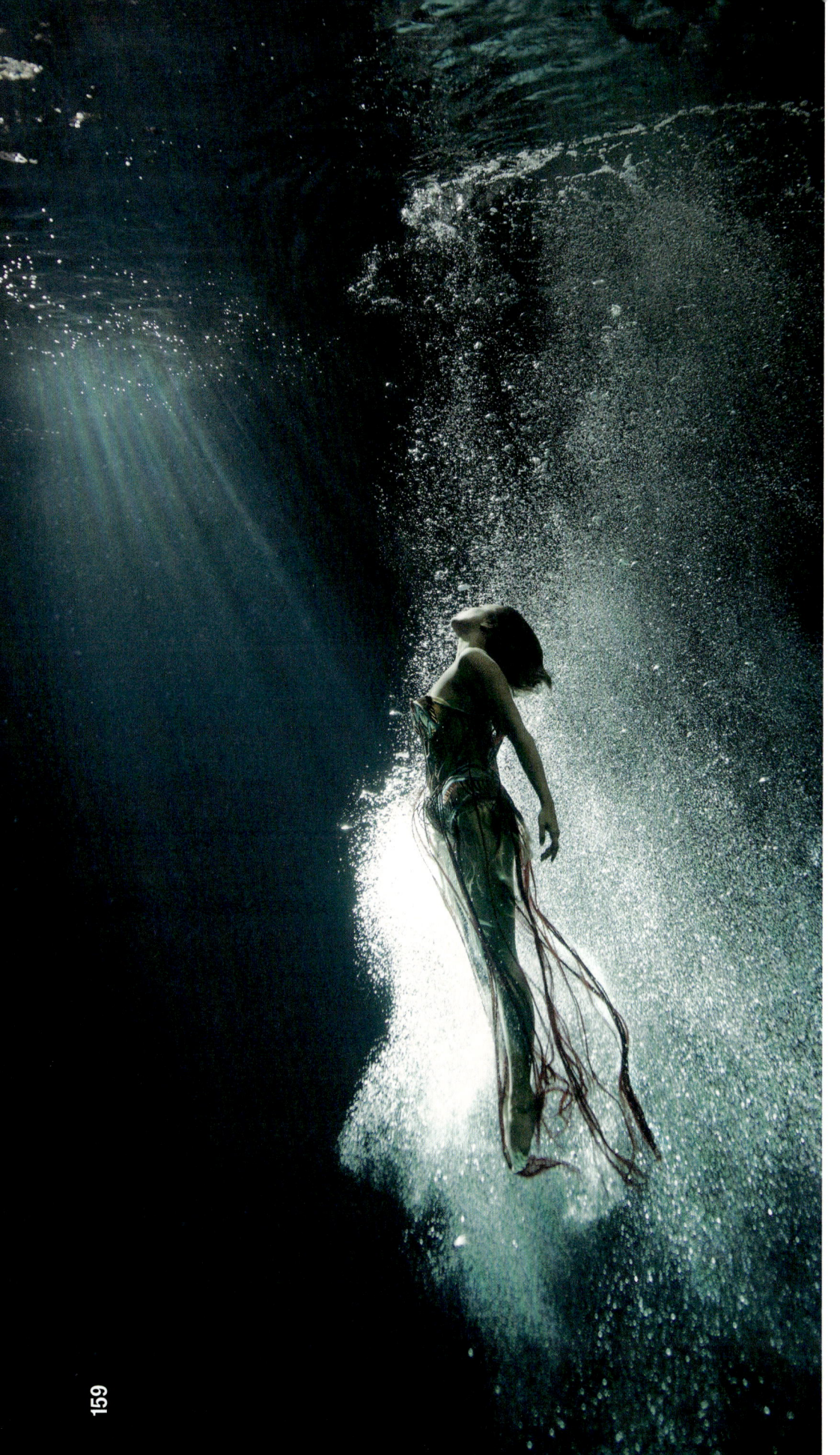

pp. 154, 159 Iris van Herpen, dress from the *Carte Blanche* collection, presented in the form of a film, January 2024 (in collaboration with filmmaker Julie Gautier). In *Carte Blanche* Iris van Herpen demonstrates the power of the female body and women's resilience, courtesy of Iris van Herpen, Amsterdam.

p. 155 Tess van Zalinge, Dress with corset structure, *Momentum* collection, 2024, courtesy of Tess van Zalinge, Amsterdam.

p. 156 Underwater image of the bow section of the Titanic, which sank on 15 April 1912; the wreckage was discovered on the seabed in 1985 at a depth of around 3.5 km.

p. 157 Dries van Noten, Blouse and collar, spring/summer 2020, private collection.

p. 158 Vintage skirt and top, suits by Bonne Suits, Amsterdam, spring/summer 2025.

Inside backcover: London newspaper seller with banner announcing the loss of SS Titanic in 1912.

This publication accompanies the exhibition of the same name at Kunstmuseum Den Haag, from 27 September 2025 to 25 January 2026.

Publishers
Waanders Publishers, Zwolle
Kunstmuseum Den Haag

Director
Margriet Schavemaker

Exhibitions department and projects office
Daniel Koep, head of exhibitions
Esther van der Minne, head of projects office
Madelief Hohé, fashion & costume curator and project lead
Tirza Westland, project assistant
Fabienne Hom, trainee curator
Fleur Blom, trainee curator

Authors
Madelief Hohé (ed.), curator at Kunstmuseum Den Haag
Marije Blaasse, collections department, Kunstmuseum Den Haag
Cathelijne Blok, art historian, journalist and founder of *The Tittymag*
Lillian Boutros, assistant curator at Fenix, Rotterdam
Ron Brand, curator at Maritime Museum Rotterdam
Frouke van Dijke, curator at Kunstmuseum Den Haag
D. Denenge Duyst-Akpem, artist, historian and cross-disciplinary designer
Fabienne Hom, trainee curator
Jacco Hooikammer, curator at the Dutch Open Air Museum, Arnhem
Kathleen Mahieu, collections department, Kunstmuseum Den Haag
Jeroen Post, historian and maker of *Titanic de Podcast*
César Rodriguez Salinas, textile and fashion conservator at Kunstmuseum Den Haag
Tom Veldhuijzen, journalist and maker of *Titanic de Podcast*
Caro Verbeek, curator at Kunstmuseum Den Haag
Tirza Westland, project assistant at Kunstmuseum Den Haag

Opinions expressed in the articles are those of the individual authors.

Copy-editing
Caroline Reilink / Van 't Venne

Image editing
Madelief Hohé
Fabienne Hom

Catalogue design
Loes Claessens

Lithography
Benno Slijkhuis, Wilco Art Books

Printing
Wilco Art Books, Amersfoort

Translation
Sue McDonnell

Jasper Abels photo series for Kunstmuseum Den Haag
Photography: Jasper Abels
Art Direction: Maarten Spruyt
Technical assistant: Alex Berger
Hair and make-up: Anita Jolles
Location: Kunstmuseum Den Haag; Zuiderstrand, The Hague
Background set featuring ice based on nature photographs by Tineke van der Pouw Kraan
Courtesy of: Maison Margiela, Paris: 53, 125, 153
Craig Green, London: 43, 57, 59, 152
Models: Jiby @ Republic Men: 57, 59, 88, 152
Kaj @ Republic Men: 43, 59, 152
Julius @ The Troopers: 125
Elza @ Exuberance Model Management: 53, 153, 157
Sanne & Sophie @ Ulla Models: 55, 154
Felice, Pleunie and Dorro Veen: 158

Photo series of Kunstmuseum Den Haag collection
Alice de Groot

Art direction, exhibition
Maarten Spruyt

Technical drawings and print design
Felipe Gonzalez Cabezas

Conservation
César Rodríguez Salinas
Bina Sheombar, workshop assistant
Daphne Reijs / 2Restore Textielrestauratie

Mannequinage (Costume mounting)
Tirza Westland, lead, costume and accessory mounting
Kathleen Mahieu, Marije Blaasse, César Rodríguez Salinas, Bina Sheombar, Fabienne Hom, Saskia Hoogervorst

Thanks to all lenders
The Walt Disney Company, Craig Green, (Londen), Iris van Herpen (Amsterdam), Maison Margiela (Parijs), Tess van Zalinge (Amsterdam), Haags Gemeentearchief, Maritiem Museum Rotterdam, Museon-Omniversum Den Haag, Stadsarchief Rotterdam, Gert Banis, Splinter Chabot, D. Denenge Duyst-Akpem, Roberto Minozzo, Particulier bruikleengever, Clarice Gargard, Munganyende Hélène Christelle, Merol, Maja Eljak, Milou Deelen, Naaz, Lewis Orchard, Stichting Reuchlin Collecties

Other photographs:
Kunstmuseum Den Haag – Alice de Groot:
18, 23, 24, 27, 28, 41, 44, 54, 76, 77, 81, 83, 84, 87, 89, 90, 93, 94, 97, 100, 102, 105, 122, 126, 130, 133, 136-137
Kunstmuseum Den Haag – Adriaan van Dam:
17, 50, 61, 74, 78, 80, 92, 106, 127, 128, 129, 134
Kunstmuseum Den Haag: 20, 40, 42, 46, 51, 77, 82, 123, 127, 135, 153
ANP Foto: 14, 15 (Mary Evans Picture Library Ltd.), 16 (Cineliz/AllPix), 19 (Everett Collection, Inc), 22 (Mary Evans Picture Library Ltd.), 25 (Mary Evans Picture Library Ltd.), 26 (Allpix Press SARL / Cineliz/AllPix), 29 (Allpix Press SARL / Cineliz/AllPi), 47 (Science Photo Library), 48 (Roger Viollet Agence Photographique), 56 (World History Archive), 58 (Mary Evans Picture Library Ltd.), 95 (Science Photo Library), 124 (Mary Evans Picture Library Ltd.), 129 (Roger Viollet Agence Photographique), 132, 156 (Science Photo Library), inside back cover (World History Archive)
Maritime Museum Rotterdam: 49 , 52
National Archives: 45
Alamy: 131 (Chronicle)
Amsterdam City Archives: 20 (Emrik and Binger), 45, 79, 79, 85, 86, 91, 92, 95, 98, 101, 103, 106, 107, 127
Gallica: 21 (Bibliothèque nationale de France, département Sciences et techniques, FOL-V-4312)
The Hague Municipal Archives: 61
Rijksmuseum Amsterdam: 135
New York Public Library: 99, 104, 108 and 109 (Augustus F. Sherman)
Courtesy of Tess van Zalinge: 155 (Bastiaan Woudt)
Courtesy of Iris van Herpen: 154, 157 (Tony Meyer)
Courtesy of D. Denenge Duyst-Akpem: p. 150, 151

Sponsorship

FONDS 21
Partner van

MODE
MUZE

© 2025 Waanders Uitgevers b.v., Zwolle / Kunstmuseum Den Haag

ISBN 9789462626423
NUR 644

This edition was also published in a Dutch edition: ISBN 9789462626416

www.waanders.nl
www.kunstmuseum.nl

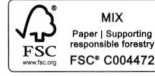

FSC MIX Paper | Supporting responsible forestry
www.fsc.org FSC® C004472